Listen to the Songs the Children Sing

A Memoir Reflecting on Some of the Major Social and Political Transformations in Liberia

Christiana Tah

LifeRich
PUBLISHING®

LifeRich Publishing is a registered trademark of The Reader's Digest Association, Inc.

LifeRich Publishing books may be ordered through booksellers or by contacting:

LifeRich Publishing
1663 Liberty Drive
Bloomington, IN 47403
www.liferichpublishing.com
1 (888) 238-8637

Scripture quotations taken from the King James Version of the Bible.

ISBN: 978-1-4897-2559-2 (sc)
ISBN: 978-1-4897-2558-5 (hc)
ISBN: 978-1-4897-2560-8 (e)

Library of Congress Control Number: 2019917282

Printed in the United States of America.

LifeRich Publishing rev. date: 2/28/2020

Contents

Part 3 – Full Circle

Author's Note

I put off writing a book for a long time, and then when I accepted the post of attorney general of Liberia in President Ellen Johnson Sirleaf's government in 2009, events began to spin around me inexorably, and I could not ignore the urge to write. During the early-evening hours, some of the staff would come to my office, and we would sit and brainstorm on a myriad of issues spanning history, politics, the economy, and the like. My favorite topic was always history. Over the years, I have come to realize that most Liberians either do not know their history, or what they claim to know remains clouded with misinformation.

Although this book is about my life's journey, it has been written to incorporate a lot of historical and social events of the past so that readers will have a broader perspective of the complexity of the social dynamism among the people of Liberia.

I have touched upon social interactions among the many ethnic groups since the founding of Liberia in 1822 by the American Colonization Society (ACS), a nongovernmental organization established in the United States in the early nineteenth centrury to repatriate free blacks to Africa. I have also addressed the indelible impact major societal transformations, such as the military coup of 1980 and the fourteen-year civil war that began in 1989, have had on the country and its people. The accounts have been drawn from my own experiences. If you ask a thousand people to recount what occurred in Liberia in April 1980, for example, you will probably get a thousand different versions. Notwithstanding, the Liberian society experienced collective pain through the years, with each person experiencing something unique that no one else can explain or interpret.

There are stories and issues I have deliberately omitted either out of respect for certain families or because of significant security implications, although unclassified.

This book was to tell my own story, not the story of anyone else. Therefore, the personalities mentioned in this book were included simply because our lives intersected at critical times and the story would be incomplete without any mention of them.

The title of the book is drawn from a common expression among some of the tribes of Liberia. "If you enter a village for the first time and want to know what kind of people live there, listen to the songs the children sing." At the end of the day when children have completed all their assigned chores, they take time to socialize before they go to bed. Often the activities involve dancing and singing—the singing of songs with words that tell of the village life, the good times and the bad times.

I wrote this memoir between 2015 and 2016 but spent the subsequent three years revising and rewriting. Knowing from the onset that writing this book would be a catharsis from some of the difficult paths I had traveled, I deliberately proceeded at a slower pace to ensure that sore emotions did not blur my objectivity. One of the primary objectives for writing this memoir is to record for posterity some of the experiences of the past that affect who we are as Liberians.

I hope that after reading this book, most Liberians will take an introspective look at themselves and determine not only how others got us to where we are but also how our commissions and omissions have brought us to where we are today. It is also hoped that our foreign friends will have a better understanding of this small but complex society.

I

The Historical and Sociocultural Context

CHAPTER 1

The Phone Call

Sometime in early April 2009, Jennie Johnson Bernard, the sister of President Ellen Johnson Sirleaf, called me from Liberia and left a message on my phone that she wanted to talk to me. I was living in the United States at the time. I had a hunch that the president had asked her to call me regarding a job offer, and that made me reluctant to return the call for a few days because I had already been down this road before.

To backtrack a little, in early January 2007, I traveled to Liberia from the United States, where I had been residing since I escaped the Liberian civil war in 1990. My trip was in response to an invitation from Ellen Johnson Sirleaf, the president of Liberia; she wanted me to join the Supreme Court of Liberia as an associate justice, an assignment I considered with some reluctance because it lacked the dynamism I needed to experience in a nation-rebuilding exercise. I, however, accepted the position and returned to the United States late January to wrap up things with my employer and family to return to Liberia before the March 2007 term of the Supreme Court began. Before I left Liberia, the Senate Committee conducted the required hearing and later wrote a unanimous report to the plenary approving my nomination. When I did not hear from the president regarding the status of my appointment by the end of February, I called her directly to inquire. She told me simply that the Senate had rejected my nomination.

I learned later from one of the senators that the president herself had lobbied the senators to reject my nomination because someone had told her, after my nomination, that I was a staunch member of the Liberty Party, an opposition political party. The focal person leading the withdrawal of the nomination was a female senator who was a member of the Hearing Committee, one of the five who had signed the committee's report to approve my nomination. Although I was not a member of Liberty Party and have never been a member of any political party, I pondered: *What if I do belong to an opposition party? Has the president not promised to form a government of inclusion? Why should any citizen be denied the opportunity to serve the country, especially if there is no showing of past involvement in subversive activities?*

The decision did not matter to me personally, as I have never viewed public service as an avenue for achieving wealth and power. Public service has always been, and always will be, about how the contribution of each citizen can improve the well-being of the greatest number of people. My greatest disappointment had to do with the fact that our country had just emerged from a devastating civil war that claimed the lives of more than a quarter-million people, and there we were engaged in the usual partisan politics.

I just simply returned to my normal life in the United States, which I had wisely decided not to alter until I had received some firm commitment from the government of Liberia.

In January 2008, upon invitation from a nongovernmental organization, I traveled to Liberia to conduct a workshop on the new inheritance law and its implications for women and was contacted by the president's office to set up an appointment to meet with the president. I accepted the invitation just out of plain curiosity and courtesy. I was curious about what her demeanor would be when we meet face-to-face after she had allegedly unceremoniously withdrawn support for her nomination of me to the Supreme Court bench. When we met, the president wanted to know if I was still interested in working for the government. I told her that I was more interested in knowing what had prompted the rejection of my nomination and why had she not fought for the nomination to be confirmed. She gave me a one-word answer: "Politics." I looked directly into her eyes and repeated quietly, "Politics? Is that all, Your Excellency?" "Indeed," she said, "nothing more." Shortly after, I wished her well and asked permission to exit.

When Jennie called in early 2009, it was truly unexpected. "Chris, I am so sorry about everything that has happened. Ellen wants to talk to you." By now, I was comfortable with my life in the USA, both regarding my job with a college as a full professor and with my general legal practice.

Although I had not spoken to the president since the meeting of 2008 and did not know why she wanted me to return her call, I already had my suspicion that she wanted to offer me another job. The thought made me feel increasingly uncomfortable, thinking about leaving a peaceful, stable environment for one that was unpredictable and action-packed. A cousin wrote, "You will be putting yourself in a hornet's nest. After what happened with the Supreme Court nomination, I just don't think you should trust anyone in Liberia." I appreciated his concern but dismissed his observation as being too cynical. While I understood his concerns, I entertained the thought that this might be the last opportunity our generation would have to save the country from further destruction and provide some hope for the youth.

One Sunday afternoon in late April 2009, I decided to return Jennie's call. Jennie and I had met during the seventies when I returned from school in the United States and worked at the Bureau of Social Welfare at the Ministry of Health & Social Welfare; she was then the chief nursing officer of the Republic of Liberia. She was many years my senior but related well to young people, and we all loved to seek her advice on personal matters. She informed me that President Sirleaf had traveled to the southeastern part of the country on a development inspection tour but that she would make sure she called me upon her return within a week. She did.

The president was very direct: "I would like for you to come and work for the government as minister of justice. Are you interested?" I asked for a few days to consult with my family and give the offer some thought. Most of my friends opposed the idea. They thought that it would be very risky to deal with this government after the Supreme Court nomination debacle. But my daughter and husband were of the view that the rejection of the nomination for Supreme Court justice had left an unnecessarily, inexplicable drama that required some action on my part to repair the damage; acceptance of the position, they felt, would greatly mitigate the damage at the least.

Ordinarily, I would not be interested in the position; I had worked many years ago as assistant minister of justice for rehabilitation and knew how difficult and thankless working at the Ministry of Justice could be, but I understood my family's position. "You cannot be remembered only as the lawyer whose nomination was rejected by the Liberian Senate," my husband said. "In the future, no one will remember the context, and no one knows how a pundit will spin this story eventually. Accepting the job as justice minister might be the only opportunity for the Liberian people to know who you are."

Several phone calls from the president preceded this decisive meeting with my family. But even after the meeting with my family, lingering doubts crossed my mind intermittently; I thought about the fact that I was not a confidante, nor a partisan, nor a relative of the president. I wondered whether I could count on the president to cover my back when the chips are down.

My cousin, Florence Chenoweth, a former UN consultant in many African countries, had been asked to become the next minister of agriculture. Like me, she was not only reluctant to accept the appointment but had been receiving calls from many Liberians suggesting that she does not accept the position. Florence and I talked on the phone frequently during late April and early May 2009 to determine whether we should take the leap.

I was satisfied with where I was in my life at the time and did not have any strong desire to make a change. By practicing law and teaching sociology and criminal justice, I was as occupied as I wanted to be. Notwithstanding, and deep within me, there was this nagging feeling that it was God's will that I return to Liberia to serve my people.

Finally, after a month of deliberations, Florence and I decided to accept the respective positions with the Government of Liberia no matter what unexpected challenges lie ahead.

I contacted the president by telephone, almost a week later, and informed her I would accept the position. We agreed I would be allowed to recommend the persons nominated for the positions of solicitor general and deputy minister of justice for economic affairs. She asked that I retain the deputy minister of justice for administration, and I agreed. It was important to me that the three departments were headed by strong, competent individuals to ease the pressure on me as minister. She gave her approbation to my request for the other two deputies, and by May 29, 2009, I arrived in Liberia.

CHAPTER 2

"You Can't Go Home Again"

As the plane landed at Roberts International Airport, I experienced the nostalgia that almost every Liberian experiences upon returning to the country after having been away for several months or years. The airport workers chattered in the unique Liberian accent, and the air smelled of palm trees and salt water blowing from the nearby Atlantic Ocean. My last visit had been in January 2009, and before that, January 2008, January 2007, July 2004, July 1998, March 1996. and June 1994. This trip was different, as my mission here was more than just a short visit. I had committed to work with the government for at least two years. Although my decision to join the government was voluntary and decisive, there were sporadic doubts about whether I had done the right thing. *How can it be wrong to serve your country?* I thought, quickly erasing any trace of apprehension.

During the one-hour drive from the airport to town, the realization hit me that I might not know many people in the country anymore, as I hardly recognized anyone at the airport. More than two hundred thousand people were killed in the civil war that lasted from 1989 to 2003, and of the survivors, most had fled into exile all over the world, with the largest numbers settling in several West African countries and the United States. Although I had returned to Liberia several times during the nineteen years I lived in exile due to the war, nothing could have prepared me for the real consequences of the war, both physical and psychological. Most of the people I knew were still externally displaced, or had been killed, or had died of some illness in the absence of basic health care. Many concrete and stylish buildings I remembered from my childhood were now in ruins, while, at the same time, many zinc shacks had popped up all over the capital city, most of them constructed illegally on public land or land owned by people in exile.

The capital city was very crowded with lots of strange faces. I learned that the population of the city had increased to more than one million, up from an estimate of five hundred thousand just before the civil war began in 1989. I also learned most of the folks had come from various parts of the interior of Liberia; some were ex-combatants from neighboring African countries who had participated in the civil war with one or more of the many warring factions. Others were former peacekeeping soldiers deployed in Liberia by the Economic Community of West African States (ECOWAS), a subregional organization, and had returned to Liberia after their respective tour of duty to avail themselves of what they saw as lucrative business opportunities.

My friend Marie Leigh Parker agreed to provide accommodation for me in her exquisitely decorated chateau until I found a place to rent. Marie and I became friends when her family, like ours, settled in the state of Maryland, USA, in 1990 upon fleeing Liberia. I figured, having all my belongings in a ten-foot-by-twelve-foot bedroom would motivate me to get a place of my own quickly.

The civil war had devastated the capital to the extent that pristine neighborhoods had become slums, and landlords were trying to rent run-down three-bedroom bungalows with neither electricity nor running water for US$2,000–$3,000 a month. The places that were move-in ready had all been taken by expatriates. The properties owned by me or my relatives were in complete disrepair and, therefore, uninhabitable. A four-bedroom split-level house I began constructing near the beach in 1989, although unfinished, was occupied by more than fifty internally displaced men, women, and children.

Marie, with a background in economics and finance, soon appointed herself as my financial adviser. She suggested that I think about constructing rather than renting a house. She promised that her financial analysis of my finances would help me determine whether or not I was in a position to construct a house of my own.

The final decision was to build a small house on a plot of land given to me by another friend when she heard I was relocating to Liberia. Our guess was that the house would take about six months to one year to construct if I budgeted well, stayed within the spending limits, and practiced deferred gratification. Notwithstanding careful planning and supervision of construction, the house was completed eighteen months after construction began in December 2009. During the construction, I reminded myself of how lucky I was to have a good friend like Marie amidst the avarice, deceit, jealousy, and selfishness that now seemed to pervade this once happy place characterized by a hospitable profile.

After settling in for a few days, I realized that I had returned to a country inhabited by people who were very different from the folks who lived here before the war. Although some of the places and faces remained the same, fourteen years of disruption and persistent experience of atrocities had taken its toll on the minds and attitudes of the people, as well as the social institutions. Liberia's 2008 *Poverty Reduction Strategy*, most aptly describes the state of the economy at the time:

> The damage and negative consequences of the conflict were enormous. Commercial and productive activities ceased as various warlords looted and vandalized the country. Families were shattered; entire communities were uprooted; and social, political, economic, and traditional governance systems were destroyed. There was a massive exodus of skilled and talented individuals from the country. The economy completely collapsed. GDP fell a catastrophic 90 percent between 1987 and 1995, one of the largest economic collapses ever recorded in the world. By the time of the elections in 2005, average income in Liberia was just one-quarter of what it had been in 1987, and just one-sixth of its level in 1979.[1]

Consequently, the unemployment rate was high, forcing a lot of young people to beg on a regular basis, engage in prostitution, steal, or sell drugs to survive from one day to the next. Even where jobs were available, the applicant would have to meet the eligibility requirement, an impediment for most who attended school during the war when the educational system was dysfunctional due to brain drain and lack of equipment and supplies to operate the schools properly. Although the government, in partnership with the international community, was doing its utmost, the situation I found on the ground when I arrived in May 2009 was dismal.

Returnees brought back cultural influences reflective of where they had lived in exile, and because our people had been in exile in so many different countries, our society had virtually become a cultural hodgepodge in terms of language, values, dress code, religion, food, you name it. In addition to English and the local dialects, many Liberians now spoke other languages, including French, Arabic, Dutch, Yoruba, Fanti, and so on. Rice continued to be the staple food in Liberia, but the cuisine has expanded to include *bankun* from Ghana, *acheke* from La Cote D'Ivoire (staples prepared from corn and cassava, respectively) *egusi* soup from Nigeria, and so forth.

There was a general breakdown in social control in the various communities, and children tended to liberate themselves from parents early. High school education no longer guaranteed that the graduate was literate, and children were no longer afraid to view a mutilated body. Norms and values that set social boundaries had been almost completely eroded, leaving the country in a state of anomie.

When I arrived, there was (and there still is) a general resentment towards Liberians who returned home after the war, especially those who returned from the United States. There was the perception that those who left the country during the war sought refuge for themselves and their family members and left the rest of the population to suffer. Nothing could be further from the truth. Only a few Liberians left at the onset of the war; most people wanted to hold out, thinking that the war would last for only a short time and everyone would return to their daily activities. When the war escalated, and the death toll continued to climb, and the various government agencies began to shut down, most of the population headed for the borders. Others had family members in Europe, the United States, and Canada who raised money to get them out. The US embassy airlifted its citizens, some of whom were of Liberian origin but had become naturalized US citizens at some time in the past.

What Liberians on the ground did not know was that some Liberians living in the diaspora suffered just as much as they tried to pick up the pieces and put their lives back together in strange lands. They regularly received news that relatives, whom they had expected to join them in the future, had been killed indiscriminately by fighters bereft of conscience. Some degree holders, now refugees, accepted and performed menial jobs to make ends meet. Older folks died while waiting for their immigration status to be adjusted so that they could receive medical benefits. Those who qualified for a work permit had to take on two or three jobs to support their families in the United States, relatives in Liberia, and relatives in refugee camps somewhere in West Africa. In addition to dealing with the intermittent hostility toward immigrants in the US, Liberians had to deal with racism, a social issue not too familiar to most Liberians.

There were more germane issues underlying the hostilities toward Liberians from the diaspora. Some citizens on the ground abused the property rights of others who were internally and externally displaced by encroaching on the property. Now they were concerned that returnees would try to reclaim their property. There was a further concern the returning professionals would become competitors for high-paying private sector business opportunities or high-profile public sector jobs.

The hostility toward the returning Liberians was more about the interference with the balance of economic and political power established during the years of war. Those who had survived the war on the ground had formed strong alliances among themselves, and they united, when necessary, to protect one another from what appeared to be an intrusion. It did not matter that no one ethnic group, interest group, or clique could rebuild the country. It was about the feeling of entitlement reinforced by the perception that their lives were sacrificed to save the country just by being in Liberia during the war.

I observed that something as insignificant as a plastic shopping bag had become a prized possession. People kept money, food, documents, jewelry, and anything of value to them in a simple plastic bag. During the war, it was important to have a plastic bag because this was what you would use to throw in your earthly possessions when you received orders from a rebel group to evacuate an area immediately. If you tried to pack a suitcase or place your property in a container that did not visibly and easily display what you had in your possession, you could lose your life for what appeared to be the concealment of valuables from the rebels.

I soon realized that, although the definitions of conventional crimes such as theft, rape, and murder remained the same on the books, in practice they all had a different meaning. People had become used to taking the law into their own hands during the fourteen years of chaos and civil unrest in the country. Very frequently, an accused thief was mobbed and killed by members of the community before the police arrived; and now, the newly elected government was asking my team to replace this state of anomie with the rule of law.

Surely, I concluded, the fourteen years of civil disorder in the country most certainly had an inordinate impact on all of us. I had truly come to understand what one of my college professors meant when he often said in the classroom, "You can't go home again."

CHAPTER 3

The Liberian mosaic

The nomination and confirmation process for my assignment as attorney general took almost six weeks. During the interim, I met with government officials and members of the international community from time to time to begin to lay a foundation for my work ahead. One afternoon, as I stood in the hallway of the capitol building talking to an old acquaintance, I heard one of the legislators ask the driver, "Who is that lady?" The driver said, "She is the new minister of justice." The legislator turned to one of his colleagues and said, "You see what is happening here? The president is bringing back all of her Congor people." I pretended not to have overheard the conversation, but the words of the legislator continued to reverberate in my mind long after I left the building.

I spoke to a couple of people later that evening about what I had experienced at the capitol building earlier that day, and each told me that nowadays ethnicity was often considered even more important than your academic qualifications and work experience. From what I observed, the general public tended to think that each Liberian belonged to one of two groups: you were either "Country" or "Congor." From my understanding, "Country" meant a Liberian of an indigenous background (educated or uneducated) who lacked the sophistication of the Western culture and was most likely to have origins in the rural parts of the country. "Congor," on the other hand, referred to a

Liberian who was not only educated but also considered civilized, heavily influenced by Western culture, and likely to be of American Negro descent or to have been assimilated into the American Negro settler community. "American Negro" was commonly used in Liberia in the nineteenth century and during the first half of the twentieth century to refer to the American black immigrant population. The community was also referred to as Americo-Liberians or Liberians.

Unfortunately, the Liberian society is more complex than just two general categories.

From the written and oral history of Liberia, I have developed my own understanding of the social history of the groups that make up the Liberian society as follows:

Black American immigrants: The American Colonization Society (ACS) was a philanthropic nongovernmental organization established and managed by white men to remove freed blacks from the United States. They were concerned that the increasing number of free blacks would soon demand equal rights and pose other social problems for the United States. Accordingly, the organization sent white agents out to Africa early in the nineteenth century to procure land for the settlement of blacks. The ACS received the blessings of the then US president, James Monroe, and several former presidents, including George Washington. The agents of the ACS decided that the Grain Coast, now Liberia, would be suitable land to settle the blacks and successfully negotiated with the indigenous tribes inhabiting the land—at that time the Bassas, the Krus, the Golas, and the Deys. There is no indication that the inhabitants at the time understood the concept of private land ownership, considering at the time Africans largely existed out of communal communities; nevertheless, the local chiefs signed treaties with the agents to alienate land. The first group of black settlers arrived in Liberia from the United States in 1822.[2]

The Maryland Colonization Society sent out agents to a contiguous area called Cape Palmas to negotiate with the Grebo tribe to settle blacks from the state of Maryland in the United States. Hence, there were two separate American settler communities in the early nineteenth century; one was Maryland, and the other was Liberia.[3,4]

Recaptured Africans: For a few decades in the nineteenth century, the British and Americans patrolled the Atlantic Ocean to enforce antislavery laws abolishing the transatlantic slave trade. In some cases, British and American patrol boats intercepted slave ships on the high seas and redirected them back to Africa; while in other cases, rescued slaves were transported all the way to the new world and kept in segregated holding cells until a ship was hired to take them back to Africa. The word "Congo" was used to categorize the recaptured slaves since most of them had, in fact, been bought from the heavily populated Congo basin area. Other slaves were bought at various points along the coast of West Africa as the slave ship sailed through its route to the new world, but the entire group was referred to as the "Congo people" when they were rescued or recaptured. The abolitionists designated Sierra Leone and Liberia as the refuge for recaptured slaves since both areas had been established for freed blacks by Great Britain and the United States, respectively. The recaptured slaves (generally referred to as Congo or Congor people) eventually assimilated into the American Negro (a.k.a. Americo-Liberian) settler community following a difficult period of maladjustment to both the black American settler society and the indigenous Liberian community.[5]

The indigenous communities: The current Liberian population consists of seventeen ethnic groups: the Bassa, Kpelle, Kru, Gio, Grebo, Gola, Krahn, Vai, Gbandi, Kissi, Mano, Mende, Gio, Belle, Mandingo, Lorma, and Americo-Liberian (including West Indians, descendants of recaptured Africans and immigrants from other African countries). When Liberia held its constitutional convention on July 5, 1847, there were delegates from only three counties, Montserrado, Bassa, and Sinoe.[6] It meant that when Liberia became independent on July 26, 1847, the Republic consisted of only three counties or subdivisions with fewer than ten tribes or ethnic groups. Grand Cape Mount county joined the Republic in 1855[7] and Maryland county in 1857,[8] signaling the gradual coming together of the Liberian mosaic. Today, there are seventeen ethnic groups and fifteen counties or subdivisions.

It did not take long for the black American settlers to recognize that there were three major language groups in Liberia by the end of the nineteenth century: the Kraa or Kru from the southeast consists of Kru, Krahn, Grebo, Bassa, Belle, and Dey; the Mande group found in the west and northwest include the Mano, Gio, Kpelle, Lorma, Gbandi, Mende, Vai, and Mandingo; and finally, the Mel is predominated by the Gola and Kissi in western Liberia.[9]

For many decades during the nineteenth century, the black settlers from the west remained on the Atlantic coast and very seldom ventured into the interior parts of Africa. Perhaps, this is partly due to the fact that the land purchased by the ACS for the settlement of black Americans was situated along the Atlantic ocean. Therefore, the tribes most familiar to black settlers for a long time were the tribes that occupied the land they settled on; tribes like the Bassa, Kpelle, Grebo, Kru, Gola, Dey, and Vai. The mandingoes came from Musardu in the north to Liberia regularly to trade and eventually found in the black American settler community a trading partner.[10]

In the late nineteenth century, when the British and French began to partition West Africa to establish colonies, the Liberian government strategically formed alliances with the northern tribes and annexed their territories (Bong, Lofa, Nimba, and Grand Gedeh) to Liberia to avert colonization. Today, Liberia has fifteen subdivisions.

West Indian immigrants: In the mid-nineteenth century, immigrants began to come into Liberia from the West Indies. They came from places like the Virgin Islands, Guyana, Trinidad, Jamaica, and Barbados. The largest single recorded voyage of West Indians, 346 in number, arrived in Liberia in April 1865 from Barbados and were specifically settled in the township of Crozierville, about twenty miles outside Monrovia.[11] It is noteworthy that the immigrants from Barbados produced quite a number of prominent citizens: two presidents (Arthur Barclay and Edwin Barclay); a minister of health (Mai Wiles-Padmore); a minister of local government (E. Jonathan Goodrige); a popular journalist (Albert Porte); several presidents of the University of Liberia (including Rocheforte L. Weeks, Sr.); Burleigh Holder, Sr. (minister of defense and minister of national security); a Liberian Ambassador to the United States of America (George Padmore); a renown chief justice (Louis Arthur Grimes), a secretary of state (J. Rudolph Grimes); a former deputy minister of finance and well respected international lawyer (Gerald Padmore); creating a legacy that has continued to increase the number of professionals and politicians in this community.

For the West Indians, their culture was so similar to the Americo-Liberians that they did not allow themselves to be absorbed by the latter; instead, they chose the process of amalgamation whereby the two cultures virtually coexisted, influencing the food, language, values, and norms of the other. To the indigenous people, these two groups were indistinguishable.

West African immigrants: Then in the late nineteenth century and early twentieth century, Africans frustrated by the conditions of colonialism in their respective colonies, especially in West Africa, began to immigrate to Liberia en masse, especially from Guinea, Sierra Leone, Togo, Ghana, and Nigeria. The immigrants from Sierra Leone consisted largely of Creoles, members of the Sierra Leonean settler community. Members of this group, particularly the Creoles from Sierra Leone, quickly assimilated into the American settler society.

The Commonwealth of Monrovia, the seat of power in Liberia at the time, was ruled by white agents until 1839, when Thomas Buchanan, the first nonwhite governor, ascended to power. It is therefore always mind-boggling to read that freed black American slaves founded Liberia. Apparently, blacks (freed or enslaved) had no intention of chartering ships and moving back to Africa on their own. It would appear, from all the information available, that blacks played no part in the plan and organization of the ACS, nor the initial negotiation and procurement of the land in West Africa for resettlement. (The "Back to Africa" movement led by Marcus Garvey, the renown black Pan-Africanist, would start almost a hundred years later, during the second decade of the twentieth century.) The ACS was not formed to accommodate the dreams of black men; rather, the participation of the blacks in the repatriation process was to facilitate the agenda of the white population, which was primarily to remove blacks from the United States. The expectation of blacks, therefore, was that they would be willing to travel to Africa and settle on the land that had been acquired by the ACS.

By the late 1890s, when the black population in the United States continued to grow exponentially, reaching more than a million, the ACS decided to give up on its "back to Africa" program, especially since in almost a century the number of black Americans repatriated to Liberia had not exceeded thirty thousand.[12]

For several decades after the arrival of the American settlers, there were sporadic conflicts between the natives and the settlers regarding anything from land disputes to politics. These conflicts were grounded mainly in distrust by each group of the other. For instance, there were reports of illegal slave trade still going on along the West African coast, including the coast of Liberia, involving some of the Liberian tribes. Overcome by fear, in 1863 the Negro American settler government enacted a law to bar the natives and Europeans from trading along the Liberian coast. Of course, this action angered the native population because the restraint on trade further impoverished their communities. According to a speech by Edward Wilmot Blyden delivered at a reception held in his honor in Monrovia on January 21, 1897, some in the Americo-Liberian community, although angry with natives for frequent unprovoked attacks on the Americo-Liberian settlement, sympathized with the natives, whom they felt were in a disadvantageous position when it came to social, economic, and political power.[13]

The inattention to the critical but unresolved matter of unification and integration would come to haunt Liberia in years to come.

What the ACS never factored into its repatriation program was the fact the settlement of former slaves in Liberia brought together in one place the descendants of slaves and descendants of some who had collaborated with slave traders. The ACS was so preoccupied with the removal of blacks from the United States it never seriously considered the difficulties and tensions that would have accompanied the forced integration of two unlikely groups. On the one hand, the black Americans worried that they might be resold into slavery since the traffic persisted illegally. Some black Americans had been taught to embrace the false notion that slavery in America was better than freedom in Africa. The culture of the Deep South socialized blacks to believe that one's stature in a higher class was achieved and maintained by standing on the back of another, and that segregation and class distinction were acceptable modes of adaptation.

The desire of the American immigrants to hold on to the Western culture, although with no harmful intention, in the midst of a majority African population, would someday prove to be unwise. It would become a weapon used by demagogues and miscreants to infuse discord in the Liberian society.

The natives, on the other hand, believed that the presence of the black Americans would interfere with the freedom of tribesmen to control their destiny. In the decades preceding the settlement of black American immigrants, they had enjoyed unimpeded trade with the Europeans, did not have to pay taxes, and did not have to subscribe to formal western rules.

How then could anyone expect that by bringing the two groups together, the native Africans and the blacks from the West, the problem of the white guilt and the black victimization would automatically vanish? These two groups (the natives and the settlers), unprepared for what seemed to be a major cultural transformation, clashed often.

During the mid-nineteenth century when the population of the recaptured Africans grew to surpass the Americo-Liberian population, the latter decided to parcel out land to incoming recaptured slaves and other black immigrants in such a way that their respective settlements surrounded Monrovia. The new land-assignment policy consequently provided social distance between the Americo-Liberian enclave and the larger indigenous population on the outskirts. This arrangement allowed for a great deal of interaction between the natives (indigenous people) and the Congo people (or recaptured slaves) on a regular basis. Therefore, I believe that this might have led to the perception that the entire black immigrant community (including those from the United States and the West Indies) was of Congo origin; to the natives, there was no distinction in culture among the people who had come to their land by ship.[14]

Eventually, the words "Americo-Liberian" and "Congor" (a variation of Congo) came to be used interchangeably. And eventually, all black immigrants from the United States and West Indies, the recaptured Africans, some immigrants from other African countries who assimilated into the black American settler society, and some indigenous Liberians who attained higher education and adopted Western culture, collectively came to be referred to as "Congor People." It means that the word "America-Liberian" or "Congor" signifies one's social class and not necessarily one's ethnicity.

For instance, President Sirleaf stated in her address to the joint session of the United States Congress on March 15, 2006, that she is an indigenous Liberian; her mother was part German and part Kru, and her father was from the Gola tribe. Aside from the German heritage, she is an indigenous Liberian. But this is not how the ordinary Liberian understands ethnicity. To the average Liberian, President Sirleaf is America-Liberian (or Congor) simply because she is well educated; light in complexion; has a Western maiden name, and has occupied many prominent positions in government (even before the revolution). She attended one of the well- known high schools in the country (College of West Africa) and had a brother-in-law and a first cousin who were two of the most prominent doctors in the country in the 1970s. Her father (although indigenous) was a member of the Liberian Legislature during the Tubman administration.

It is interesting to note here that a lot of tribal families, especially those on the seacoast, bore Western last names either assigned to them by some missionary, black immigrants, or ship merchants doing business along the Liberian coast. The most popular Western name, even today, is "Johnson," a surname found in almost every subdivision in Liberia. Other Western names used by some indigenous people are Freeman, Bryant, Harmon, Baker, Greaves, Sharpe, Brown, Diggs, Thompson, and Sherman. Quite frankly, a lot of Liberians, ex-slaves and indigenous alike carry borrowed names.

When I was growing up, there were also prominent indigenous names such as Togba, Beysolow, Nagbe, Sayeh, Massaquoi, Boayue, Tamba, Sackor, Tweh, Nah, Fahngalo, Bropleh, Dukuly, Sirleaf, Kromah, Kamara, Tarpeh, Kiawu, Fahnbulleh, Gbarbea, Gbalazeh, Badio, Acolatse, Ziama, Toweh, Sackor, and Nimely. Most of the people who bear these names are directly or indirectly related to America-Liberians through marriage, especially those from the seacoast where the interaction with immigrants has persisted for more than a century and continues to persist. These are names you are likely to find in some of the best private and parochial schools in the country; these are names of people who held prominent positions in government alongside America-Liberians and other immigrants historically. Some could also afford to send their children to boarding schools abroad.

People may have contorted their faces or mispronounced the name, but they had no choice but to accept it.

If your last name was Western, you had to constantly answer questions about your relationship to some prominent America-Liberian person with the same last name, and that could be very annoying. In fact, no matter where we went to school, my mother always had to explain that our last name was Hammond and not Harmon. One day in 1977, my coworker, Joyce Mends-Cole, and I were discussing family, and we discovered that we both were related to "Cousin Fannie" (Fannie Speare) who resided on Carey Street in the heart of the capital. I said, "But she is Grebo; she is my father's first cousin." Cousin Fannie studied home economics and did a lot of catering from her home. People came in to pick up food of some sort throughout the day. Although she was fluent in English, she spoke Grebo in her home all the time. Her husband, Nathaniel Puo Speare, was the assistant postmaster general, and he was also Grebo.

"So how are you related to Cousin Fannie?" I asked.

She said, "My mother is a Harmon, and Cousin Fannie is related to the Harmons." She was right; a lot of the Harmons who came from Maryland County to Monrovia lived with Cousin Fannie until they got on their feet. So now, you must be as confused as I am. The point is, we are more intertwined in Liberia than we know.

Why should any of this matter anyway? Except for a few people who know my family background, most Liberians refer to me as Congor or America-Liberian, which I often acknowledge. Our father died when we were young, therefore our America-Liberian mother raised us the only way she knew how.

It is also interesting that by the turn of the twentieth century, intermarriage between America-Liberian women and indigenous men increased because for a long time most tribal families did not allow their girls to attend school for fear that they would become arrogant and disrespectful to their husbands. Instead, most indigenous girls were sent to "bush school" to learn to take care of their husbands and raise a family. Consequently, the well-educated indigenous men, with limited choices, married America-Liberian or other immigrant girls whose parents did not object to the union. Alternatively, the indigenous men chose a spouse from among the few educated indigenous girls whose enlightened and farsighted biological or foster parents sent them to school. I believe this trend, which steadily developed between the 1930s and 1960s, eventually became the catalyst for the emergence and expansion of the social stratification system in Liberia.

From the perspective of the general Liberian population, Congor people are the following:

1. The descendants of black immigrants from the West, as well as recaptured slaves, who have good formal education and access to wealth and power. Some of them have inherited wealth or accumulated wealth on their own. Usually light in complexion, they speak standard English and tend to study abroad.
2. The descendants of blacks from the West, as well as the recaptured Africans. They have a similar ethnic background as those in the first category, but some may have little money and little formal education. They tend to hold middle- and low-level government jobs or operate small businesses. They may be identified by physical appearance (such as fair complexion) and are likely to have a Western last name and a distinct accent.
3. Indigenous (or native) Liberians who have become successful. Individuals in this category tend to have good formal education, wealth, and sometimes power. The last name may or may not be indigenous. It appears that lifestyle is a major determining factor in this category.
4. Then there are those who are part-immigrant and part-indigenous. Individuals in this category tend to have a good formal education. They may or may not have an indigenous last name (especially if it is the mother who is indigenous). Some also have wealth and power.

It would seem, then, that the social designation in Liberia is not based solely on ethnic background, as in the past; instead, it is based on a combination of factors, including education, money, job, physical appearance, and lifestyle. Of course, we know that education and income are major determining factors for lifestyle.

Hence, the simplistic dichotomy we harbored as our understanding of social class in Liberia, based on ethnicity, has been gradually eroded by intermarriages, education, and the steady change in social behavior, significantly blurring the lines that used to distinguish between natives and immigrants.

CHAPTER 4

Fond Memories of Growing Up

Our parents were of different ethnic background, but there was never a reminder of the dissimilarity because they got along so well. My mother's paternal ancestor, Albert Chenoweth, from Muscogee Indian Territory in Arkansas, USA, arrived in Robertsport, Grand Cape Mount County, in 1887 with other immediate relatives. They were part-African and part Native American. My mother's maternal ancestor, Dublin Harvey, who also arrived in Liberia in the late nineteenth century from Virginia, quickly integrated with the Vai tribe in Grand Mount County and ended up with two sets of children, a total of fifteen, in both the Vai and Americo-Liberian communities.

My paternal grandfather, Yude Hammond, who was from the Grebo ethnic group, left his home at Hoffman Station, Maryland County, and relocated to Monrovia when he was a young adult. He operated a small launch along the St. Paul River, delivering supplies to the American settlements along the St. Paul riverbanks. Soon he met Lucelia, a young businesswoman from the Kru tribe who traded in gold and fine fabrics. They got married, bought land in downtown Monrovia, and constructed a two-story frame house on pillars, representing the popular architecture of the day introduced by the

American settlers. My father, John Payne Hammond, Sr., their only child, was born and raised in Monrovia.

We did not know our paternal grandparents. Our paternal grandfather died while my father was a young schoolboy, and his mother had to take over the reins to see him through Liberia College. After school, she sent him to tailoring classes to occupy his time. She lived downstairs with her relatives and gave my father the entire top floor, where he allowed some of his friends from the out-of-town settlements to live free and attend college. Upon graduation, my father worked for the Internal Revenue Service as assistant director, while also operating his tailoring business, a popular trade at the time. For some reason, he only made suits and preferred to order shirts from Bella Hess and Montgomery Ward in the United States.

I recall that Liberians were industrious when I was a child. We went to the seamstress and the tailor to make clothes and hairdressers to get our hair done for special occasions. We bought our raincoats, rain boots, and umbrellas from Mr. William Ketter on Randall Street and good-quality shoes from Mr. James L. York down near the waterside. Both men were members of the African Methodist Episcopal (AME) Church, like my father, so he felt he had a duty to support their businesses. We often bought retail foodstuffs from Ernest Dennis on Randall Street, or Mr. Brownell, a Grebo merchant (a.k.a. Solo baby) on Carey Street. If you forgot to buy all your groceries on Saturday, you could count on one of these merchants to crack their back or side door open and slip out a loaf of bread or a can of tomato paste. Back then, the Blue Laws introduced by the American settlers did not allow commerce and sports on Sunday.

My paternal grandmother died four years after my father met my mother. According to my mother, the day my grandmother died, her Kru relatives were digging all over the yard to find the pots of gold the old lady had buried in various places around the front yard. There was no access to banks in those days. Therefore, the folks used to save money and valuables at home under the mattress, or place them in the care of merchants, or just simply bury them in the ground. Unfortunately for the relatives, they did not find any gold.

We knew when we were very young children that our parents placed a high value on education. Both parents walked with my brother, John, and me to the Assemblies of God Mission School (AGM) at the corner of Carey and Buchanan Streets the first day we enrolled, and they kept coming each day until they were satisfied that we were fully adjusted and would remain in school. Missionaries operated some of the best schools, perhaps because they reinforced a lot of the values taught at home. The government itself seemed to rely a lot on missionaries (both local and foreign) to run the educational system. In addition to public schools, there were many parochial schools funded by the National Baptist Convention and the AME. Church (both African American organizations); the Southern Baptist Convention; The Catholic diocese; the Methodists; the Episcopalians; and the Lutherans (most of whom were from Europe and various parts of the United States).

My first-grade teacher, Louise Gittens, would inspect our clothes, hair, face, nails, and shoes before we entered the classroom. All the students had to greet her, pledge allegiance to the flag, and then say a prayer (all in unison) before we began our lessons. You did not have to be wealthy to enter the classroom, but you had to be neat. At recess, we would play *na foh* (a local foot game) or run across the street to Miz Eugenia (Eugenia Cooper Shaw) to buy popcorn and Monrovia rock (a local hard candy). Na foh was fun, but it ruined the sole of our shoes. We played anyway, due to peer pressure, and just simply inserted a piece of cardboard paper, cut in the shape of the sole of the shoe, as a stopgap measure until the next shopping trip to the shoe store. The cardboard was a major disappointment on a rainy day.

I used to stand near the sidewalk in front of the house to wait for my father to ascend the slope on Benson Street toward Randall Street around two fifteen each weekday afternoon, at the end of his workday. The government workday went from 8:00 a.m. to 2:00 p.m. The government office hours ran straight through from 8:00 a.m. to 2:00 p.m. without lunch. I always knew when to expect him to get off work because the local radio routinely played "Tequila" at two o'clock as the introduction to a program. First, I would see the top of his hat as he ascended the slope and, gradually, his entire body. He was always well dressed and always wore a hat. As he made it up the slope toward Randall Street, I would jump and clap, anxious to tell him what had happened at school that day. He would have lunch, take a nap, and then help us with homework.

Our parents allowed us to go out and play with other children in the backyard when we had done our homework and chores. At age six, my main chores were to clean my room and help my mother set the table for dinner. After dinner, we went out to play. There were no fences. Every backyard in the four-square block of houses formed a common area. We would sing, dance, or play hopscotch. The songs we sang reflected the diverse culture in which we lived. We sang "Nana Kru," a song about a young man pleading with his bride, for whom he had paid a dowry, to get into his canoe; we sang "Mary Mack," a song about a little girl who asked the maid for fifty cents to see the elephant jump. The elephant "jumped so high, it touched the sky, and did not come back until the Fourth of July." And we sang about how an aunt called her niece who liked walking about the streets and advised her to take time in life because she had a long way to go.

Other times, we would sit in groups under the silver moon and listen to tales from the village. We sometimes pledged to share our food, especially meat, to hear these traditional stories. We knew that the storytellers sometimes made up tales to get the food, but we would sit there attentively listening to every word and enjoying every animation. My favorite tale was always about "Why Spider Has a Small Waist."

The storyteller would begin with "Once upon a time." you had to say, "Time," for the storyteller to continue. Spider lived in a village situated between two other villages. One day, Spider received an invitation from each of his two neighbors to attend a feast to be held on the same day at the same time in their respective villages. He wanted to attend both, so he tied a rope around his waist and gave one end to the village on his right, and the other end to the village on his left. He asked each neighboring village to pull the rope when the meal was ready. He gambled on the fact that Africans were never on time. Therefore, it was not likely that both parties would start at noon. His calculation was wrong. Both villages finished the preparations on time and began pulling the rope with what seemed like equal strength. Spider did not move from where he stood in the middle of his village. He tried to call out for the neighbors to stop pulling the rope, but no one could hear him due to the noise of drums at the respective parties. All the people in his village had already gone to one of the two parties. As his neighbors pulled, Spider's waist got smaller and smaller, and he eventually dropped to the ground. When the people in his village returned late at night, they found Spider unconscious but still alive. The moral of the tale is do not be a greedy spider. Learn to prioritize and make choices instead of trying to grab it all.

Both parents were disciplinarians, and both disciplined us when we did something that would become an impediment to our moral growth. They were kind and loving parents, but very firm about the need to respect the rights of others. Neither parent could tolerate stealing or lying. My mother used to say, "A liar is a thief, and a thief is a murderer."

There was a lot of time to play, but there were also a lot of little rules and admonitions that parents often reminded us of in the following expressions: "Do unto others as you would have them do unto you." "Don't talk about others unless you have something good to say." "Don't talk with food in your mouth." "What goes around comes around." "Don't wash your dirty laundry and waste the water in the front yard." "If you cannot hear, you will feel." "Don't go to a party hungry, so you don't act greedy." "Be satisfied with what you have, so begging and stealing do not become your habit." "The wall is not your napkin." "Make your bed and clean your room in the morning before you come out to start the day." "Don't leave dirty dishes in the kitchen sink overnight." "Always wash your hands after you use the bathroom." "If you need or want something that belongs to someone else, ask the owner for permission and get approval before you take or use it." My mother used to say, "You need to learn universal rules so that you will be able to live anywhere in the world."

My mother also used to say that she did not like to punish us for breaking the rules, but if she were derelict in her duty, she would be like the mother of a young man hanged for the commission of murder. I still don't know whether this is a real story or just an urban legend. But as it goes, this young man had been sentenced to death by hanging for homicide; he was asked by the chaplain whether he had anything to say before his death. He replied, "Yes," and asked for the noose to be removed from his neck so that he could bend down and whisper what he had to say in the ear of his mother. When the mother leaned forward to hear what her son had to say, he bit off her ear and said, "Every time the people see this woman with one ear, they will remember that she is the mother who failed to discipline her son." He concluded by saying, "If my mother had corrected my behavior as she should have done, I would not have been condemned to die today."

CHAPTER 5

Off to Boarding School

When I was only seven years old, my father suddenly took ill. After spending a week at home in bed, he asked my mother to take him to the hospital. I stood on the stairs and watched as my mother and my godmother, Maylue Reeves, walked my father to the waiting vehicle. After two weeks in the hospital, he passed away. Miz Maylue had white dresses made for my sister, Lucelia, and me for the funeral and took us to live with her family for several months after the burial so that my mother could have time to grieve and readjust. I did not understand death; I thought that my father would wake up after a while. But it did not happen.

My mother was now a thirty-four-year-old widow with six children, faced with the challenge of going to court to assert her rights and the rights of her children to property that our father had inherited from his parents. Each of our paternal grandparents left the documents for properties they owned in the care of their respective traditional family head. My mother eventually prevailed in the cases that involved properties that she could easily identify. Although we inherited land owned by our grandparents as private property, as well as communal land commonly owned by extended relatives, my mother, in her good judgment, only sought to claim the rights in property owned free and clear by our father at the time of his death.

My mother decided that it would be best to send us to local boarding schools, which she did on a staggered basis over a period of three years. She also decided that we should be sent to different schools to broaden our social network. I received a scholarship, with the help of my mother's pastor, Rev. Samuel Stubblefield, to attend Ricks Institute, a Baptist mission school, about twenty-two miles outside the capital city. I was ten years old, in the fifth grade, and could barely take care of myself. My mother arranged with an older student to help me take care of my clothes and hair. It was not unusual to have classmates five or six years older. Students whose family did not have the financial means tended to start school very late.

The single largest group of students on Ricks were from Monrovia, but the beauty of it all was that the student body was representative of every subdivision and every tribe in the entire country. There was so much to learn from all these different students; I saw a creek for the first time, and my new-found friend, Lady, from Bensonville, showed me how to draw water from a creek without falling in. We learned to open cans on concrete, open a soda bottle on the door lock, boil cassava in a bucket with a portable water heater, and make hair conditioner from plants in the forest. Some girls knew how to make quilts and do embroidery work, and others could bake and cook very well. Although it was obvious that students from the capital city had a social edge since they had more access to extracurricular activities, the school administrators discouraged discrimination of any kind. You could get punished for name-calling or bullying. All students were required to wear a uniform to class and eat the same food in the mess hall.

There were girls from the settlements (also called Upriver) who would conduct informal or mock trials when clothing or textbooks went missing. I was always fascinated by how they were so adept at getting students to confess to the act and return the property. Perhaps this was the beginning of my interest in justice.

On one occasion, I went home for clothes my sister and I needed to wear to a special upcoming event, but my mother said she had already sent the clothes by a young girl who claimed that we had sent her for the clothes. The girl had specifically described the dresses she wanted my mother to give her; it was our Sunday best. I then recalled that a few months back, we had attended an event in Monrovia during the holidays, and a girl I barely knew had complimented my clothing. Somehow, she fit the description my mother gave me. At age fifteen, I had become a private investigator. I set out to find this girl. I finally came across someone who knew where she lived. As I approached the yard, she fled. I knew then that I was right. I walked up to her mother and explained my suspicion; the mother quietly left me, went into the house, and returned with the clothes. I was shocked. In the end, the girl admitted to deceiving my mother. Later that evening, the girl's parents brought her to our house to apologize for what she had done. We accepted the apology, but my mother subsequently donated the clothes to a local orphanage, and that ended the story.

My first two principals at Ricks Institute, Joseph Ellworth DeShield and Augustus Marwieh, were Liberians; they received financial support mainly from the Liberian Baptist Missionary and Educational Convention (LBMEC) and did their utmost with very limited funding. Each served for a year, consecutively, after I enrolled.

The third principal, and the one who would remain until my graduation from high school, was T. Eugene Oody from Tennessee, USA. Other missionaries from various parts of the United States joined him within a short time after his arrival. Most of the missionaries had master's degrees. The Southern Baptist Convention provided the financial support for the school, augmented by what was already being provided by the LBMEC. The increased funding suddenly transformed the school. In addition to academics, the new management introduced extracurricular activities in agriculture, music, business, and competitive team sports. A yellow school bus was provided to transport students to sporting events off- campus. The dietician packed brown-bag lunches (e.g., ham and cheese sandwich, punch, and a candy bar) to take to off campus events, so we did not have to run the risk of consuming food or drinks that would make us sick. Students used lawnmowers, replacing hoes and other manual implements used to cut grass. Academic excellence was prioritized; consequently, Ricks became a first-rate school under the leadership of Mr. Oody. The basic difference between Mr. Oody and his Liberian predecessors was that he had the financial support to do what was required.

From the sixth grade, I had always had the second- highest average in the class, and that was just fine. But one day during the first semester of the junior year of high school, Mr. Oody summoned me to his office. He told me that the male student who usually topped the class had returned after being out sick for several weeks, and it did not appear that he would be able to pull up his grades enough to resume his position in the class. Therefore, he was telling me, as he had already told two other young men in the class, that any one of the three of us could become the dux if that person outperformed the other two. The dux of the junior class became the senior prefect of the school during the senior year; this required the student to assist the administration with matters of student affairs.

At the end of the junior year, I took first place in the class and became the senior prefect. The senior class was more challenging than the year before. I needed time to focus on my studies rather than being bogged down with students' attendance at assembly and the like. I asked the principal if I could be relieved of my post as senior prefect. He flatly denied my request. He said something to the effect that the responsibility came with the territory.

By this time, I had an A grade in every subject, except physics. I contacted a Sudanese immigrant student in the class, called Joe, to help me with physics after school so that I could pull up my grade in that subject from a B to an A. He agreed, and the next test we took, I earned an A in physics. When the word got out that I had become the frontrunner, the pressure came to bear. President Tubman, the head of the nation, had accepted the invitation to be the keynote speaker at our graduation, and some of the students had openly expressed their disapprobation of a girl being the valedictorian on this auspicious occasion. It was the first time I became aware that gender was a serious social issue.

I went home for the weekend and explained to my mother what had happened. She smiled and said, "You think those guys will help you get ahead of another guy?"

"What should I do?" I asked her.

She said, "It depends on what is important to you at this time. Do you want to be liked by everyone, or do you want to be head of the class? The way it looks, you cannot have both in this situation. It is not to suggest that you abandon your friends; rather, it is to suggest that when you have to make a tough choice, you might want to prioritize by considering what is more important at a particular point in time."

I went back to campus even more determined to head the class.

On Monday afternoon, following my weekend at home, I went to the library to meet Joe, my physics tutor, but he was unusually absent. When I finally got in touch with him it was clear to me that he would no longer be able to provide tutoring sessions for unspecified reasons. I stood on the mezzanine of the administration building thinking, *"Yeah, my mother was right; this is a gender competition, and from now on I am on my own.*

In the end, I did become the valedictorian of the class.

On the day of my graduation, I was sick with malaria and could barely stand due to a very high fever. I didn't know what to do; *my mother would have a fit if I did not show up*, I thought. The guests had started arriving on campus, and I was still in bed. One of my roommates, Rita Cooper, came over and encouraged me to go into the shower and drench myself in cold water to break the fever. The fever immediately went away. I knew that I was still not well, but I now felt strong enough to attend the program and deliver my speech.

I recall that the topic was the dignity of labor in education; I don't recall much more than that. I remember that the audience clapped at various times, and in the end, I received three scholarship offers, one of which afforded me the opportunity to attend school in the United States The following year, I matriculated at Cuttington College in Suacoco (Liberia) for a semester and then transferred to Carson-Newman College (CNC) in Jefferson City, Tennessee, in the fall. At CNC, I would later discover that the experiences during my senior year in high school had adequately prepared me for adjustment to life in a strange land with even more challenging social issues.

CHAPTER 6

College and my Bout with Race Relations in the US

Mr. Oody, the principal of my high school, his wife (Betty Oody) my mother, and my siblings were all at the airport to see me off to the United States. Before then, I had only traveled to the neighboring West African country of Sierra Leone. The anxiety was high, as I did not know what to expect when I finally arrived in this great United States of America. Mr. Oody's daughter, Arvilla, who was also on her way to Carson-Newman College (CNC) to begin her sophomore year, boarded the Pan Am flight with me. I don't recall where Arvilla stayed for the two weeks while we waited for school to officially open, but the Oodys arranged for me to stay with Mrs. Oody's sister, Louise Cannon, and her family in a small town called Loudon, Tennessee, a community populated predominantly by whites. We went out to several places around the town, including church, and I don't recall seeing more than one black person just walking randomly in the street. The family was very kind and warm and did their utmost to ensure that I was comfortable.

One day as I sat at the kitchen table looking through the Christmas catalog, I felt a sudden sting on my upper left arm; when I turned to look, the three-year-old boy sitting next to me had taken the butter knife and scraped my skin off by a half of an inch. The mother had her back turned, as she washed dishes in the kitchen sink; she turned quickly to see why I had said, "Ouch!" When she saw that the kid had scraped my skin, her face became flushed. "Why did you do that, Kevin?" she asked. He replied, "I am just trying to scrape the dirt off Chris. She has all this dirt on her skin." The mother said, "But that is how her skin is. She is a different color from you. Her parents are like that too." "No," he said, "she is not supposed to be like that." The mother just stood there not knowing what else to say or do. I broke the impasse and said, "It is all right; I know that his actions are completely innocent. He is only trying to understand the world around him, as I did when I was just as young."

Then I recounted to her how when I was five years old, my parents enrolled me at the Assemblies of God Mission School operated by white missionaries. It was the first time that I recalled seeing a white person. When I returned home at the end of my first day, my parents wanted to know whether I liked the school. I told them that I liked the school, but I did not like the principal. "What's wrong with the principal?" my mother asked. I said, "He bathed himself in Clorox bleach and straightened his hair with a hot comb, and his eyes are blue." My parents laughed raucously. When they were done laughing, they tried to explain that this is how white people are supposed to look and explained how people in various parts of the world have different physical characteristics.

I did not believe the explanation they gave. My impression was that these were black people who had done strange things to themselves. Therefore, I wanted to go to another school. It was not until I became an adult that my mother told me how she and my father had had to escort me to school for a whole month before I accepted that the principal and a couple of other missionaries were normal people. So, like me, this little kid in Loudon, Tennessee, was doing his best to understand the world. At this point in the child's life, he was not exhibiting behavior that he had learned; rather, he had developed a perception attributable to his limited understanding of the world around him. It would be up to the parents to shape his perception. It was my first lesson in race relations in America.

When I finally moved on campus, I quickly realized that there were a lot of "Kevins" around, except that they were young adults. A lot of the girls in the dorm often called me by the name of another black female commuter student, irrespective of the fact that I was the only black female in the dorm. Often, the student whose identity was mixed up with mine was an entirely different shade of black. I wondered, *How could they mistake me for someone who is much darker or much lighter?* It didn't take long for me to realize that I had the same problem; all white people looked alike to me. To distinguish the girls in the dorm, I had to go by the color and length of the hair. I looked in a magazine to learn how to identify the various hair colors, like blonde, brunette, auburn, platinum blonde, and the like. Like the situation with Kevin, it would have been unreasonable to become offended by what seemed to have grown out of ignorance or innocence.

But then, other forms of racism were not so innocuous and just simply could not be tolerated. A Cameroonian student by the name of Mbong Valentine, a former student of Ricks Institute, had been at CNC for a year and was very popular because he played soccer. He said to me, "Look, you will be asked a lot of foolish questions about Africa. Don't bother to explain. Just give back a foolish answer." He told me a story of how during his first few weeks on campus, a group of boys used to come and stand in front of the shower stall as he showered himself. He would see them, through the opaque shower curtain, walk out of the bathroom just as he cut off the water.

One day, Mbong decided that after he completed his shower, he would let the water continue to run and then abruptly open the shower curtain while the group was still standing there. There must have been about five or six young men standing there when he opened the curtain; all ran out except two. He stood in front of them, completely nude, and in his deep bass voice, he asked, "What are you looking for?" He said one of them stood as though he was a statue; the other stammered slowly and said, "The rumor around is that you have a tail." He smiled and looked at me in amusement as I anxiously waited to hear how he responded to the guys. He said, "I just told them, yes I did have a tail, but I had surgery to remove it." "Did they believe you?" I asked. "I don't know, and I don't care. I am here to learn and not to teach."

I could tell that Mbong was concerned about me since I was the only black in a dorm of 250 girls. Mr. Oody's daughter, the only person I knew, was in another dormitory. The five African Americans females enrolled at CNC were commuter students who did not concern themselves with what happened in the dormitories, because at the end of the school day, they went home. My home was about nine thousand miles away.

In high school, there was not much concern about racism, tribalism, and the like. Even where it flared up, the school authorities took action to quell it. Therefore, living in a place where restaurants did not want to serve you because you were of a different race was hard to understand and accept. Young black men could not go to the only barbershop in town to get a haircut. The storekeeper wanted you to pay for clothes without trying them on, and a young black man would get arrested for driving below the speed limit if a white female passenger was in his car.

A couple of weeks later, Mbong came looking for me in the cafeteria and wanted to talk. When we got outside, he turned to me asked, "Does your roommate cry a lot?" I said, "Yes, why?" He looked at me for a few minutes and said, "She is afraid of you because you're an African." That was the craziest thing I had ever heard. "What do you mean?" I asked. He said, "When you go back to the dorm this evening, ask her about what I have told you." My knees were shaking as I walked back from the cafeteria to my room. *How do I handle something as crazy as this situation?* I thought. *What does he mean that my roommate is afraid of Africans?*

The dorm room was a small nine-foot-by-twelve-foot space with the window positioned directly opposite the door as you entered. On the left wall was a twin bed, and at its head near the window, there was a small bookshelf mounted on the wall, with a desk and chair below. At the foot of the bed, near the door, was a closet and the chest drawers. On the right side of the room, the space assigned to me, was a replica of what was on the left. As I entered the room, my roommate was making up her bed and sobbing. I greeted her and sat on my bed. "What's wrong?" I asked. She wouldn't answer. I asked if she was homesick. She sat on the bed and opened up in a way I could not have imagined.

"Homesickness is just a part of it," she said. "I feel that I am the only unfortunate student in the dorm since I am the only one with a black roommate. I am from a family that held slaves; therefore, I am not used to sharing anything with a black person. In fact, this is the closest physical contact I have had with a black person. Not only do I dislike blacks, but I am particularly afraid of Africans because all of my life I have been told they are cannibals and live in trees. At night, I am afraid to sleep because I think that you will get up to harm me."

At this point, I had heard enough. "So, what do you want me to do?" I asked.

"It is best for you to move out," she responded. I told her to wait, and I would be back.

I had heard that there had been only one black female boarding student (African American) enrolled a couple of years before my arrival, but she could not handle the racially charged environment, so she left the school after just one semester.

I walked down the long hallway and headed to the apartment of the dorm matron, Mrs. Day. I had been taught to think carefully before taking action and to always defer to authority when a situation got out of control. At the end of the hallway, I made a right turn, walked ten more feet, and stood in front of the door to my left. I wavered a bit before I knocked on the door to Mrs. Day's apartment because my short stay in the States had taught me that the mind-set of Mrs. Day might not be too different from my roommate's, and if this was true, then I would be embarking on an exercise in futility.

Mrs. Day welcomed me in the living room of the small apartment and offered me a seat. As I explained to her what had transpired between my roommate and me, I could tell that she was most embarrassed. We sat at a right angle, and she positioned her left hand on her left cheek, almost as though to hide her face. It was dusk, and she had not turned on the lights; therefore, it was difficult to read her facial expressions. After I explained, and it was evident that she did not know what to say or do, and probably had no solution, I told her that I had already thought of a solution. Relieved, she said, "What is the solution?"

"I want my roommate to move out tonight," I said, "because it would be easier for her to find a roommate since she has told almost everyone that she suspects that I am a cannibal; if she does not move out tonight, I will eat her." Mrs. Day flew out of the room before I could complete my sentence. As she left, she told me to wait, and she would be back. I stood up and switched on the lights and sat back down for what appeared to be fifteen or twenty minutes, and still Mrs. Day had not come back. I decided to go back to my room to see what was going on; perhaps Mrs. Day was reading the riot act to my roommate. As I approached the room, I realized that Mrs. Day and my roommate had nearly moved all of her belongings out of the room.

The next day, when I saw Mbong, he was beaming. "I hear you were planning for a big feast last night, huh?" We both burst into laughter.

"News certainly does spread quickly around here," I said. "I must give you credit, Mbong. You are a good teacher." I walked away.

In the next few months, Joe, another Liberian student, introduced me to an African American commuter student named Rebecca Wells, popularly called Becky. She lived across the train tracks with her parents, William and Geneva Tate, whom she called Unkie and Gega, respectively. Gega was the mispronunciation of Geneva by Becky when she was only three years old, and the name stuck. All the other African students on campus, including me, also called Becky's parents Unkie and Gega.

After class one Friday afternoon, I walked home with Becky, whose parents immediately took to me and suggested that we go back to my dorm to get some clothes so I could spend the weekend. It was the beginning of my home away from home. There was something about the food (the collard greens, corn bread, potato salad, and fried chicken); the language (I ain't, y'all, etc.); the old spiritual songs ("Steal Away to Jesus," "Climbing Jacob's Ladder," "Gimme dah Ole Time Religion"); and the general mannerisms that reminded me of the Americo-Liberian settler community back in Liberia.

Almost everyone in the little black community was related somehow, and it was not unusual to go next door to borrow anything you needed urgently. Gega's house was on the top of the hill. Therefore, if I walked to her without stopping by the other houses to say hello, they would already have a complaint on me by the time I got to the top of the hill.

I was so fortunate that Gega was a hairdresser. Almost every weekend, she would help me shampoo my thick, long hair and straighten it with a hot comb. I could not manage it myself.

For short holidays like Easter and Thanksgiving, we would sometimes receive invitations from missionaries, formerly assigned in Liberia, to visit with them for a couple of days, or travel home with other students. In response to one of such invitations, Joe Weah, Ben Harris, and I went to visit the former vice principal of Ricks and his wife in a small town in South Carolina. It was an invitation we could not turn down, for they were such delightful people. We rented a car for the trip. We arrived in South Carolina on Thursday and spent Friday and part of Saturday sightseeing. On Saturday evening, the missionary couple left us at the home of a black family because they had to attend an important church meeting. They picked us up after several hours, and we all called it a day.

Then, the next morning as we sat eating breakfast, we noticed that the vice principal was not eating his food. He kept poking his fork in the scrambled egg. The three of us stopped eating and stared at him. Then he finally broke down and told us that he stayed a long time at the church meeting on Saturday evening because there was a disagreement among the members as to whether we should be allowed to attend the Sunday morning service. It was an all-white church, and the majority of the members decided that they did not want blacks worshipping with them. He said that he wanted to be defiant and take us to the worship service, but he thought about the four black girls who were bombed in the church basement in Alabama only a few years back and decided that he did not want to expose us to danger. The only question we asked was "Was that the same church that sent you and your wife to Liberia as missionaries?" When he answered, "Yes," we thanked him for the invitation to visit and left.

While Joe drove us back to East Tennessee, we could not stop talking about what had happened in South Carolina. We were debating as to whether the missionaries were as prejudice and hateful as the majority of the members of the church. "How could the missionaries be members of the church and not be like those people?" one of the guys asked. He had a good point. But I think that missionaries often think that they go to Africa to change us; most often, we change them. I felt that those missionaries may have been like the members of the church before they left for Africa, but their interaction with us broadened their perspective of people beyond that little town in South Carolina. I truly believed that when they returned from Africa, they realized for the first time that the people who needed religion were those right in their church and their little town.

Within a few weeks, I had joined a few organizations on campus and made friends with a lot of people, irrespective of race. I figured if I had to live in a predominantly white college town, I might as well make the best of it until I decided otherwise. Obviously, all my friends in the dorm (Donna, Linda, and Ellen) were white, since I was the only black female boarding student during my freshman year. We did a lot of things together, on and off campus. I recall how they followed me around to see how I would react when I saw my first snow. I was also very anxious because I had never seen snow before. When it finally snowed, I left class early so they would not take pictures of me looking stupefied. Little did I know, they were trailing me from a distance, observing closely and giggling in anticipation of the unusual.

Suddenly, I approached a slope and continued to strut as though I had lived with snow all my life, not wanting to be identified as one of the students who had never seen snow. Before I knew what was happening, I had landed on my butt at the bottom of the slope with both feet in the air. My books were scattered all over the huge parking lot. Each time I tried to get up, I fell back down, not understanding that my smooth-bottomed shoes provided no support. Finally, I looked up and saw Donna and Linda standing over me, fighting to hold back the laughter. Then, the three of us just started laughing out of control. When we were done laughing, they helped me to my feet, and we headed for the dorm. After I connected with these girls, I realized that once you are willing to move past the color barrier, you will find that there are people in other races who are just like you, with the same interests, ideas, feelings, and concerns. The more we connected, the less conscious I was of the color of their skin. They disliked racism as much I did and would often walk out of a restaurant with me if it appeared that the proprietor was racially biased.

Within a few weeks, I had gotten used to the bland food and heavy chunks of soft chicken flesh served in the cafeteria. I learned quickly that chicken tetrazzini was a casserole dish put together with leftover chicken. I also learned that *stay put* meant just stay where you are and don't do anything, and that *rock bottom* meant to drop in prices. I stopped trying to find the meaning of certain phrases in the dictionary when I discovered that even professors used slang in the classroom. Both white and black students picked up on some of my strange vocabulary, such as *scobee* when I meant "sneakers"; *dash* when I meant a "tip" (gratuity); *chunk* when I meant "throw"; and *I am coming to go,* instead of saying "I am leaving" or "I am about to leave."

Early in the second semester, my estranged roommate approached me in the cafeteria, very apologetic for what had transpired at the beginning of the school year; she wanted to make amends. My African Americans friends who sat with me for lunch were furious and quite astounded that I would be so tolerant and forgiving of behavior that they termed "despicable and unforgivable." In the end, we decided to hear her out, release her of her psychological burden, and let her go her happy way. One of the guys just simply said, "Let go and be happy."

CHAPTER 7

A Glimpse of yet
Another America

At the end of my freshman year, I decided that I would go to live with a relative in Washington, DC, work part-time, and attend summer classes at Howard University, a historically black university. A couple of my friends who attended Howard had convinced me that at Howard I would not have to deal with racial issues. When I left Tennessee that summer, I planned on not going back to Carson-Newman College (CNC) but instead transferring my credits to Howard, or another school in the Northeast, and enrolling in the fall as a full-time student. My mother tried to convince me to remain at CNC. She believed that if I could overcome the hardships at CNC, as I did during my senior year in high school, I would become a better and stronger person and would be more prepared for more challenging times in the future. That was a hard sell for an nineteen-year-old.

My relative lived in a one-bedroom apartment in a building called the Diplomat at 2420 Sixteenth Street, Northwest. I was introduced to a Liberian girl, named Matilda Green, who had also registered for classes at Howard University for the summer and who lived with her parents at the corner of Sixteenth and U Streets, four blocks from where I lived. She instructed me to get on the S-2 bus in front of my building and then get off at the corner of Sixteenth and U, where she would join me to take a transfer bus along U Street all the way to Seventh Street, and then another transfer bus to the Howard Campus. U Street was known at the time to be an area infested with drug and prostitution activities, and each day we stood at the bus stop at the corner, we said a prayer.

As we stood in line waiting to register for our classes on the Howard University campus, I recall thinking that this was the first time since I left Africa that I had seen so many black people in one place. But as we began to attend classes and interact more and more, I realized that even Howard had its share of problems; that even at Howard, prejudice and discrimination lurked in the crevices of the campus. Even Howard had students who judged other students by the color of their skin and by nationality, although it was certainly not the school's policy.

Before I left Tennessee for the summer, I had confided in my friend Donna that I might consider transferring to a historically black college or university. She tried to discourage me, arguing that black schools discriminated against Africans and dark-skinned African Americans. She specifically mentioned that a historically black university in Tennessee was known for encouraging what she called the "blue vein society." "What is that?" I asked. She explained that this was where opportunities would be available only to a black person whose skin was so light that the veins showed through the skin, appearing dark blue. I recall being very defensive and dismissive of what she was saying as propaganda to divide the black race.

Now at Howard, I observed firsthand what Donna meant. Interestingly, there were layers of segregation. The students first segregated themselves by regions, then nationalities, and then skin color: there were the Africans, the West Indians, and the Afro Americans (the generally preferred designation at the time). One young African student told me that his father was a wealthy African chief and had deliberately sent him to a black school so that he would not experience the humiliation of racial discrimination in a predominantly white academic environment. He was trying to figure out why other blacks did not embrace him. I was reluctant to tell him that what he was experiencing was not deliberate; our brothers and sisters in the US were haunted by the vestiges of slavery, like all of us.

Then among the black Americans, students were segregated by skin color and social class; the less privileged ones were more likely to be dark-skinned, first in the family to attend college, and lived in the inner city. At times, a few African Americans from each of these groups would venture to break the social barrier (especially those who considered themselves Pan Africanists), but generally, and sadly, the mode of adaptation was subconscious or unintentional segregation. I often wondered how much of the segregation was imposed by the culture of our host country and how much of it grew out of our primordial tendency as humans to be drawn to people who are similar to us.

At the college in Tennessee, the Africans and African Americans were a close-knit group. Perhaps because we were a small subgroup in a predominantly white population, we felt the need to unite and protect one another.

During the rare occasion at Howard when blacks of diverse background would get into a discussion on the slave trade, Africans would often be blamed for the plight of blacks in the diaspora because, as the argument goes, "the Africans sold us into slavery." Every time I heard this allegation, I wondered whether the African Americans realized that victims of the slave trade remained in West Africa just as there were those transported on the slave ships. For centuries, generation after generation, many families cried and mourned for their young children who went out to play, or to run an errand, or bathe in the river and were never seen again.

I recall a story told by one of my Liberian friends whose family is originally from Yoruba land, now part of modern-day Nigeria. She recounted that her family had, over several decades in the nineteenth century, traveled to Sierra Leone to follow up on leads of a sighting of their very young daughter who had been kidnapped from Yoruba land and taken into slavery. Because most of the reports of her sighting had been somewhere in Sierra Leone, where many believed the ship first docked after her abduction, the family settled there for many years, hoping to find the little girl. At the end of the nineteenth century, they finally gave up the search and immigrated to Liberia. Perhaps, today, some of the descendants of that little Yoruba girl live somewhere in Europe, North America, or the West Indies, but the pain of her abduction continued to be passed down from one generation to the next among the relatives she left behind.

Interestingly, one of the two classes I enrolled in at Howard that summer was a course in black literature, and one of the heated topics of discussion was the concept of *Negritude*. Negritude was developed and introduced by Leopold Senghor of Senegal, Aime Cesaire of Martinique, and Leon Damas of French Guyana, three young black intellectuals pursuing an education in France during the early 1930s. Professor Eleanor Turpin told us how these three young men of diverse backgrounds came together and developed a philosophy that would focus on the shared values and physical characteristics of the black race to the extent that it would become an affirmation of the "self.". In my understanding of the mandate from these black scholars, it was not a call to indict and hate the white race but, rather, an urging for blacks all over the world to become introspective on the path to discovering the inner self.

But a more explosive discussion on one of those hot summer days in Professor Turpin's class was the discussion of the poem, *The Middle Passage*, by Robert Hayden, an African American poet. A portion of the poem reads thus:

Aye lad, and I have seen those factories,
Gambia, Rio Pong, Calabar;
Have watched the artful mongos baiting traps
Of war wherein the victor and the vanquished

Were caught as prizes for our barracoons.
Have seen the nigger kings whose vanity
And greed turned wild black hides of Fellatah,
Mandingo, Ibo, Kru to gold for us.

And there was one King -Anthracite we named him –
fetish face beneath French parasols
of brass and orange velvet, impudent mouth
whose cups were carven skulls of enemies:

He'd honor us with drum and feast and conjo
and palm-oil-glistening wenches deft in love,
and for tin crowns that shone with paste,
red calico and German silver trinkets

Would have the drums talk war and send
His warriors to burn the sleeping villages
and kill the sick and old and lead the young
in coffles to our factories.

I was shocked and visibly shaken as I listened as another student read this graphic poem about the pain and suffering surrounding the kidnapping and lengthy and horrific experiences of the transport of human cargo across the Atlantic Ocean. I had never heard about the role of African kings and chiefs in the slave trade. I sat there thinking, *The fact that the Kings participated in the slave trade automatically institutionalized this scourge. If the leader was leading the pack, then where did the ordinary citizens go for redress? To whom did parents in the village go to report that their children may have been abducted while playing out in the field?* I kept wondering, "*How could millions of Africans just sit by and allow a few leaders and a handful of their lieutenants to terrorize the entire West African region?"* The answer is simple; the villagers and townspeople were powerless and helpless.

I had wanted to believe that the Kings and Chiefs were brave men who went all out to defend their territory and people with primitive weapons but were overpowered by European slave traders who had more sophisticated weapons; but that did not seem to be the case. In any case, I sat there thinking, as though in a desperate search for reassurance of some sort: *there must have been only a few kings and chiefs like King Anthracite.*

The professor spoke of the "nigger king" with such disdain you would have thought that he is still alive today and still wreaking havoc on his people in exchange for cheap material goods.

Oftentimes in college, I realized that other students in the class expected African Americans or Africans to defend or clarify issues pertaining to their respective ethnic group or nationality. As a nineteen-year old, this topic was too overwhelming for me. Besides, I was not prepared to defend that which was indefensible. Instead, I sat quietly and listened knowing that my maternal ancestors, who returned to Liberia from the United States, had also experienced what Robert Hayden had so vividly described.

The topic was tough, but the students behaved maturely, and the professor moderated well.

Although the topic was too emotionally burdensome for me, I appreciated the openness of the professor and the students. You cannot avoid discussion of an issue simply because it is too difficult. I learned for the first time of the role of some African leaders in the slave trade and my classmates learned from me that there were more victims than predators or collaborators in Africa.

At the end of the summer, I told an African friend that I would go back to school in Tennessee to complete my college education. Of course, he wanted to know why. "Well," I said, "I think integration helps the whites more than we realize. It gives most of them the opportunity to interact with people of other races and acquire firsthand knowledge of others in a way that the books and magazines cannot articulate. Besides, I want to see more blacks in the dormitory for women at CNC."

When I told my mother of my decision to go back to Tennessee, she quipped, "I knew that it wouldn't take you long to discover a noble cause."

I felt that by remaining at Carson-Newman College, more black girls would be encouraged to move in the dormitories and properly integrate the school. The last year I spent at the college, more than two dozen black girls were living on campus. I also felt that by remaining at Carson-Newman, many white students, removed from the reality of life in a racially and ethnically diverse country, would have the opportunity to experience close interaction with blacks and realize that we are all part of the same human species.

I did not have the solution for race relations in the United States, but I felt empowered in a small way to make a difference. I had spent my freshman year developing coping mechanisms for survival in a racially charged environment, and one of those mechanisms was maintaining a healthy self-esteem. I was determined that no matter how difficult the experience, in the end, I would emerge as a stronger and better person.

Having spent my undergraduate years in a predominantly white environment, I now know that there will always be whites who dislike blacks no matter what you attain in life, but I firmly believe that whites with this narrow mind-set are in the minority. I also learned that it would be foolish to live my life constantly anticipating acceptance from others. Therefore, I often choose to do what is best for me so long as it does not infringe on the liberty and happiness of others.

I believe that there will always be disagreements along racial lines in America, but we need to ensure that race does not dominate the soul of every social institution in society. We cannot legislate kindness; it should be natural. Likewise, antidiscrimination laws do not make us compassionate; they only impose a duty on us. An imposition is a burden and not a solution. We must learn to live as though civility is second nature and caring is divine.

CHAPTER 8

My First Job and My First Boss

After I completed my undergraduate work at CNC, I matriculated at Kent State University in Ohio, USA. It was a much larger school with several campuses. The main campus, where I lived, had a population of about fourteen thousand students. It was a more racially and culturally diverse environment and much more liberal than CNC, politically and socially. For the first time, I had the time to include parties in my schedule.

After eighteen months at Kent State, I attained a Master of Arts degree in sociology from the Department of Sociology, although my area of specialization was corrections (a component of the criminal justice system). The school had only an undergraduate Department of Criminal Justice at the time. Therefore, students pursuing a graduate degree in criminal justice had to enroll under the Department of Sociology. My program included a six-week summer internship as a probation officer trainee under a Law Enforcement Administration Assistance (LEAA) grant from the United States government.

Although I returned to Liberia with a specialization in corrections, I was told by the government of Liberia that I was too young to be an assistant minister of justice for rehabilitation, the person responsible for the management of the prison system in the country. Instead, I was appointed director of social welfare at the Ministry of Health and Social Welfare, with focus on developing and monitoring programs for delinquent children and children with physical disabilities. Apparently, the government was unsure of how to utilize my skills, but I decided that I would accept the job and do my best.

After a little over a year at the Ministry of Health and Social Welfare, Oliver Bright, Jr., the then minister of health and social welfare, was appointed minister of justice. Although he was a transactional lawyer with experience in foreign affairs, most people felt that he would make a good justice minister because of his broad understanding of the law, his sharp mind, and his firmness as an administrator. He recommended me for the position of assistant minister of justice for rehabilitation, the same position the government had said I was too young to occupy the year before.

Now that the government offered me the job, I was not interested. I wanted to remain at the Ministry of Health and Social Welfare for another year to complete the frameworks I had begun to develop. Minister Bright and Honorable Burleigh Holder, the minister of state for national security, negotiated with me for more than a month before we reached a decision. Essentially, I told them that I wanted to reform the correctional system, but I did not want to be an assistant minister. I argued that a political appointment would distract me from what I needed to do. I finally agreed for my name to be submitted as a nominee when I learned that it was the incumbent in the position, Rudolph Sherman, who had recommended me to be his successor.

Mr. Sherman told Minister Bright that I had, in the immediate past, provided him with helpful consultations; therefore, he felt I could handle the job. I was astounded that someone in government would be so selfless and so open-minded to recommend another person to take his job. I had not met Mr. Sherman in person before my appointment, but he had called on the phone quite a few times when he had issues with the prison system. He said that he would be doing the country a disservice to remain in the position when there was someone else in the country with specific training to do the job.

Everyone said that Minister Bright was a difficult person to work with; therefore, I should decline the offer to go to the Ministry of Justice. I understood their concerns, but I had to think about my career plan; first, the prison reform, and then my enrollment in law school. The environment at the Ministry of Justice would help prepare me for law school, I reasoned. Besides, over the several months at the Ministry of Health, the minister and I had grown to understand and respect each other, although reaching this point was preceded by some disagreements. A case in point: usually, I received instructions for work through my direct supervisor, the assistant minister for social welfare. Then one day when my supervisor was out of the country, and I was acting in her stead, the minister gave me verbal instructions to make up a list of students to be hired for vacation jobs, selecting eight students from each of the eight counties in the country at the time. In all, we selected sixty-four students, most of whom had never worked before and were desperately in need of financial assistance.

About a week later, the minister asked for the list and said he needed to remove some of the names to accommodate officials who wanted to employ relatives and friends. I told him that we had already committed to hiring the sixty-four young people around the country; therefore, it would be wrong to cancel the list. He then asked me who gave me instructions to make commitments to the students for employment. I said, "You did, Mr. Minister." Then he asked if I had any evidence that he had given me instructions to employ the students. I answered in the negative because I had no witness and no written instructions to hire the students. He canceled the list and put the burden on me to call the superintendent in each of the eight counties to inform them that the minister had rejected the list I had generated for employment.

Some weeks later, the minister apologized and said that it was a lesson for me to know that anytime you make an important commitment, especially one that has financial implications, make sure it is in writing; either request the instructions in writing or send a written memo to your boss recapitulating the verbal conversation. It would be the first of many lessons I learned from Oliver Bright, Jr.

The Ministry of Justice was even more challenging. I drafted most of the letters on matters pertaining to Corrections for the minister's signature. No letter was ever perfect. I kept all the letters with his comments in a special folder and reviewed them often to make sure I did not make the same mistake twice. One day when I thought I had written my best letter for his signature, he crossed out almost all of the paragraphs and yelled at me. That day I thought about leaving the job and going to law school full-time or returning to the United States to pursue a career in criminal justice. I graduated at a time when there were very few blacks and very few women in the United States with a graduate degree in the field.

But before the day ended, the minister summoned me and told me how he had grown up with my mother in Robertsport. His father was the assigned circuit judge to the area, and they had rented a house just across the street from my maternal grandfather's house, where his brother and he had many meals. "Your mother was kind to my brother and me, so I feel I owe her. Maybe you haven't noticed, but your mother calls me Prince. Only my family and people who really know me call me by that name. I am doing all of this for your own good. You have potential, and I believe one day you will be minister of justice." I was astounded! I went back to my office and just sat in the chair, staring at the wall in front of me. Perhaps no one wanted to tell me how well the families knew each other so I wouldn't take the minister for granted. *Small world*, I thought.

The Ministry of Justice is a very busy place; there is always one crisis after another. But with all that was going on in the ministry, the minister took time a few weeks after I started the new job to sit with me and offer some help in planning my future. He said, "It is easy to get caught up in the rigors of the job and forget about yourself. Your income has increased threefold since you took up the assignment with the Ministry of Justice. I advise that you invest the extra income rather than increase your expenditure." *Only in Africa would someone be so brazen to delve into your personal affairs*, I thought, but I was grateful.

I told Minister Bright that upon advice from a secretary (Olga Harris) at the Ministry of Health, I had acquired two parcels of land in an area called Duport Road and had begun construction. My brother John Hammond, an architect, designed a three-bedroom, two-and-a-half-bath bungalow for me. His friend Joshua Davies, a construction engineer, put a small team together, and for several weeks we worked on constructing the foundation and the walls. Unfortunately, funds ran out, and we put the project on hold while I waited for approval of a $30,000 bank loan from the newly established National Housing & Savings Bank. After listening intently, the minister said that I was on the right track.

By the time the loan went through, my brother and Joshua were occupied full-time with government assignments and could not devote much time to my project. Again, I turned to Minister Bright, who promised to check with his wife, Violet, to see if their construction team would be available; fortunately, the team was available. The contractor and his nephews were Ghanaians, very professional, and very reasonable in their charges. When I completed the construction, I still had $13,000, of the $30,000, left from the bank loan.

Minister Bright advised me to lease the newly constructed home and let it pay for itself; that would free up my salary, he said, and then I could use the $13,000 to start the construction of a second house. I was very grateful for the advice. It seemed very elementary, but I would not have thought about that at that stage in my life. Left to me, I would have bought a car with the $13,000.

I cannot close this chapter without briefly mentioning why the establishment of the National Housing & Savings Bank was such a godsend to the ordinary Liberian citizen. Before the seventies, only a few Liberian families had access to the banking system. Most working families, especially those employed by the government, would borrow much-needed funds from Lebanese merchants to build a house, start a business, or finance the education of their children. The borrowers would execute a legal power of attorney (LPA), authorizing the merchant to collect their government paycheck over the life of the loan, which was usually for a ten-month period. The families kept their paychecks unencumbered during the months of November and December in order to be able to do holiday shopping for their children. In January, families went back into LPA. Sometimes it took as long as ten years, on the average, for a family to complete the construction of a modest home under this system.

Other families, as in the case my family, would lease a parcel of land to the merchants to construct a commercial building with a store space on the street level and rental apartments on the top floors. The annual ground rent was determined by location and the size of the lot.

Some citizens kept money under the mattress, while others entrusted their meager financial resources with the Lebanese merchants. Before the nineteen seventies, banks required a minimum of US$100 to open an account, making it difficult for market women, students, and others with nominal income to open a savings account. The new National Housing & Savings Bank required only twenty-five dollars to open a savings account.

This commercial arrangement between the Liberian landowners and foreign merchants who brought in the capital was the beginning of a system that would eventually empower the Lebanese community in Liberia economically. Today, the best real properties in the capital are controlled by Lebanese nationals, a system that was fostered and strengthened by previous governments in their failure to empower their own citizens economically.

CHAPTER 9

Organizing the Bureau
of Corrections

The Office of the Bureau of Corrections (then the Department of Rehabilitation) consisted of only the assistant minister, a secretary, and a messenger. My team and I had to build the bureau from scratch. Like everything else I do, I sat down and listed the things my staff and I had to achieve in the first three years, and if there was time left after that, we would update our plan and do more. My goals were as follows:

1. Develop an organogram for the proposed Department or Bureau of Corrections.
2. Build capacity of the central office: Recruit and train senior staff to run the central office. Those recruited as senior staff members would go to the United States to participate in a six-month course in criminal justice and return so that together we could introduce the necessary reforms. The recruits included Elizabeth Catherine Toh, Francis S. Korkpor, Ruben Sidifall, Freddie Yancy, all graduating seniors from the Department of Sociology, University of Liberia; Sayon Washington, recruited from the Special Security Services; and

an older gentleman named Wilmot Mason, who had been strongly recommended by the director of police.

3. Build capacity nationwide: recruit and train corrections officers locally to replace soldiers who had historically provided security for all jails and prisons across the country, including those operated by the Ministry of Justice.

4. Inspect all prison facilities around the country to determine where renovation work was needed and where new construction of detention or prison facility was imperative. Concurrently, assess the food and medical services and determine how best to upgrade the quality of service.

5. Introduce rehabilitation programs (especially agriculture) in the prison facilities, where inmates had been convicted and were serving sentences, to defray the cost of operating the prison system.

6. Ask the government to shut down Belle Yalla and the Post Stockade, the only two detention facilities operated exclusively by the Ministry of Defense where both civilians and military personnel were detained; or discontinue the commitment of civilians to military facilities.

The senior staff left for a six-month training at North Carolina Criminal Justice Academy in the US in 1977. While they were away, reforms involving legislation, construction, renovation, and local training had all begun in earnest, bringing us to a target date for visible changes between late 1979 to early 1980. The minister used to jokingly call us the "Bureau of Children" since we were all in our twenties, but he always qualified it by saying, "I know you all mean business." We had planned that after completing the initial goals by 1980, we would introduce probation and parole among the next set of goals, but this was not to be.

While the staff was abroad for training, I also used that time to develop an organizational chart for the bureau. I worked with the Ministry of Public Works (specifically Minister Gabriel Tucker, Deputy Minister Aaron Milton, and Granville Dennis) to revise the blueprint for the first modern rehabilitation center under construction in Northern Liberia (Grand Gedeh County). The government had already begun construction when I was appointed, and I asked to make a few necessary revisions before the Ministry of Public Works proceeded with construction, and they agreed. Oddly, we could not agree on the need to include toilets in the cellblocks, but on the whole, the engineers did a great job with the designs.

A few months into the project, President Tolbert and Minister Bright asked me to take over the full project, construction and all. Most of the workers were on government payroll under the Ministry of Public Works, and they believed that was slowing the work down. They figured a private contractor would complete the work on time. I thought it through and concluded that this would take me off my timetable. I had to leave in early 1980 to attend law school. Supervising construction and developing a new bureau would be too much for my staff and me. Besides, the private contractors I consulted with wanted an increase of 50 percent in project cost to complete the work. I respectfully declined. I decided to take my chance with the Ministry of Public Works. All I would have to do, going forward, was inspect the progress of work more frequently and memorialize all conversations and meetings with the Ministry of Public Works pertaining to the project. That worked.

I asked why the government had chosen Grand Gedeh for the project. I was told that the superintendent of Grand Gedeh County, Albert T. White Sr. had lobbied for the project, arguing that the government had been unfair to his people by taking development projects everywhere else in the country, except Grand Gedeh. He specifically wanted the project in his county because it would create much-needed jobs for his people. All of that made sense to me.

Superintendent White and his wife, Kate Urey, were not originally from Grand Gedeh County. He was an army general assigned to that area in 1950, even before the area became a county, and he adopted it as his home.

By the end of the six-month period, the senior staff returned from the United States, after completing the training course, and the prison reform agenda began. The staff had been trained well. They had much to contribute, and I was so glad that the government had agreed to invest in their training.

We traveled around the country often to inspect ongoing construction and renovation work in the various counties. But our biggest challenge was the Monrovia Central Prison (MCP), the largest detention facility in the country at the time, with an average of eight hundred inmates in a facility built for 350 persons. With the completion of the project in Grand Gedeh, the convicts in the MCP would be transferred to Grand Gedeh to help reduce the overcrowding. We also needed to introduce programs to occupy inmates on a regular basis to replace boredom, frustration, and idleness as well as prepare them to return to normal daily living upon release.

At times, I would be told in the morning when I went to work that there had been a riot at the prison the night before, but the minister and the director of police showed up and quelled the violence. I could not understand why the soldiers did not call me, except that they did not believe that I could handle the inmates. I decided that I needed to either take charge of my work or just simply quit the job.

One day, the minister asked me to screen three hundred inmates who were detained at the Monrovia Central Prison (MCP) for minor offenses so that he could recommend at least fifteen of them for a presidential pardon during the Christmas holiday. I went to the MCP and set up a screening area in the prison yard with a large table and three chairs for myself and the two assistants. We asked the soldiers to escort the inmates out to the yard fifteen or twenty at a time. As we began the interview process, the inmates were very noisy and rude. One of them said, "If this chick lets me out, I will take her on a date; I have my own car." I just went on working and ignored the unwanted, annoying comments.

As I interviewed the third person in the second group of men, I noticed that he did not look well, so I asked what was wrong. He said that he had a hernia. Before I could say anything more, someone yelled from the back of the line, "Take your trousers down so she can see." I was quiet and expressionless. I looked at the young man and saw he did not want to disrespect me by taking off his pants, but he was also afraid that if he disobeyed his cellmates, he would face problems when they all went back to the cellblock. He would pull the pants just below the butt, look at me, and then look frightenedly at his fellow inmates. I felt pity for him.

After a few minutes of intimidation of this young man, I spoke out. I asked, "Who said this man should pull down his pants?" No one answered. I asked again, and no one answered. I looked at the young man and told him to take his pants down, but when he was done, everyone on the line would have to take their pants off and go on display. The whole place went silent. The sick young man hurriedly pulled his pants up and zipped it. I ordered him to leave the line and go back to the cell and retrieve his belongings, as he would be among those recommended to be released that day. Thank God he had been arrested and charged with some minor offense. Then I continued to interview and screen the rest of the inmates. The unruly behavior had abruptly stopped, and I received the utmost respect and cooperation going forward.

Although I had been responsible for the prison system for nearly a year, it was the first time I realized that the inmates took me seriously. The soldiers also seemed to be impressed that I had handled my situation without asking them to intervene. I do not know how I would have taken off the pants of fourteen unruly young men, but what was important is that they believed that I had the power to do it. It was the first time I felt I was in control of the situation. After that, when there was a problem in prison, the soldiers contacted me before they called the minister or the director of police.

CHAPTER 10

The Ghost of the
Village Entertainer

No matter how much you learn in school, you are never able to properly measure your understanding of the discipline until you go into the field to work, especially when a matter involves age-old cultural practices and customs.

On a sunny day in 1977, when one of my colleagues called and informed me that a group of individuals, some of whom were prominent citizens, had been arrested for the ritualistic killing of a young man, I was quite shocked and could not speak for nearly ten minutes. The ritualistic killing of another human being was just too far-fetched and unthinkable. It was beyond what my brain was willing to process. Murder, in and of itself, is horrific, but the cutting of parts from the body while the victim is supposedly still alive, to be used in witchcraft to attain political power, or money, or enhance relationships, is just incomprehensible.

Maryland, the county where the murder was alleged to have been committed, is notorious for ritualistic murders. In the mid-sixties, a group of people were convicted by the circuit court in Maryland County for the ritualistic killing of a man named Wahtoe. In 1967, the Supreme Court discharged the defendants because the evidence was insufficient.[15] Also, in

1966, the Supreme Court convicted several persons of beheading a woman named Madam Korlu, while she was asleep, and extracting parts from her body. This time the murder took place in Margibi County.[16] Both cases involved individuals of both America-Liberian and indigenous backgrounds. Although ritualistic murders occur sporadically across the country, Maryland County is known for a disproportionate share.

In the 1977 case, the government accused the suspects of the ritualistic killing of a young traditional entertainer, named Moses Tweh, who traveled from village to village singing and playing his musical instrument. Villagers discovered the body of Moses on the beach with his armpits, eyeballs, genitals, and some internal organs missing. The superintendent of the county (the political head) was among eleven individuals arrested. They were tried and convicted. However, the Supreme Court overturned the conviction because the police violated the constitutional rights of the defendants during their arrest by physically abusing them to induce a confession. After a second trial, the defendants were convicted in the Fourth Judicial Circuit Court of Maryland County and sentenced to death by hanging, a decision that was subsequently upheld by the Supreme Court of Liberia.

It was just too difficult to conceive of the fact that the superintendent could participate in the commission of such a horrific crime. He was well educated, from a well-to-do family, and had a pleasant demeanor. A few months before the arrest, I was a government guest of the superintendent and his wife. The superintendent often volunteered to host officials of government in his private home since public and private accommodations were very scarce.

I recalled that as we sat at the dining table for supper on the first day of my visit, the superintendent asked about my mission to Maryland, and I told him that I was there to inspect the prison to determine what kind of renovation work was needed. After renovation, we would furnish the facility with beds and other furniture. "Beds!" he exclaimed "What do you mean by beds? Have you ever heard prisoners sleeping on beds?" I was visibly shaken and felt disappointed that we did not share the same vision for corrections.

Then another man at the table, Fulton Dunbar, said, "The world is changing, Supe (short for Superintendent); that is not a bad idea." Mr. Dunbar later told me, and I agreed, that the Supe's reaction to my view of running a prison was reflective of how the general public felt about prisoners. People saw prisoners as people who had harmed society and therefore should be put away and punished. Other than that, we both agreed that the Supe seemed to be a nice man with a great sense of humor.

The week after the Supe and others were arrested, we traveled to Maryland to make sure that all was well so that allegations of mistreatment by the police would not spill over into corrections. I went to each door and put my face close to the square glass window in the cell door and greeted the inmate. By then, the renovation work was completed, and the facility was furnished. Each inmate was in a separate room, equipped with the basics, including a bed. As I walked away from the former superintendent's door toward the door of another prisoner, he called me back. We looked each other in the eyes through the small glass square in the securely locked door. He smiled and said quietly, "I just want to thank you for the bed." I did not know what to say. The whole experience was so surreal and painful for me. I smiled slightly and walked away.

For two weeks in January 1979, the former superintendent sent to ask for an audience with me, and I kept putting it off. Then one day in late January 1979, we were told that the government would execute the defendants in the ritualistic killings on February 9, 1979. Shock waves went through the ministry. No one could believe that the government would follow through on this judgment.

During a discussion with the former Liberian ambassador to the United Kingdom during the Samuel K. Doe administration, Willie A. Givens Sr., he recalled that he was present when the death warrant was signed. The father of the superintendent had asked for an audience with President Tolbert to plea for his son. Four cabinet ministers, all men, were present. Ambassador Givens, who was then deputy press secretary, at the Executive Mansion, had been called in the meeting since his boss, Henry B. Cole, was out sick that day. After the father made his passionate statement, the president asked everyone to bow for a word of prayer. When he was done praying, he announced that it was God's will for him to carry out the wishes of the people. As he took the pen to affix his signature to the death warrant, the superintendent's father walked out of the office, according to Ambassador Givens.

"What did the cabinet ministers do or say?" I asked the ambassador.

"Nothing," he said. "I guess everyone was in a shock. I really don't know. They did not comment; they just stood there. Perhaps, they conducted a conversation after I left. I was just a junior official, so I excused myself to go and start preparing the press release."

I was always of the opinion the outcome of this case would be influenced by the usual Liberian connections. After all, the superintendent's father was a former senator and the national chairman of the True Whig Party, the leading political party in the country at the time. I felt even if there were a conviction, the death sentence would never be carried out. The superintendent's father was also well connected through his affiliation with the Masonic order. He knew the president, members of the legislature, and the chief justice very well.

The superintendent himself was the contemporary of key ministers, including the minister of justice, the minister of defense, and the minister of national security. Therefore, there was no reason to believe that the ultimate sentence was likely to be carried out. Even the superintendent himself assured his cohorts that his father would come through for all of them; therefore, when the government announced a date for execution, everyone was stunned. For those of us in corrections, each execution virtually diminished the purpose of our mission, which was to rehabilitate the convict and return him to society better than he was before incarceration.

But there was another concern. The decision of the president to sign the death warrant signified a disintegration in the fabric of the Americo-Liberian society. It seemed imprudent to take such an action at a time when the society was marred by dissension, with politicians pitting indigenous Liberians against Americo-Liberians, notwithstanding that those convicted of this heinous crime included individuals of both ethnic persuasions.

I finally mustered the courage to go to the Central Prison. I had procrastinated because I just did not know what to say to a man, nearly twice my age, who had gotten himself entangled in a terrible predicament. I had planned to go to see him without alerting the minister or the director of police, both of whom I knew would try to stop me. But then, on the afternoon of Wednesday, February 7, 1979, the minister sent for me to join the meeting of the Joint Security Committee (JSC) in his office. The invitation caught me off guard since the Bureau of Rehabilitation (now Corrections) was never invited to the JSC meeting. The JSC wanted me to be aware that the prisoners in the ritualistic killing case would be transferred to Maryland by road on the following day. Apparently, the officials had made all their decisions and wanted to ensure the information would be transmitted properly to those in charge of the prisons in both counties (Montserrado and Maryland). The minister and the director of police had always deliberately tried to keep me out of what they perceived as difficult situations; I never knew how much of this had to do with my age and gender.

When I arrived at the prison compound, the head of the facility, James N. Tarpeh, who had been waiting for me, quickly followed me into the cellblock, insisting that I should not meet with the inmate alone. We both sat in single chairs across from the inmate, who sat at the edge of his bed.

Once again, the superintendent and I were meeting; however, the circumstances were very different this time. No matter how much I searched my brain, I could not think of what to say during the meeting. But then I remembered that it was he who wanted to talk, so all I had to do was listen. Very apprehensive, I sat there waiting for the former superintendent now inmate to speak. He talked about how he had spent so much time reading his Bible and getting closer to God, something he wished he had done before. But he repeated several times that his "soul was right with God." He wanted his mother and her identical twin sister to visit his cellblock. He wanted assurance that the handwritten will he had prepared in prison would be given to his family and would be honored by the government. He wanted me to take the Bible from his hands after his execution and give it to his son named after him.

He said he was thankful the prison authorities had not mistreated him or his friends. We promised to do our best to have his requests granted, except that someone else would have to collect the Bible, as I had no plans to attend the execution. The head of the Central Prison, James N. Tarpeh, and I had tears streaming down our cheeks. I felt helpless. I just wanted to get out of there and run, and run, and run.

I left the prison compound, went home, and fell across the bed. I wanted to think that once I fell asleep and woke up, I would discover that the whole experience was a dream. But before I could fall asleep, the phone rang; it was Mr. Tarpeh calling from the prison. He started by saying, "I just want you to know that I have received instructions to transport the prisoners to Spriggs Payne, the local airport, immediately. The Ministry of Defense plane will fly them to Maryland County within a few minutes." So then, what was the purpose of inviting me to the JSC meeting to explain to me this elaborate plan to transfer the prisoners by road the following day? Did they think that my disapproval of capital punishment would motivate me to derail the executions? Or was there some concern, as I observed throughout the entire process, that I might be biased because of my paternal link to Maryland County? Or what?

I sat there staring at the telephone and thinking that perhaps my mother was right, I should have gone directly to law school from undergrad.

CHAPTER 11

The Rice Riot of 1979

During the administration of President William V. S. Tubman (1944–1971), the hallmark of the government security services was called the public relations officer (PRO) system. Essentially, almost every family in the country had one or more persons on the government's payroll as a public relations officer (PRO). The PRO was expected to report to the president or his security apparatus any negative statement or plan against the government. A lot of people went to jail because of what a family member or friend had reported to the government. Therefore, people were afraid to express themselves publicly or privately.

When William R. Tolbert Jr. came to power in 1971, he discontinued the PRO system and often had his informant and the accused confront each other in his presence. Consequently, many Liberians were discouraged from divulging useful and credible security information to the president or his security officials. It would turn out to be one of President Tolbert's biggest mistakes.

Instead, President Tolbert encouraged Liberians to engage in business enterprises to become self-reliant. He wanted citizens to be more nationalistic and to focus on infrastructural, economic, and social development. The government invested in road construction, affordable housing, agriculture, education, the banking sector, the health sector, and so on. The speed of

President Tolbert just simply overwhelmed some Liberians, and for others, all of this was just not enough.

More importantly, once President Tolbert showed a little bit of tolerance for free speech, the public's expectation went high; he was now expected to cure all the socioeconomic disparities that had existed since the founding of the country. President Tolbert encouraged dialogue, but that did not appease the people; to them, the dialogue would lead to nothing but unfulfilled promises.

Just as the nation was trying to recover from the public executions of those convicted for ritualistic killings, a new political issue was brewing. On the streets, the talk was around that a hundred-pound bag of parboiled rice, then sold at twenty-two US dollars, would soon be increased to thirty dollars, and that after 1980, no more imported rice would be allowed in the country. These two actions, the president believed, would stimulate local rice production.

Behind the scenes, the then agriculture minister, Florence Chenoweth disagreed, but publicly, she took the fall. She wanted the government to delay these two policies and, instead, increase the budgetary allocation to the agricultural sector so that constraints on the local production of rice, such as lack of access to microfinance, poor quality of roads, lack of information to farmers, and more could be addressed. The Progressive Alliance of Liberia (PAL), an opposition group, headed by Baccus Matthews, decided to make political mileage of the rice issue. He promised the masses (students, workers, street vendors, market women, etc.) that he could bring rice in the country at the cost of no more than nine US dollars per hundred-pound bag.

One day in March 1979, the minister of justice summoned me to his office and asked whether I knew Bacchus Matthews and whether he had visited my office. In amazement, I answered, "Yes, I do know him, but I rarely see him; and yes, he stopped by the office some weeks ago and wanted to talk, but I was very busy, so he left some literature, which I have not yet read."

"Well," he said, "Matthews is inciting citizens to rise against the government. Therefore, he is being monitored by the security. MOJA (Movement for Justice in Africa), whose members consist largely of university professors and students, are providing moral support to him, from what we have gathered. There are also government officials who are supporters and sympathizers."

Why did the minister ask me about Matthews? I thought. Either he thinks that I am working with Matthews clandestinely, or perhaps he thinks I might be able to talk Matthews out of the demonstration. Whatever it was, I was not interested in pursuing the conversation. I knew that the government had become a bit paranoid because rumors abounded that some government officials were members of PAL and were passing information on to Matthews. I was never one to subscribe blindly to what everyone else is doing. I would consider the opinion of others, but in the end, I would weigh my options, weigh the costs and benefits, think of the consequences that I was willing and able to bear, and then decide. I simply assured the minister that I was not engaged in subversive activities.

Many young, educated Liberians, like me, were ambivalent about the air of change that was impending, to the extent that ambivalence transformed easily into complacency. Almost every young person who was not from the oligarchy wanted to see change—but positive change, not the kind of change where you change the driver but keep the old car. Young, educated Liberians wanted to control their destiny and not continue to feel that they were working only to provide better lives for the privileged; they were concerned about the uncertainties, the consequences, and the what ifs. What if, figuratively, we were jumping out of the frying pan into the fire? A student from the University of Liberia once complained that the Progressive professors had organized a party and entertained the students in the yard with cheap local liquor (cane juice), while the professors socialized in the house and drank imported whiskey. The student said that it was not a good sign from people who were concerned about inequality among the citizens.

President Tolbert was making a lot of strides in the quality and pace of development in the country, but it was perceived by the public as too little too late. The political activists (commonly called "the Progressives") had convinced the public that "the time of the people has come." The Progressives had more credibility than the government, which derived from the fact that they were young and highly educated and represented a cross section of the population.

Moreover, most of the Progressive leaders either belonged to the privileged class or enjoyed the benevolence of the privileged class, and most of all, Liberians knew very little about their character flaws and their background. For instance, both Matthews (a descendant of an Americo-Liberian president) and Ellen Johnson Sirleaf (daughter of a legislator) were considered by the poor as members of the elite class. Dr. Boima Fahnbulleh and Dr. Togba Nah Tipoteh (a.k.a. Rudolph Roberts), although of indigenous background, their parents were well educated, and each of their fathers had held high positions in government. Therefore, they too were considered a part of the elite class by Liberian definition. But the Liberian population, beaten down over the years by poverty, despair, and unfulfilled promises, was mesmerized by the political rhetoric and fearless demeanor of the Progressives and, therefore, followed them blindly. The masses became more emboldened by the fact that the children of the establishment were leading the charge against the government. To the general population, Progressive Alliance of Liberia (PAL) and the Movement for Justice in Africa (MOJA) were the same: same people, same rhetoric, and same objectives. Until today, the general public has never really tried to make a distinction between the two political groups.

The educated young Liberians had also realized by now that the underlying class tension that had brewed for years, since the administration of the predecessor of President Tolbert, might soon come to a head, but they wanted to change without bloodshed. In fact, Liberians were a nonviolent people and, therefore, hardly ever entertained the thought of attaining power "by all means necessary." Many expected that President Tolbert would end his term in 1983, and the wind of change would then begin to blow. Many foresaw a problem only if the True Whig Party (TWP), the ruling party, attempted to replace President Tolbert by another member of that party undemocratically.

In its March 31, 1979, publication entitled "The Voices of the Revolution," PAL gave an account of events leading up to the Rice Riot. And in a special edition of the same news organization dated, simply, September 1979, the PAL activists again recounted its exchanges with the government just before and just after the Rice Riot. According to the publications, the PAL leadership met on March 17, 1979, for two reasons: (1) to decide on the need to inform the legislature about the adverse economic effect the increase in the price of rice would have on the poor; and (2) to reach a determination that it was necessary for its members to stage a demonstration at three o'clock in the afternoon on April 14, 1979. The purpose of the demonstration would be "to dramatize their opposition to an increase in the price of rice."

Following the March 17 meeting, Matthews, as chairman of PAL, wrote a letter to the minister of justice, Honourable Oliver Bright Jr., dated March 20, 1979, in which PAL requested a permit to march on April 14, 1979. The minister of justice referred the letter to the attention of the president of Liberia. The president left the country for France on March 21, 1979, but not before referring the same letter to Honorable E. Reginald Townsend, his minister of state, for action. On March 22, 1979, Minister Townsend convened a meeting in his office that included the minister of justice, Mr. Baccus Matthews, and Mr. Oscar Quiah, the secretary-general for PAL. Minister Townsend told Mr. Matthews that the president would meet with him upon his return from France. There was no definitive response to the request to march. In fact, according to PAL, at the end of the meeting, the

PAL representatives were left with the impression that the government would unleash security forces on the demonstrators if they were defiant, in spite of the fact that the government had expressed its willingness to dialogue. To call off the demonstration, PAL wanted assurance from the government that it would not increase the price of rice and that security forces would not harass people who came out on the streets to demonstrate.

According to the Progressives' newsletter, when the president returned from France, he met with Mr. Matthews, as promised, and indicated in a meeting on March 28 that he would announce a decision on the Rice issue by April 7, 1979. The president and Mr. Matthews met again on April 2, 1979, at which time the president said that there would be a delay in the announcement of his decision because some members of the Rice Committee had gone to America on a mission but that the announcement would certainly come before April 14, 1979. Mr. Albert Porte, a veteran writer on political issues, volunteered to meet with the president on April 13, 1979, acting as an intermediary, to try to broker a compromise between the government and PAL before April 14. According to the PAL leadership, Mr. Porte told them that the president was unwilling to compromise and unwilling to instruct his security apparatus to exercise "restraint and caution."

I do not know whether the demonstrators went out on the streets first, or whether it was the police that first went to the headquarters of PAL looking for its leaders. But on the morning of Saturday, April 14, 1979, people began to mill around the streets, seemingly to witness the impending showdown between the government's forces and PAL's supporters. The minister of justice went on the radio to warn citizens to remain indoors but to no avail. Young people started looting stores, and the police came out to try to quell the riots. Shots rang out from both the police and the crowd. Gabriel Scott, a professional police officer, was shot and killed. Several civilians lost their lives, but people continued to come out and loot. Even women carried large refrigerators on their backs.

The government had never before experienced this level of civil disorder and obviously did not know what to do. In the weeks and months preceding the Rice Riot, there was growing frustration in the government manifested by crankiness and confusion among top officials. The president would yell at his ministers; then the ministers would go back to their offices and yell at the deputies, and the deputies would then yell at their subordinates, and so on. Now that the tension was reaching its peak, real leadership seemed to be lacking.

The public's perception was the president did not know whom to trust anymore. All of his trusted associates had predeceased him. Steve Tolbert, his brother, who was also the finance minister, died in a plane crash on April 28, 1975. His childhood friend, the then national chairman of the True Whig Party and minister of local government, E. Jonathan Goodridge, died on August 15, 1976, after a brief illness. His loyal vice president, James E. Greene, died on July 21, 1977, after a protracted illness. On September 9, 1978, McKinley A. DeShield, the secretary-general of the True Whig Party, postmaster general, and a trusted adviser passed away. Then, when President Tolbert gave his approbation for the execution of the superintendent, son of the national chairman of the True Whig Party, that further alienated him and caused a split in the True Whig Party and the Americo-Liberian community. All of these, I believe, were contributing factors to the disintegration of the century-old oligarchy.

Apparently, all of Saturday and Sunday, the security officials were meeting and conferring with the president. I did not see the minister until Monday morning, April 16, 1979. He was busy, but he agreed to stop what he was doing to see me. He looked up and said, "Please give me your honest opinion of the Rice Riot on Saturday." He looked perplexed.

All I could muster the nerve to say was "In my opinion, I believe the government (meaning, the security forces) truly underestimated the level of rage that had built up due to the unresolved rice issue." I also felt, but did not say, that the government knew that the rage was there but did not know how to handle it.

The government now knew that although Matthews did not control the army or police, his actions were widely supported by the ordinary citizens. The masses or grassroots citizens were captivated by Matthews. They liked his message of hope; they understood and believed the message. According to some of the young people who often discussed their experiences at the rallies, the Americo-Liberian settlers had come back to Africa in the nineteenth century and had taken their land illegally and subjugated them. Matthews would make things right again, and life for them would be much better. This was the simplest version of Liberian history I had heard, and it was scary, especially when the public did not seem to be able to distinguish between facts and propaganda.

The message of economic exploitation and human rights abuse was repeated over and over by various opposition politicians, but the government officials did not counter or challenge the authenticity of any of the information. They were only concerned about crowds gathering and milling around the streets, not about the message. This led the public to believe that everything

Matthews and other opposition politicians said about the government or the America-Liberian community was true.

Within days, after the riots subsided, soldiers from the Republic of Guinea were deployed at the Executive Mansion in Monrovia. It angered the Liberian soldiers and allowed politicians of the progressive movement to spread rumors that the president did not trust his soldiers. After a few weeks, the government of Guinea withdrew its soldiers. At the end of the first cabinet meeting after the Rice Riot, the minister of agriculture, Florence Chenoweth resigned, claiming that she could not continue to be the fall guy on the rice issue.

Within three months after the incident, the minister of justice, Oliver Bright Jr., was replaced by Counselor Joseph J.F. Chesson, who had been attorney general a couple of decades prior and was, at the time of his appointment, the lead defense lawyer for opposition leader, Baccus Mathews. Unlike Bright, who was primarily a transactional lawyer and an administrator, Minister Chesson's strength was in prosecution; but Minister Chesson had now inherited a major security challenge. Security is not prosecution. Perhaps the president's selection of Counsellor Chesson to succeed Minister Bright was indicative of government's determination to dialogue with Mr. Matthews and his organization.

What is so odd about the exchanges between PAL and the government officials between March 20, 1979, and April 14, 1979, is that neither party was serious about backing down from its position. PAL did not take any convincing stance to show that it did not want to carry out the demonstration, and the government, with the various delay tactics employed, did not seem to want to deviate from its intention to increase the price of rice. Therefore, the two parties engaged in a cat and mouse game until the situation erupted into violence on April 14.

CHAPTER 12

Our Struggle to Understand the Liberian Class System

E ach time Baccus Matthews spoke at his rallies in Monrovia, he talked about the "masses" and the "oligarchy," elite, or privileged class. A vast majority of the people who had gone out on the streets during the Rice Riot were young adults who were unemployed, self-employed (such as market women, street vendors, etc.), and students. Where, then, did everyone else fit if, in fact, by masses he meant the very poor, and by privileged he meant the few relatively wealthy citizens? Somehow, by hammering his designations at each rally, he had succeeded in creating a clear divide between the rich and the poor in the minds of the masses. To them, there were two distinct social classes of Liberians: the haves and the have-nots. I do not know of any empirical research on social stratification in Liberia; therefore, if you ask a hundred people to define social class, you just might get almost a hundred different answers to the same question.

In Liberia, we call someone rich because of the lifestyle of the individual, not because we have made some accurate assessment of what assets the individual has. In fact, officials have historically hidden assets (especially cash) from the government and even from their immediate family members. Therefore, we often come up with an approximation based on what we observe, or what is in the public records, or what is voluntarily made public by the individual. Is the individual educated? What is the level of education? What is the quality of education? Did the individual attend a second-rate public school or a private school in Liberia, or an above-average school abroad? Does he or she own a house? Is the house large and well-constructed, with electricity and an indoor plumbing system? Is the house tastefully furnished? Does he own a car? Is the car new and on the high-end regarding price and model? Does he hold a high public office? Does he own and operate a very successful business? Did he inherit money? This is how I tried to understand the class system in the 1970s when Liberia was relatively stable.

I believe that those are some of the factors considered by the average Liberian in determining where a person falls on the stratification ladder. But then, we also must consider that some people have more than one car, more than one degree, and more than one house; they even have stocks and bonds and farmland producing commodities for export. Then there are those who focus on one's ethnic background. If you are light in complexion and well spoken, you are presumed to be an Americo-Liberian (or Congor) and, therefore, a member of the privileged class, even if you have few or no assets.

If we display the Liberian class structure in the form of a diagram, I think it would look more like a pyramid. The smallest portion on the very top would represent the wealthy class; the largest portion at the bottom would represent the poor (perhaps two-thirds of the population); and the second largest group in the middle would represent those who are neither rich nor poor. The wealthy class has historically been very small and predominantly occupied by Americo-Liberians, other black immigrants, and a few indigenous citizens, while the lowest class, or the poor, has consistently been predominated by indigenous people and a few Americo-Liberians and other immigrants of little means.

The second largest class, the one in the middle, was the most diverse, most educated, and most interesting group. It was the class that grew larger in the fifties, sixties, and seventies due to the increase in inter-ethnic marriages and relationships, as well as the expansion of educational opportunities under the Tubman and Tolbert administrations to the rural areas. It was the class where one was most likely to find marriages between Americo-Liberians and indigenous citizens, or marriages between two highly educated indigenous people (sometimes of different tribal background). It was the class where one found the largest number of professionals such as doctors, lawyers, college professors, engineers, accountants, owners of large businesses, the clergy, and so on. It was the group that was most likely to have attended school from kindergarten through twelfth grade in Liberia and traveled abroad for higher education. It was the group that was likely to have attended boarding or parochial day schools in Liberia and developed an array of solid life skills by interacting with students from all backgrounds. It was the group whose parents held middle-level positions in government, or owned and managed small businesses such as shops, public transportation, and small farms and vowed that their children would do better than they did. Members of this class not only focused on education as other classes did, but they encouraged their children to become professionals and commit to public service.

Also among this middle group, you would find the educated (and sometimes wealthy) indigenous citizens from the seacoast whose ancestors engaged for centuries in various trade activities with Europeans. Some of their ancestors worked on the slave and merchant ships and, consequently, traveled to many parts of the world, learning new cultures and languages. They tended to have relatives in Europe and other countries along the West African Coast. In this group are also some indigenous families from the interior whose ancestors were successful farmers, businesspeople, and local leaders who continued to do well and who invested in the formal education of their children.

Because of its diversity, this middle group consisted of many subclasses. Some of its members did extremely well and sat on the top of the pack. While those at the bottom of this group were not necessarily poor, they tended to live from paycheck to paycheck and used their contact with more successful members of this class to stay afloat. This middle group was the group with the largest and fiercest number of social climbers, or wannabees (want-to-be), as we say locally.

But there was this other subgroup within the middle group that straddled somewhere between the middle and the lowest group: those were people raised by people other than their own families. Some Americo-Liberians raised other Americo-Liberians who were less fortunate. Some indigenous families took in indigenous relatives or other indigenous children with whom they had no blood relationship. However, the most common arrangement involved an indigenous Liberian raised by an Americo-Liberian or some other immigrant family, or missionaries. The fate of the beneficiary child was always left to chance since, unfortunately, the government did not formally regulate the care of children before the 1960s. Many families treated their wards (meaning nonbiological children) disparately compared to their biological children.

Often the wards spent more time serving their benefactors than attending school. Those who were fortunate to have fallen into the hands of kind people were likely to become as successful and sometimes more successful than some children who had been raised by their biological parents. There were those who ended up in the wrong household but turned out very well, anyway, because of their ambition and self-determination. They tended to end up in one of the two top tiers. But those who did not fare well from the intervention of the benefactor (s) were likely to end up among those on the lowest stratum of the ladder.

It was in the middle group, with all of its diversity, that one found the greatest amount of discrimination. The middle group took their social class status seriously. They discriminated against students from low-income families who dared to attend school with them when they didn't have the proper uniform or enough money for recess. They discriminated against folks in their own class who had a funny last name or were an out-of-town Americo-Liberian or Congor student who spoke with a funny accent and wore outdated clothes. Similarly, the seacoast indigenous discriminated against the indigenous from the rural areas, whom they considered less sophisticated or less civilized. There were all these overlapping dramas and overlapping hierarchies that often culminated in a love-hate relationship among the members of this class. Sometimes it looked like the struggle was between city dwellers and rural people; other times, it looked like a struggle between indigenous and nonindigenous groups. But when there was a ball game, it all boiled down to whether your favorite soccer team was the best in the country.

More interestingly, a few Liberians in the two top tiers of the social class structure described above had never seen areas beyond the outskirts of the capital. For example, when I told some of my friends that my mother had sent my brother and me on an errand to West Point, a large urban ghetto just about a mile from central Monrovia, they were shocked. Most of them told me that they had never been to West Point before. I could not understand that someone could spend their entire life in Monrovia and never see West Point. Others told me that they had never been outside of the capital city or outside Montserrado County, the seat of power for the country.

It is important to note here that although some families had the means to send their children abroad, they chose to educate them in Liberia with everyone else; and although some of the wealthy students put social distance between themselves and other students, most of them interacted with their schoolmates and formed lifelong bonds. It was this group, the second tier, or middle wrung on the social stratification ladder, that was poised to take control of the government, through a democratic process, when President Tolbert stepped down in 1983, as he had promised.

But there was the younger generation of the True Whig Party, some of whom were children of the elite, who felt that power would quite naturally devolve upon them. Then there were some contemporaries of President Tolbert, some of whom were officials of his government, who were waiting in the wings to replace him. But, of course, there was Matthews, and the Progressives, who had professed to the masses that "the time of the people has come," a message taken literally by poor, desperate Liberians.

The Rice Riot of 1979 had exposed the weakness in the government security and given Matthews the resolve to step up his momentum. The poor people, who looted homes and businesses during the riot, now had new clothes, an abundance of food supply, television sets, stereo players, mattresses, refrigerators, and extra cash for the first time in their lives. They now saw marked improvement in their lifestyle just after a few hours of looting and were, therefore, more energized to follow Matthews and his compatriots blindly.

Somehow, I had the feeling that everyone, except perhaps a few members of the elite class, thought that Matthews was working hard to make life better for them. There were rumors that some Americo-Liberians, including some government officials, supported Matthews secretly.

Even some educated indigenous Liberians, who were already making positive strides in society, applauded Matthews for his courage and wished him well. Somehow they expected that Matthews would not only make their lives better, but he would do for their people (especially the population in rural Liberia) what they had not done themselves. They had attained a good education, in some cases a PhD, and had held high public offices but had not looked back at the people in their villages. Now they too claimed to be part of the "suffering masses" and joined to cheer Matthews on and, at the same time, showed indignation for members of the oligarchy who had theretofore been their benefactors.

CHAPTER 13

Approaching the
Denouement

It seemed like the Rice Riot in April 1979 was a wakeup call for President Tolbert. He called a meeting of young people sometime around August 1979, established a task force, and appointed Emanuel Shaw as its chairman. The mandate was for the Task Force to travel around the country and engage citizens, especially the youth, in a dialogue. The mandate from the president to the Task Force was to find out what had gone wrong in the country and submit recommendations on what could be done to rectify the problem in order to avert what seemed to be an impending political turmoil looming over the country.

It was the first time I had attended a political meeting. I had never voted before and was not a member of the ruling True Whig Party or any other political group; politics was just not my interest. But I decided that it was important to participate in this meeting, especially since the government seemed willing to engage the citizens in a dialogue. We agreed that a two-man team would travel to each of the nine counties and report back to the task force within two weeks so that the chairman (Emanuel Shaw) would have time to prepare a report for the upcoming True Whig Party Convention in October 1979. George Boley and I were designated to go to Grand Gedeh County.

Grand Gedeh County was one of nine political subdivisions in the country at the time. Today, Liberia has fifteen subdivisions. This part of the country lagged in social and economic development, not only because it was one of the last areas to become part of the Republic of Liberia but also because successive governments failed to provide the requisite social and economic development to the area. Although there are other tribes in Grand Gedeh, such as Gio and Mandingo, the dominant tribe in the county is Krahn. Although Boley and I had attended the same high school, I did not know until this assignment that he was from the Krahn tribe. The school did not encourage tribalism.

When Boley and I arrived in Zwedru, Grand Gedeh County, we contacted the superintendent, General Albert T. White Sr., who agreed to convene a town hall meeting in the auditorium of the multilateral high school.

As I mentioned in an earlier chapter, General White first went to Grand Gedeh in 1950 as a military commander, and after his tour of duty, he returned to live in the county to help with its development. He engaged in agriculture, operated a general store, and contributed personally to the education of many young people in the county. He had only been called back to public service to serve as superintendent a few years before my first visit to Grand Gedeh in 1977. Because of their warmth and hospitality, I became endeared to General White, his wife (Kate Urey), and their children during my various trips to the county to inspect the construction work on the correctional facility. Some of the family members and I would stay up late at night playing scrabble, eating venison sautéed with onions and hot pepper, and drinking icy cold club beer (the local beer).

After Superintendent White introduced Boley and me to the more than two hundred people, mostly youth, packed in the auditorium, we told them briefly that we had come to Grand Gedeh to hear their views on the various problems facing the country.

When the young people opened their mouths to talk, we were taken aback. We did not expect to find so much rage and hostility toward the government. At least, I did not. They talked about how the Americo-Liberian citizens, a numerical minority of less than 5 percent of the 2.5 million population at the time, had dominated the society and controlled the government for more than a hundred years. The youth felt that it was now time to remove them by force, even if it meant that they had to burn down the cities. They mentioned that they would chase into exile those who survived the uprising. After the takeover, they asserted that the wealth of the country would be distributed equitably among the masses. Everyone would be able to go to school and get a good job and live well. They went on to say that they would prosecute the big shots for corruption and confiscate the properties of those found guilty. The ranting went on and on, often using the words "Americo-Liberians" and "Congor" interchangeably. As I mentioned in the author's note, there is an expression in Liberia: "if you want to know what kind of people live in a town, just listen to the songs the children sing."

Those pronouncements were truly disturbing. It was eerily similar to what we heard from young people who attended Matthew's rallies or MOJA meetings. That evening, as I sat on the porch at Superintendent White's house talking to him and trying to make sense of the meeting, he also expressed concern and confusion about the trend of thought of the young people in his county. I told him how I had thought that the problem was only in Monrovia. "No," he said. "People come from Monrovia to talk to people here. Those young people in the auditorium were unusually aggressive." The superintendent mentioned that some activist group had even opened a farm down the road in a place called Putu and often had meetings with the villagers under the guise of providing training for farmers.

The outcome of the meeting with the young people was worrisome. There was too much rage, and the experience of the Rice Riot earlier that year had taught me that we could no longer take peace for granted.

For me, the excitement in anticipation of change had now turned to fear, fear that either the young people must have misunderstood the message for change, or they had been deliberately misinformed. What could have triggered this level of anger? It did not appear that the anger was directed at us personally, nor did it appear that the anger had emerged just before we arrived in Zwedru that day. After all, Boley was a son of Grand Gedeh. As for me, I had recruited more than two dozen young people from Grand Gedeh in the previous year to train as corrections officers at the Police Training Academy in Monrovia. Therefore, we were familiar to them. It appeared that the anger and rage had been built up over a period of months or years. They were not rude to us, but they were bold and blunt in their deliberation and allowed intolerance and impatience to overshadow reasonableness. It was like going after the right thing in the wrong way.

I left the meeting with the impression that these young people had defined the enemy of the people to be anyone (wealthy or not) who was fair in complexion and spoke good English; and if you happened to have money and a high government position, or of an Americo-Liberian ancestry, then you were doomed. With this impression, I was concerned that if any violence erupted again, as we witnessed during the Rice Riot, innocent people would get hurt for no reason. Like me, most of the people I knew had one indigenous parent and one parent of American ancestry, or some other immigrant background, including Matthews himself. How then would the masses know who the enemy was just by perceived ethnicity, especially since the various groups in the Liberian society had intermarried and assimilated over several decades? Only a few families still insisted that their children marry within a specific ethnic or tribal group.

The norms of the past were changing rapidly, with the increase in exposure of young people studying in other countries. Young people of all backgrounds were now exercising the freedom to choose who they wanted to marry. The number of qualified young people of indigenous background in high government positions was increasing. For instance, the following is from the 1979 cabinet roster: Ellen Sirleaf (Gola), minister of finance; James Y. Gbarbea Sr. (Kpelle), minister of defense; Binyah E. Kesselley (Mandingo), minister of internal affairs; Johnny McClain (Bassa), minister of information; Cletus S. Wotorson (Kru), minister of lands, mines, and energy; Bernard Blamo (Kru), minister of education; John Sherman (Vai), minister of commerce; Kate Bryant (Grebo), minister of health and social welfare; Trohoe Kparghai (Krahn), minister of post and telecommunications, and the list goes on. The same was true in the legislative and judicial branches of government, as well as the public corporations. Therefore, the stratification or hierarchical system that used to exist along ethnic lines seemed to have been transformed into a social class structure, with education being the major determinant.

Obviously, my knowledge of sociology was beginning to have some relevance; but first, we needed to get to Monrovia and find the chairman, Mr. Emanuel Shaw. We told Emanuel that things did not look too good in Grand Gedeh; I felt that we needed to return to Grand Gedeh and engage the people some more. I predicted that if we had any trouble in the country, it was likely to come from Grand Gedeh. The other teams from around the country had sent in reports of disgruntled citizens in various places, but we could not compare reports from anywhere else in the country to the rage we had witnessed in Grand Gedeh. Emanuel suggested that if it was that bad, then we needed to inform President Tolbert. It was after six o'clock at night, and we were debating whether we should not wait until the next day; in the end, we decided to see the president that evening.

I was astounded that the government had focused so much on Monrovia, the capital, and had not paid as much attention to the voices of the people living in the interior parts of the country. The young people in Zwedru had spoken loudly and clearly. There was no way the government could ignore their supplications.

We went to the Executive Mansion, the official residence of the president, but we were informed that the president had gone to Crozierville, a settlement about twenty or more miles outside the capital, to attend the wake-keeping service of the mother of his national security adviser. We went to Crozierville and explained to the chief of security that we had to see the president urgently; he reluctantly escorted the president out of the church to where George Boley, Alfred Kulah, Emanuel Shaw, and I stood in the churchyard. After we explained our findings to the president, he agreed that it was serious and promised us that he would refer the matter to the cabinet, as well as personally follow up on the grievances of the people of Grand Gedeh.

From the various reports received from around the country by the task force, a general mode of discontent permeated the entire country. In other places, citizens were not as vocal and aggressive as we had seen in Zwedru. The rumblings were not just coming from the indigeneous population, the students, and the workers; it was coming from the Americo-Liberian community as well. Except for a handful of people, (like Matthews, for example), most Americo-Liberians were discreet in their support of the opposition. There appeared to be a lot of infighting among government officials. The talk in the ministry of justice was that the chief justice and President Tolbert did not get along, notwithstanding the chief justice's daughter was the widow of the president's late brother. One minute we heard that the minister of state, E. Reginald Townsend, would replace the deceased vice president, James E. Greene. Then we heard the next pick for vice president would be Jackson F. Doe from Nimba County. In the end, the president selected Dr. Bennie D. Warner, bishop of the United Methodist Church. Then the word on the street was that President Tolbert had promised to back Robert I. E. Bright, a successful businessman, in his bid for secretary-general of the ruling True Whig Party. Instead, President Tolbert supported Clarence L. Simpson Jr., a former attorney general and a member of the oligarchy. Surely, these were bad signs.

The following week, sometime in October 1979, during the True Whig Party (TWP) Convention in Buchanan, the chairman of the Task Force, Emanuel Shaw, was given a slot on the program agenda to report on our cross-country dialogue with the youth. He spoke extensively about the findings of each of the committees that had been dispatched around the country and about the amount of anger and rage that had built up among the ordinary citizens nationwide. I recall that it was a brilliant speech, but I do not recall all of what was said. What I do remember was that at the end of the speech, and somewhat fortuitously, Emanuel admonished the True Whig Party officials and its members to pay heed to all of the information and concerns he had brought back from the people. If not, he continued, "The October 1979 Convention will be the last convention of the True Whig Party."

CHAPTER 14

The 1980 Military Coup

On January 1, 1980, I prayed that the year 1980 would be less eventful than 1979. I prayed that there would be no more riots and no more executions.

The school year ran from March to December at the time. My mother would be delighted to hear that I was finally enrolling in law school in March 1980. The plan was first to open up the new correctional facility in Grand Gedeh County that had been under construction for four years. It would be the first rehabilitation center for convicted inmates and the first time in the history of the country that a prison facility would be run entirely by a civilian staff. Then the next plan would be to enroll in law school; and, finally, I would resign my post by July 1980 and devote full-time to the study of law.

Notwithstanding, I had accomplished the first two parts of my plan by March, the political landscape of the country seemed to be going helter-skelter. One did not know what to expect from one day to the next, or what story the newspaper would carry. Rumors circulated again that some government officials were supporting the opposition and that one of them would ascend to the presidency upon the removal of President Tolbert. There were names of presidential hopefuls coming from all three branches of government and the private sector. Rumors without supporting evidence always remain just rumors.

But then I had a few encounters during March 1980 that I now understand, in hindsight, to be signs of the time to come:

- Julius Hoff sold and installed communications equipment. He often came to the office to try to convince me to procure communications equipment for the correctional system, as it was the only component of the entire criminal justice system that had no communications network. He was right, but I could not convince Honorable Chesson, the new minister of justice, to approve the request; he cited budgetary constraints. After numerous visits from Julius, who said that the system would only cost US$50,000, I met with the solicitor general, Ephraim Smallwood, on April 11, 1980, and asked him to persuade the minister to approve the request. He promised to have a conversation with the minister on Monday, April 14, 1980.

- Early in March 1980, Jonathan Reffell, a prominent radio and television personality, called and asked if I would appear on television on his Sunday Press Program. I declined. He kept calling every other day, and one day he said to me, "You know, some of the political opposition members, like Matthews, have been arrested and jailed. There are rumors that they are being mistreated by the government, meaning the ministry of justice. Since you are in charge of the prison system, the public will assume that you are responsible for everything that is happening to them. I know that the key leaders of the activists are in the Post Stockade, under the Ministry of Defense, but the public does not know that. I am trying to give you the opportunity to exonerate yourself." On Sunday, March 16, 1980, I appeared on television with Reffell and gave all the clarification needed in response to his very direct questions. Reffell was right. The next day, almost all of the newspapers published the clarification surrounding the detention of top opposition leaders. The public now knew that Matthews and his cohorts were in detention at the facility run by the Ministry of Defense and not the Ministry of Justice.

- Also, sometime in March 1980, I left my office and returned by mid-afternoon only to be told by Reuben Sidifall, a staff member, that someone had come to visit me. He giggled as he described how this visitor was raving and ranting about corruption in the government and the determination of the Progressives to bring about change, and that officials spend so much time out of office on personal errands. Reuben said the visitor had promised to come back. I asked who the visitor was, and he said, "Chea Cheapo." I had heard about this man but had never met him. I knew that he was a lawyer, that he was cantankerous, and that he was the foster son of my boss, Minister Chesson. Ten minutes after I received the message, I heard a knock on the door, and in walked Cheapo, even before I invited him in. He took his seat and began ranting about "the corrupt, useless government working against the interests of the people."

I just sat there listening to him, partly amazed and partly amused. As we had never met before, I decided to keep my cool and listen. When he did not get a reaction from me, he calmed down and told me that he had come to ask for a pass to visit the prison, as the political detainees were entitled to legal representation. I told him that I had no authority to give him a pass to the military facility but that I would issue a pass to the Monrovia Central Prison, the facility under the Ministry of Justice, where some activists (not part of the leadership) had been detained. I warned him that with all of the confusion going on, the authorities at the prison were also receiving direct instructions from the president and the minister. Therefore, if the authorities at the prison questioned the pass from my office, he should not get into an argument; just simply return to me, and I would seek clarity from my bosses. Cheapo did not come back to my office. About a week later, I heard that he had been arrested and detained along with others accused of engaging in subversive activities.

- In early April 1980, Baccus Matthews's mother came by my office with a huge plastic bag containing at least a dozen blankets. She said that she had bought enough blankets for her son and his friends, but the authorities, specifically the head of the Post Stockade, would not allow the detainees to have blankets but would rather have them sleep on the bare concrete. She asked if I could convince the head of the facility to allow the inmates to have the blankets. I worried that the government would soon misunderstand and misinterpret my constant intervention, although her request was valid and reasonable. I picked up the phone and called the head of the military detention facility. After a few minutes of persuasive back-and-forth conversation, and a promise to share my ration of government's gasoline, he agreed to allow the inmates to have the blankets. One of the corrections staff members, John Smole, volunteered to deliver the blankets to the Post Stockade.

The week of April 7, 1980 was somewhat eventful but not too out of the ordinary. The Baptists were celebrating a one-week commemoration of the hundredth year of the founding of the Liberian Baptist Missionary & Educational Convention (LBMEC); President Tolbert as head of the LBMEC attended the last day of the program on the evening of April 11, 1980. The Joint Security Committee, under the minister of justice, continued with its frequent but random meetings at odd hours during that week. The newspapers reported sometime during the week that the government had planned to indict Matthews and others on Monday, April 14, 1980. My husband, Dr. Augustus P. Tah, and I, just married in January 1980, traveled to Buchanan, a two-hour drive from the capital, to visit his mother on April 11 and returned the same day. On our way to Buchanan, we noticed a large group of young men jogging in the vicinity of the soldiers' barracks in Schiefflin; they wore sporting clothes of various colors. Therefore it was difficult to determine whether they were civilians or soldiers, but, for some reason, they claimed our attention.

On the way back from Buchanan, we stopped by a roadside market and bought palm nuts for the prisoners at the Monrovia Central Prison. We decided to donate the palm nuts to the prison since it was cheaper than the ones sold in the city and could make enough palm sauce to feed a lot of inmates. When we arrived home and turned on the television, a fictional movie about the overthrow of a head of government was showing; the setting of the movie was somewhere in the West. My husband seemed visibly disturbed that the network was airing the movie at a time when the public was agitated about the impending indictment of Matthews on the anniversary of the Rice Riot. His mind went back to the strange groups of young men jogging and walking along the highway near the Schiefflin soldiers' barracks during the morning. Then he suddenly reminded me that his high school classmate, Carney Johnson, and his wife, Ophelia, had invited us to lunch the next day, April 12, 1980.

Around three o'clock in the morning on April 12, 1980, the phone rang. The loud ring of the black rotary telephone startled me. The call was for my husband. When he ended the conversation and placed the phone on the receiver, he said, "This is strange; a young lady from the radio station called to ask if I had the phone number for Jonathan Reffell."

"This is strange," I echoed and tried to fall asleep again.

Within half an hour, my husband woke me up and said he could not sleep because of the sound of gunshots coming from nearby. We lived on Cheeseman Avenue and Tenth Street, about one and a half miles from the Matadi Housing Estate, a new government housing project under construction at the time. I told him that someone in my office had said that the soldiers assigned to the estate to provide security were in the habit of shooting in the air sporadically to ward off thieves. He said, "Listen carefully; it is not sporadic shooting. It sounds like machine guns, and the sound is coming from the opposite direction, as though from the center of the city." I left the bed and sat in the La-Z-Boy chair three feet away from the bed, against the wall, and listened intently. Yes, indeed, the shooting was incessant.

I started to make some calls, first to the Minister and then some of the security officials, to find out if they knew what was happening. Minister Chesson's phone kept giving a busy signal. Then I tried the police director and the commissioner of immigration and got the same busy signal. At this time, it was clear in my mind that something was wrong. I sat for at least twenty minutes, and then I said, "Why didn't I think of the Monrovia Central Prison?" I picked up the rotary phone and dialed 222216, and a soldier answered, as soldiers were still in charge of the prison, soon to be replaced by corrections officers in training. I had to hold the phone receiver away from my head, as the sound of gunshots was so loud that it seemed like the shooting was occurring in the prison compound. I identified myself and asked the man on the other end of the phone if he knew what was happening. Liberians love to be the bearer of bad news. The man started speaking so fast in broken English that I could hardly understand what he was saying. Did he say the President was "there" or "dead"? These two words are pronounced "deh" in the Liberian vernacular. I begged him to calm down and speak slowly, and he did. "A man name Duo killed the president. He is a master sergeant in the army. He is a Krahn man from Grand Gedeh." We would learn later that day that the correct name of the leader of the coup makers was Samuel Kanyon Doe, not Duo. The sound of the gunshots, he said, was from the Post Stockade, the military prison almost adjacent to the Monrovia Central Prison.

After what seemed like a three- or four-minute phone call, I relayed to my husband what the man on the phone had told me. We sat down speechless for what might have been one or two hours. After every half an hour or so, the soldier who answered the phone at the Central Prison would call me back with updates. We just sat there helpless with all the information, not knowing who to call, what to do, or what to think. You just don't pick up the phone and call someone and say, "A soldier just killed the president." It is not a conversation that most Liberians ever imagined they would be having; the whole thing seemed so unreal. The security officials, who were supposed to know all the answers and give instructions on the next step in a situation like this, were not answering their phones, and the fate of each was unknown. It felt like a heavy rainstorm had carried the roof of the house.

The soldier called me again around six thirty on the morning of April 12 and said that some people had come to the prison with instructions from the new Liberian leader to release all Krahn people from the prison. "So why did you call me?" I asked.

"Because you are in charge of the prison," he said.

I said, "Go ahead and comply with the instructions, but please do not call me again." A few days later, when I saw the soldier in person, he told me that the soldiers who brought the message for the release of prisoners pointed their guns at him menacingly as they waited for a response from me. I guess that the soldiers went to the prison to release inmates on their own, but there was no way to investigate anything in this chaotic situation.

By seven o'clock that morning, the barrage of calls started to come in from family and friends. For the first time, we heard how the president died. One caller said that he had been shot and then disemboweled with a bayonet. Some of the callers were crying, and others were still in shock and disbelief like me. My husband and I were wondering what happened to the security guard who should have reported to us at six thirty that morning to end his shift. We lived on the top floor of a two-story apartment building, and there was no place for a security guard to stand or sit. When the minister insisted that I accept a security guard, I suggested that the guard sleeps across the street at Warner Avenue and Eleventh Street in my husband's clinic, where he would have access to comfortable vinyl-covered chairs, a television, and a refrigerator with soft drinks and water. All of the security guards loved the arrangement. The area was crime-free; therefore, the guard effectively had nothing to do. At dawn, the guard would come across the street to the apartment and turn in the .38-caliber pistol and the keys to the clinic and go home.

When the guard assigned on the night of April 11 did not show up at seven o'clock on the morning of April 12, we became concerned. Trucks were passing up and down crammed with soldiers and unruly civilians singing "Who Owns Papa's Land?" (a popular West African revolutionary song by Sonny Okosun). My husband, from the Bassa tribe, dressed inconspicuously in a short-sleeve shirt, jeans, and slippers, and walked across the street to see what had happened to the security guard. He used his spare keys to enter the clinic and found that the place was clean and in order, but the guard was not there. The only thing found in the clinic, on the floor, was a piece of notebook paper folded. He opened the paper, and it was a letter, addressed to no one in particular, but it contained a vague message forwarning of darkness that was moving across Africa and was about to land on Liberia. My husband asked if I recognized the handwriting. I said I did. It was the handwriting of the security guard; he used to be my messenger before he became a corrections officer, and as the messenger, it was his job to write down all the messages left for me during my absence from the office.

As we sat at the dining table wondering where the security guard was on a day like this, the doorbell rang, and it was the security guard unusually dressed in plain clothes. His pants had blood stains in various places, and he walked in with a limp. He told us of how a truck full of soldiers had picked him up, just as he was about to cross the road to come to the house to turn in his gun. They drove off in the direction of the military barracks in Schiefflin, more than five miles from where he had been picked up. They beat him up, took the gun, stripped him of his uniform, and were attempting to stab him with a bayonet when a soldier intervened, saying, "Although he is dressed in a government security uniform, he is one of us; we cannot kill him." Then they dropped him off at the ELWA junction, from where he walked about two miles to his house on the Old Road. He said that although he was in so much pain, he could not retire to bed knowing that we might be wondering what may have happened to him. We showed him the note and asked if he was the one who wrote the note. He denied it vehemently, and that baffled me.

We waited at home all day Saturday and Sunday for someone from the new government to contact us, especially me, for whatever reason, but no one came. By then, the new government had arrested almost every official in the Ministry of Justice and other security agencies, and that made it all the more disconcerting for me.

On Monday, April 14, 1980, my husband suggested that we get dressed and leave for work as we usually did. "If they plan to arrest you," he said, "it will be better for it to happen at the office, where there are a lot of people, than at home where you will be alone. I have to go to the hospital to help with all the injuries from rape, gunshot wounds, and God knows what else." He drove to the Ministry of Justice at the corner of Center and Ashmun Streets to drop me off before going to the hospital. We parked at the side of the building on Center Street and walked toward the front on Ashmun Street. As we approached the front, there was a huge crowd standing on the sidewalk all the way to the top of the stairs, with attention toward the front door. Chea Cheapo stood at the top of the stairs, holding the doorknob and complaining that all the Justice Ministry officials had run away and taken the key, and he needed to enter to begin his work as the new minister of justice.

My husband and I stood on the sidewalk quietly behind the crowd. In a few seconds, after we stood, Cheapo's eyes went over the crowd and into my face. My knees got weak, and I could feel a knot in my stomach. *Now*, I thought, *he will publicly order my arrest*. Instead, Cheapo's face lit up, causing the entire crowd to turn around and look at me. The crowd started to clap for me spontaneously, but I was still very unnerved standing there. Then Cheapo called the attention of the crowd and said, "This lady is my friend. She is brave! All the men have run away, and here, she has chosen to come to work. She will be my deputy." Now I was really confused. In the first place, I knew that to be a deputy minister of justice, one had to have a law degree, unlike being the head of corrections. Second, I was not part of this revolution and was confused as to what would be expected of me, especially since I had worked for the now-defunct government.

When Minister Cheapo finally opened the door to the building, I went first to the rehabilitation office on the lower level to check on my staff. Then I went upstairs to try to talk Minister Cheapo out of placing me in the deputy minister post. His office was locked. A young man, who introduced himself as Richard, said Cheapo and Matthews were in a private meeting. I stood beside Richard in the foyer, waiting for the meeting to be over. He looked at me and said, "I know you, but you do not know me."

I said, "How so?"

"We are not going to bother you for several reasons: we used to monitor the security meetings from the College of West Africa building across the street from the Justice Ministry, and we never saw you attend any of those meetings; we never heard your voice on the security communication system. We have several police handsets that we used to monitor the security officials. Each time a police officer brought a handset to the radio shop for repair, we told our agent in the shop to repair the radio and hand it over to us and then tell the government that the handset was beyond repair. As a result, we had several security radios, but we did not have one for Corrections. Either you did not have access to a communications network, or you never used it." I said nothing.

While standing there, looking at Richard in bewilderment, Matthews walked out of Minister Cheapo's office, and when he saw me, he embraced me and said, "Thank you for the blankets, my sister." Already, the encounters with Cheapo, Richard, and Matthews on the morning of April 14, 1980, helped me understand and appreciate the unusual experiences I had leading up to the military coup.

When the announcement of my appointment by Minister Cheapo came on BBC, President Doe sent for Minister Cheapo and chastised him for unilaterally taking such a major decision. Within forty-eight hours, I was back in the post as assistant minister for rehabilitation (now corrections and rehabilitation). I went back to my basement office where I felt safe and did not have to worry about drunken soldiers coming in the building on the top floor, brandishing guns, and threatening everyone in sight. I did not know that I would be so happy to be demoted to my previous position.

The True Whig Party government was truly gone. The People's Redemption Council (PRC) was now at the helm of power.

The major concern for most Liberians was: how were the seventeen young soldiers (turn coup makers), mostly in their twenties and thirties, with very little education and experience, going to run the country? The news report was that the leader was a mere master sergeant, twenty-eight years old, with less than a high school education. Historically, soldiers were assigned to provide security in nearly every sector in the country, and very little attention was given to their educational pursuits and personal well-being.

The other concern was that having a head of state with less than a high school education would lower the bar for the highest office in the land. Now, almost every adult in the country, hereafter, would feel that he or she was qualified to become president of Liberia, and mediocrity would become commonplace. Our only consolation was that the Progressives, such as Dr. Amos Sawyer, Dr. Boima Fahnbulleh, G. Baccus Matthews, Madam Ellen Sirleaf, Dr. Byron Tarr, Dr. Togba Nah Tipoteh, Dr. George Boley, and others were reported to be the mentors and principal advisers of the coup makers. They were known to be some of the most educated people in the country. It gave us some assurance that the country would indirectly benefit from their collective knowledge, experience, and wisdom.

On the morning of April 22, 1980, ten days after the military coup, everything appeared to be calm as far as the general public was concerned. The day seemed like a regular day—regular in the sense that women and children, for the tenth day, continued to dance in the streets as an expression of gratitude to the soldiers for redeeming them from the oppressors. Regular in the sense that the usual stream of people kept coming into my office to ask me to intercede for Minister Cheapo to issue them an exit visa to leave Liberia, as no one was allowed to leave the country without approval from the government. Regular in the sense that all through the morning, people stopped by my office to tell me the story of a neighbor or a family member who had been raped or found dead in random places.

Little did I know that around three thirty or four o'clock that afternoon, gunshots would ring out from the Post Stockade (the military facility at South Beach), less than a mile from the Ministry of Justice, and that the entire city would eerily be clothed in darkness. But it happened. We soon learned that the PRC or military government had just executed thirteen former officials of the Tolbert government. A kangaroo military court, headed by a lawyer in the military called Frank Senkpeni, summarily tried the officials a few days before the execution. The main crime the officials were charged with was "rampant corruption." Those executed included the chief justice, James A.A. Pierre; the president pro tempore of the Liberian Senate, Frank Tolbert Sr.; the minister of state for presidential affairs, E. Reginald Townsend; and the Speaker of the House of Representatives, Richard A. Henries. The government also executed the former minister of finance, James T. Phillips; the minister of planning, David Neal; and the minister of commerce, John Sherman. Others included the minister of justice, Joseph F. Chesson; the minister of agriculture, Cyril Bright; the minister of foreign affairs, C. Cecil Dennis; and the director of the Budget Bureau, Frank Stewart Sr.

To the amazement of the public, the government executed two private businessmen, Clarence Parker and Charles King, along with the officials of government. The soldiers learned after the executions that Henries, Sherman, Stewart, and King were of indigenous background. Only nine poles were available to carry out the executions of the thirteen men. Therefore, four of the thirteen knew what their fate would be as they waited for the bodies of the first nine officials to be removed and carried to a mass grave.

The former minister of justice, Oliver Bright, was out of the country at the time of the coup. Only God knows what his fate would have been had he been in the country. There were many inquiries from the new government of the People's Redemption Council (PRC) about his whereabouts.

The people in the streets resumed the dancing, dancing that had started on April 12, 1980, the day of the coup. Even some very educated people, in both the private and public sectors, rejoiced at what appeared to them to be a major victory. Some close associates of the former government officials rushed in to provide the PRC government with information on the officials that would have, otherwise, been difficult to obtain.

---◆◆◆---

CHAPTER 15

---◆◆◆---

Trying to Make Sense of the New Normal

When the military coup occurred in April 1980, our generation had just completed college and was making plans for the future. For example, some had embarked upon their respective careers; some had recently married or were planning to get married; and others had started construction of their first home and had already started to have children.

Except for the few who were involved directly or indirectly in the coup, the rest of us were unprepared for such a major, unprecedented transformation in our society. We were unprepared for the loss of lives, valuable lives to the country and their respective families. We were unprepared for the level of intentional and deliberate personal injuries and property damage. We were unprepared for chaos and unprepared for leaders who were unreasonable and ill-advised on major national issues. We were unprepared for the level of hatred and anger directed against the innocent. And most of all, no one could have ever been prepared for the adverse consequences of what may have begun as a well-conceived idea with good intentions.

Some Liberians left the country in 1980 and vowed never to return under any circumstances, not even to bury a loved one or to collect much-needed income from inheritance. Others vowed to stay in Liberia no matter what the situation, even if it meant the loss of limb or life. Some stayed because there were simply no other options. Others left the country to wait and see from the outside, living in limbo, and eventually choosing to live between two countries, as though the choice provided a cure for uncertainty. In my own family, you will find all the scenarios I have just described.

Everything those young students had spewed out in the auditorium of the multilateral high school in Zwedru, during our fact-finding mission back in 1979, played out during the coup and was still playing out as in a movie. People who saw themselves as having been disadvantaged in the past were lashing out at those perceived to have been the rich and privileged. Even some well-educated indigenous Liberians, who had benefitted from the benevolence of the Americo-Liberian oligarchy, were now laying the red carpet for the soldiers and openly expressing gratitude for their redemption.

But the fundamental question is, what would cause an ordinarily calm, happy, and hospitable people to become so angry, hostile, and violent? In almost every country in the world, there are rich and poor people; privileged and underprivileged people; educated and uneducated people; happy people and angry people. Nevertheless, this is not how people normally resolve the disparities among its citizens.

For some of the unruly crowd in the street, the outburst was merely a spontaneous reaction to chaos; it presented an opportunity to vent anger against perceived injustice, or simply presented an opportunity to steal. But for others, the event was calculated and driven by a prepared indoctrination strategy (which I will refer to as the three Ds strategy) designed to lead to public disorder and chaos. People who seek to brainwash or indoctrinate first identify the target group against whom the strategy is planned, usually the establishment class. Then the next step is to bombard the public especially the young and uneducated, with negative messages by the continuous *dissemination* of information. The information is often false and misleading. The messenger is not interested in the truth; he or she is only interested in ensuring that the recipient group believes the message. The message is usually intended to bring discord and *division* among the people; in other words, all that matters is that the message engenders anger and hatred sufficient for the recipient to develop the perception that the target is responsible for everything and anything that has gone wrong in the life of the recipient. *Destruction* becomes easy to achieve, once the recipient harbors ill will toward the target. At this stage, the recipient of the message can only find solace in violence against the target, the perceived enemy.

Many days after the coup, I sat and pondered on what all of this now meant for the country going forward. I concluded that it meant that the society had changed forever. I was not sure whether it was for better or worse, but I was sure that we would never be the same again. Here, we were experiencing a monumental transformation in the country, with no apparent consideration for a smooth transition. The well-educated political activists were standing in the background. Some Liberians felt that the Progressives did not want to own the coup since it was so brutal; others felt that they put the soldiers in front because they were afraid of backlash from the defunct government. Whatever the theory, the truth is Liberians did not seem to have a plan for the future.

As the new leader, Samuel K. Doe, became more and more comfortable with his new position in society, it was clear that our understanding of fiscal governance and fiscal responsibility would have a different meaning in Liberia. We were now dealing with leaders who had not studied economics or finance and who just recently earned $200 a month. We were dealing with leaders who may have never owned a bank account and leaders who strongly believed in instant gratification (some of whom had become instantly rich by simply pointing a gun in someone's face or cracking open a vault or safe).

Education now had a new value since friends and relatives of officials were appointed to jobs they could not perform. For instance, the elevator operator at the JFK Hospital applied to become the chief engineer, a position that required a degree in engineering. The night watchman at the Rehabilitation Center in Grand Gedeh lobbied to become the assistant minister of justice for rehabilitation, and he was eventually appointed after I departed the country in July 1980. Going forward, young children would believe that one did not need a good formal education to excel.

People were unashamed of their appointment to positions they were unqualified to occupy. This situation does not just devalue education but creates what is commonly referred to by sociologists as *status inconsistency*. It is a mismatch between the qualifications an individual possesses and the position they occupy on the social stratification ladder; in other words, those at the upper stratum of the stratification ladder are expected to have a good education. But when you ascend to a position of power, for instance, and you have no education, it creates status inconsistency, a clash between what the job requires and the ability of the person to perform in the position. We observed that almost every new appointee in government had to hire an assistant to write letters and, sometimes, make decisions. We saw more and more of these kinds of appointments as the country experienced a post-coup brain drain. Fortunately, President Doe quickly realized the huge performance gap caused by the lack of the appropriate academic training, and not only did he become more inclusive in his appointment of officials, but he also enrolled himself under the tutelage of professors at the University of Liberia.

Then there were the women on the streets singing, "Country woman born soldier; congor woman born rogue," while at the same time military officers hammered the message on the radio that the accused officials of government had committed rampant corruption. They repeated that the descendants of the black American settlers stole their land and enslaved them for more than 133 years. Of course, none of this is true if you read history, and read it within the proper context. But no one corrected the misinformation, even those who knew better. By allowing this sort of misinformation to go unchecked for so many months and years, we deepened the hatred between the immigrant blacks and the indigenous people and erased the bond of trust that had gradually formed for more than a century.

What place in the world have immigrants settled among indigenous people and there were no conflicts and rumblings? So what are all those Liberians of mixed heritage expected to do now that their relatives on both sides are enemies? There is a common expression in Liberia that "you do not burn down your house just to kill a rat." But what is most important is that by promoting this type of misinformation, we lost the context of what the black American settlers encountered, what they endured, and what they had to overcome. By promoting this sort of atrocious propaganda for political gains, not only did the black American settlers unfairly lose their greatest legacy, the defeat of colonialism in Africa, but Liberia lost its enviable stature among the nations of the world.

Today, most young Liberians do not know that Liberia was a founding member of the United Nations and that Angie Brooks, a Liberian woman, was president of the United Nations General Assembly in the early seventies. Most Liberians do not know that Liberia's President William V.S. Tubman invited the leaders of the first two African countries to gain independence from colonial rule (Ghana, 1957, and Guinea, 1959) to Sanniquelle, Liberia, in 1959 to begin discussions regarding the establishment of the Organization of African Unity, now the African Union. Most Liberians do not know that Liberia was a founding member of the Economic Community of West African States (ECOWAS). Most Liberians do not know that Liberia proposed the establishment of the African Development Bank and wrote the draft for its first charter. The list goes on.

As of April 22, 1980, the date of the public execution of the thirteen former officials of the defunct government, I began to make plans to leave Liberia, even if it was only for a while. Sadness, fear, and uncertainty filled the air. Laughter was no longer spontaneous and from the soul. Even those who felt that they were counted among the victorious soon became concerned that the coup makers might not be able to chart a sustainable course. For me, amidst all the chaos, the only source of laughter was the radio and television drama produced by Peter Ballah, a very talented Liberian producer and actor whose local plays took over the prime-time slots from American reruns like *Hawaii Five-O*, *Peyton Place*, *I Spy*, and *Gunsmoke*.

I went to the law school to inform Dean Tuan Wreh that I was dropping out of the program for a year. He would not accept my request and spent the next couple of days trying to talk me out of it. I did not want to tell him, or anyone else, that staying in law school was impossible, as I was planning to leave the country for an indefinite period. In June 1980, I left the country and remained abroad until I was certain that someone else had been appointed to fill my position at the Ministry of Justice.

II

Facing a Future of Uncertainties

CHAPTER 16

Post-Coup Liberia under President Doe: The Decade of the Eighties

In early 1981, my husband (a.k.a. Doc) and I decided that I should return to Liberia, notwithstanding the constant rumors of human rights abuses by the government of President Samuel Kanyon Doe. Doc had just returned to Liberia permanently in 1978, after living and studying in the Republic of West Germany for sixteen years. He was reluctant to return to Germany or relocate to another country and start his medical career all over. So we decided to give President Doe the benefit of the doubt.

In March 1982, I re-enrolled in the Louis Arthur Grimes School of Law at the University of Liberia. Although many professionals left Liberia right after the military coup in 1980, the law school still had great teachers like Professor Tuan Wreh, former commissioner of immigration and dean of the law school; Philip A. Z. Banks, III, who would later become dean of the law school, attorney general, and an associate justice of the Supreme Court of Liberia, consecutively; Counsellor Henrietta Koenig, former commissioner of Internal Revenue Services; Counsellor David Kpomakpor, who would later become an associate justice of the Supreme Court and then head of an interim ruling body of the Republic of Liberia; Counsellor S. Raymond Horace Sr., former associate justice of the Supreme Court of Liberia; Counsellor Charles W. Brumskine, who would later become president pro tempore of the Liberian Senate; Counsellor Ephraim Smallwood, solicitor general of the Republic of Liberia and later an associate justice of the Supreme Court; Counsellor Emmanuel Wureh, former assistant minister of justice for commercial transactions who would later become an associate justice of the Supreme Court; Counsellor Edward Moore, a former ambassador; Counsellor George Henries, former Associate Justice of the Supreme Court of Liberia, and Counsellor Johnnie N. Lewis, former circuit judge who would later become dean of the law school and chief justice of the Supreme Court, Republic of Liberia.

The law class was vibrant, and students were ambitious and curious about the legal profession. We challenged our professors to provide more and more information, and we challenged ourselves to enhance our analytical and critical thinking skills by forming study groups and brainstorming legal issues for hours. Benedict Sannoh, Snonsio Nigba, and I formed one of such study groups, and gradually six or seven other classmates joined. The full-time students in the class would have graduated at the end of 1984, but a significant disruption on the university campus that year resulted in school closure for several weeks, shifting the graduation calendar to the first quarter of 1985.

Sometime in mid-1984, we learned that the Doe government arrested Dr. Amos Sawyer, professor of political science at the University of Liberia, and George Kieh, a former president of the University of Liberia Student Union as they took steps to register their newly formed party, the Liberian People's Party (LPP), for the ensuing presidential elections in 1985. When students boycotted classes and protested against the government's action, the government ordered the university shut down. Notwithstanding, some students returned to campus daily and continued to protest, ignoring warnings from the government to stop the protest. Then on August 22, 1984, while students were protesting on campus (the campus is diagonally across the street from the Executive Mansion), carrying what they claimed to be the casket of President Doe, several armed soldiers jumped over the fence onto the university grounds and stormed the campus. Students scattered and began to run in different directions; some left the campus, and others hid in buildings on the campus.

I had not returned to campus since the closure but had gone to town to purchase an item for my three-month-old daughter when I saw the students carrying a casket. They chanted that the casket represented the demise of

President Doe. The students appeared agitated and aggressive. Therefore, I immediately became concerned about my brother, John Hammond, who was then the director of planning and development at the university. I parked my car near the Catholic school, situated contiguous to the university property, and got out to go on campus to find my brother when, suddenly, I saw the first group of soldiers jump over the fence, onto the university premises, about a hundred feet from where I stood. I got back in my car and sped away. When I arrived home, I called my brother, and my heart sank when he told me that he was in his office on campus. I asked him to leave, but he said that it was too late, as the soldiers had taken over, and he could hear people running and screaming. He told me not to worry, that he was communicating with another professor, Dr. James T. Tarpeh, who was also holed up in his office in another part of the same building.

Several hours after the commotion began, the bishop of the Episcopal Church of Liberia, Dr. George Brown, risked his life, amidst the havoc, and drove on campus to see what he could do to stop the madness. Dr. Tarpeh came out of the first door the bishop knocked on and informed him that my brother and others were still holed up in their respective offices. The bishop, along with Dr. Tarpeh, went to my brother's office, and each of the other offices, and rescued all of the people they found. My brother said that as they walked out, he did not see dead bodies but saw blood on the floors and walls.

Unfortunately, at the end of the rampage on the university campus, many students (I have never been able to ascertain how many) lost their lives; students and faculty members suffered physical injuries, and there was substantial damage to buildings and other properties. One of my classmates at the law school, Ernest Morgan, disappeared during the upheaval, and to this day, no one has seen or heard from him.

The student protest was an offshoot of the student revolutionary movement of the seventies that boldly challenged the government and demanded respect for fundamental rights guaranteed by the Liberian Constitution. To President Doe, the action of the students was simply not the exercise of constitutional rights but, rather, a display of utter disregard for authority. More than that, to President Doe, the action of the students, professors, and political activists registered, in his mind, as a public rejection of him as a leader.

Just a few years before, the public revered President Doe. They called him a hero. Others called him their redeemer. Now, most of the same people who had put him on this pedestal wanted to see him dethroned; he could not understand and accept that. To him, it was deceit, sycophancy, and betrayal—not politics—and that enraged him more. He appeared to have little mercy for people he perceived had turned on him. President Doe would often issue threats by suggesting if you do this, that, or the other, "you will not live to tell the story." He also often said, "You have a long life, but you are careless with it."

A couple of days after the university incident, my brother's wife, also the sister of Dr. Amos Sawyer, came over to our house and asked if we could hide Dr. Sawyer's car in our backyard, amidst indiscriminate arrests and detention being conducted by the Doe government. I told her the request was difficult not only because she lived just next door to me, but I only had a carport and not a garage. Also, there was no way that Doe's soldiers would come to search her house without searching mine, knowing the relationship between us, especially since the car would be visible from the road. I told her it would be better to find a third-party custodian, rather than for either of us to risk the wrath of the ruthless soldiers. I do not think she or her family ever understood or accepted my position on this.

The university reopened a couple of months later, and our class graduated from law school in April 1985. Within a week after graduation, Counsellor Varney Sherman, a senior legal counsel at Maxwell & Maxwell (a first-rate law firm in the country at the time) recruited me to work for the firm at the urging of the managing partner, Christian D. Maxwell. It was exciting to launch my career in a firm that was engaged in a broad range of legal activities, encompassing transactional matters and litigation. I began work around July, and a couple of months following, Counsellor Maxwell sat me down and said that he had to leave Liberia, as the Doe government was targeting him because of his close association with Ellen Johnson-Sirleaf. He wanted to know whether, in addition to my work as legal counsel, I could manage his companies in his absence. It was a tall order; he had four other companies besides the law firm: a real estate company, a quarry, a restaurant, and a travel agency. His wife, Janet Snowden Maxwell, managed the latter four companies but she had already left the country for an indefinite period. Varney Sherman would manage the law firm.

Other than helping my mother in her provision store when I was in middle school, I had never really run a business. When I was in law school, I started a small real estate company and managed a taxicab business, but neither one did well because my studies took up most of my time. Other than lack of business experience and the infringement on my legal assignments, I was concerned about the political dimension. As much I wanted to help my employer, I did not want to get caught in the crossfire.

From 1980, President Doe and a majority of the seventeen men who carried out the coup began to fall out; the government had executed a few of them for various unsubstantiated allegations by 1985. The 1985 fallout was with Thomas Quiwonkpa, nicknamed "strong man." People who knew Quiwonkpa and interacted with him said that he was energetic, intelligent, and one of the most reasonable among the seventeen coup makers. The word on the street was that in 1980, Doe and his cronies had promised to hold power for only five years and return to the barracks by 1985. Instead of living up to his promise, Doe decided to contest the presidential election in 1985. That did not go down too well with the Liberian public, especially the opposition political parties like the Liberian Action Party (LAP), where Ellen Sirleaf was the standard bearer.

Quiwonkpa, one of the closest to Doe of the seventeen coup makers, and who wanted the soldiers to live up to their commitment of 1980 to return to the barracks, was accused by President Doe of being influenced by the opposition, especially Ellen Sirleaf. The Doe government also believed that Christian D. Maxwell was a financial supporter of LAP therefore, it was understandable that he had to leave town. Quiwonkpa escaped the country after the bickering between President Doe and himself continued to escalate. In October 1985, elections were held. A couple of weeks later, Doe was declared the winner amidst grumblings and allegations of fraud.

On November 12, 1985, sometime during the morning, it was announced on the public radio General Quiwonkpa had returned to Liberia and had taken over the government, and the whereabouts of President Doe was not known. I called a friend to verify what I had heard, and he said, "Anytime a leader is overthrown, and he has not been captured or killed, you do not have a coup d'état." Because of what the friend said, my family decided to remain at home and wait to see what would happen.

Then sometime during the day, we heard on the radio a list of names of people who had been selected to work with the Quiwonkpa administration. Shortly after that, perhaps around two o'clock that afternoon, we heard the voice of President Samuel Kanyon Doe on the radio, announcing that the coup against his government had been foiled and that he was still in charge. Everyone in our house was speechless; we looked at the radio as though it had malfunctioned. People were confused. They were calling us on the phone to interpret what everyone had heard on the radio in plain English. "Doe is still president," I said on the phone to one of my relatives who insisted that I explain what Doe means by saying, "I am still the president."

A few days later, we learned that those who had gone out on the morning of November 12 to cheer General Quiwonkpa and those whose names

Quiwonkpa announced on the radio as likely officials of his government were targeted as enemies of the Doe government and arrested for questioning. A popular television newscaster, Charles Gbenyon, was out on the morning of November 12, 1985, to collect the usual news stories as the event evolved. After the Quiwonkpa plot failed, Mr. Gbenyon was arrested and taken to the mansion for questioning. To date, his whereabouts are still unknown.

One day in mid-1986, Robert Tubman, a lawyer, an economist, and former deputy minister of justice in the government of President Tolbert, came by the Maxwell & Maxwell law offices to see me. He told me that he had accepted the position of minister of finance and wanted to know if I could become his special assistant. My heart sank, and I could feel a knot in my stomach. My answer was a resounding no. He kept coming back to talk to me, and I kept refusing to change my position. Then one day I sought the advice of the late Ambassador Eugenia Stevenson, a respected diplomat and public servant. She simply said that when she found herself in a similar position in the past, she sought the advice of an aunt who said that "anyone who accepts a government job is accepting to serve the people, not the head of the government."

When Counsellor Tubman came back again, I asked, out of curiosity, why he had accepted the job. He said, "We cannot and should not just sit by and see our country go to waste without trying to do something to help." Besides, I asked whether President Doe was aware that I was being recruited to serve in his administration, since I had worked for the previous government. He answered in the affirmative and said, "If you accept the job, then I will take you to meet President Doe formally."

A lawyer told me, "You are between a rock and a hard place. You work for an office that is considered an ally of the opposition political party, Liberian Action Party, and the owner of the law firm, Christian Maxwell, is a personal and longtime friend of Ellen Sirleaf; if you refuse the job, the government will give a political interpretation to your response. If you accept the job, then you run the risk of alienating all the anti-Doe people out there."

In essence, what should have been the beginning of a budding law career had now left me preoccupied with resolving an unanticipated quagmire. Neither a law firm sympathetic to an opposition party nor a government uninterested in the rule of law was the proper arena for advancing my career, but I had to proceed cautiously. In Liberia, there is a common saying that when your hand is in the leopard's mouth, you have to pull it out slowly; otherwise you will lose the entire arm.

I justified my decision to accept the job with the thought that we all had suffered grief and pain, but Liberia's problems were much bigger than our personal pain. Every argument made sense at this point, but what was most important to me was to make my small contribution to keep the country from spiraling into an abyss. Mr. Tubman was right; we had to save this country at great personal sacrifice. I commenced work sometime in July 1986, but before my appointment, we visited President Doe, as was required. I recall that the meeting was uneventful, brief, and formal. In the end, he thanked me for accepting the position. That would be the only time I would see him up close.

The Ministry of Finance, the nerve center of the government, was everything I imagined it would be, a busy place with challenging work. The Ministry of Finance had to interact with every institution of government almost on a daily basis. Whereas my education and previous employment activities (except the Maxwell Law Firm) involved the social sciences, the Ministry of Finance was a different ball game. The job description covered the realm of international banking, debt management, contract negotiation, procurement of goods and services, revenue collection, expenditure, and so on. All of this was not only new but also interesting and challenging. The core team on fiscal matters consisted of Robert Tubman, minister of finance; Paul Jeffy, minister of planning and economic affairs; John Bestman, governor of the Central Bank; and Antoinette Sayeh, economic adviser to the minister of finance.

Notwithstanding the few qualified officials in top government positions, there were serious capacity problems in the government occasioned by the human resource outflow after the 1980 coup, resulting in substantial brain drain. The opportunity to gain vast experience was unparalleled, but inadequate governance structures and corruption overwhelmed the few who were educated and committed. Security and judicial services continued to deteriorate in the country; very little funding was appropriated to strengthen those institutions. President Doe, who had had complete trust in the Progressive intellectuals in the early days of the coup, had now made a 360-degree turn, relying on his own understanding and the advice of only a few trusted friends and relatives. In my opinion, he had become distrustful of the Progressives, particularly those whom he perceived had deceived him.

President Doe and his closest associates had unfettered access to revenues collected by the Ministry of Finance and public corporations. It appeared this government hated to hear that money was in the bank. It was not surprising to me, considering that our new leaders were only recently living from paycheck to paycheck, most of whom never knew what it was to have a savings or checking account. They traveled a lot, bought real properties, opened businesses, and bought very expensive vehicles. The popular vehicle at the time was the

Japanese-made Nissan Pajero sports utility vehicle (SUV). Because of the violent means by which this government came into power, the citizens were afraid to question the actions of public officials openly.

In September 1986, Joyce Mends-Cole contacted me with what she called good news. She said Yale Law School was awarding fellowships, and she thought that I might meet the requirements for admission. I didn't know whether I wanted to go back to the classroom, but Joyce reminded me of how important it is to have options in an uncertain environment. I concurred. After all, it was the breakthrough intervention I had hoped for to resolve my dilemma. So, by December 1986, I had submitted the full application.

In March 1987, just when rumors started to spread that President Doe might relieve the minister of finance of his post, I received an acceptance letter from Yale, informing me not only of my admission but also that I was a recipient of a fellowship. Off to Yale I went, where I would discover the few months at the Ministry of Finance had provided me a strong foundation for a focus in international business transaction courses such as International Banking, International Commercial Arbitrations, Transnational Investments, Bankruptcy, Secured Transactions, and so forth.

When I returned to Liberia after my graduate law studies, I sensed that President Doe did not have a strong grip on the country as he did during the early eighties following the military coup. His administration appeared to be moving in a slow downward spiral. The opposition to the Doe administration had grown larger and stronger and President Doe had become more dictatorial in his desperation to maintain control of the country.

Nevertheless, I was audacious enough to establish a private law office with very little resources but a lot of determination. I soon realized how essential it was to build a new professional network. Although the country had changed more than I was willing to admit, it did not take me long to build a support team. I received some financial assistance from a relative, Willie A. Givens, Sr.; professional assistance from a former professor, Counsellor Phillip A. Z. Banks, III, who assisted me with my first major corporate case; Francis S. Korkpor, a former co-worker from the Bureau of Corrections, connected me with key officials in the judiciary; Thomas Hanson, the governor of the Central Bank of Liberia, did not know me but willingly enlisted me as one of the retained lawyers for the bank; John S. Morlu, Sr., a former co-worker from the Ministry of Finance helped me set up the accounts for the firm. The fact that all of these individuals were willing to assist me, in spite of the diversity among us, gave me assurance that the vestiges of the military coup would not dampen hope for a better Liberia in the future.

I went on to slowly build up the law practice in spite of all the warnings I received that that the country was somewhat unstable. I was even daring enough to commence the construction of a four-bedroom house near the beach. After the military coup, everything I did in Liberia appeared to be *pure chance*; planning your future seemed unrealistic. We lived from day to day not knowing what to expect.

CHAPTER 17

The Charles Taylor Incursion

On Christmas Day, 1989, we heard on the radio that Charles Taylor, the former head of the General Services Agency during the early days of the Doe regime, had invaded Liberia from the Ivory Coast. Taylor had entered through Nimba, a county in the north, on Christmas Eve, with several armed young men for the singular purpose of overthrowing the government of President Samuel Kanyon Doe. There were rumors that Dr. H. Boima Fahnbulleh, a University of Liberia professor, had also planned to invade the country with a following of fifty men, but Taylor upstaged him. A few of my friends and I had planned to have breakfast together on Christmas morning, but when we met, no one had the appetite to eat; we kept saying, "This has to be a joke."

No, it was not a joke; we eventually heard Charles Taylor on the radio. President Doe had accused Taylor of absconding with nearly a million dollars of government funds when he was director general of the General Services Agency in the early eighties and had vowed to have him brought back to Liberia for trial. To the best of our knowledge, Mr. Taylor was in jail in the United States in connection with these allegations. Now, we were being informed by the media that he had broken jail in Massachusetts, left the

United States, gone to Libya and trained his army, and was now on his way to the capital to overthrow the Doe regime.

The more Mr. Taylor taunted President Doe on the radio (with words like "I know what you are wearing; I know what you had to eat today," etc.), the more the president and his officials became paranoid. There were speculations about Liberians who may have backed Mr. Taylor. Doe's first suspect was always Ellen Johnson Sirleaf and members of the Progressives. On January 4, 1990, we woke up to the sad news that Robert Phillips, a construction engineer, whom the Doe government had accused of being an opposition member, had been brutally murdered earlier that morning in his home on Payne Avenue and Fourteenth Street, Sinkor, an upscale suburb at the time. Everyone suspected that the government was responsible for the assassination, but no one was brave enough to speak up.

Two of my clients from Europe, who lived diagonally across the street from Mr. Phillips, said that as they returned home from the nightclub on foot during the early morning of January 4, they were stopped by "very nervous" government soldiers. The soldiers questioned them about their presence in the neighborhood at one in the morning, and after the soldiers realized that they were completely harmless and disinterested in what was going on, they ushered them into their house. Later, during the morning of January 4, when my clients woke up, they noticed a huge crowd on the street looking into the direction of Mr. Phillips's house and conversing inaudibly. They went across the street to inquire and learned that their quiet neighbor had been brutally murdered a few hours earlier, perhaps just about the time they were returning home from the nightclub.

Following the death of Robert Philips, Mr. Charles Taylor appeared to have stepped up his aggression; his rebel groups were advancing quickly, and some people I knew had started to leave the country to take up residence abroad until the conflict brewing between Doe and Taylor either subsided or come to a head. All sorts of disconcerting events began to unfold. A couple of months after Robert's tragic death, a local newspaper published a story about how several young men from Nimba had been rounded up and taken away by government soldiers, and no one heard from them again. But the newspaper displayed photos of the decapitated heads of three young men that had been found near a railroad track, suspecting they were among the young men who had gone missing.

As I stood at my office window on Mechlin Street one afternoon in March 1990, I saw a pickup truck loaded with wounded government soldiers come to a stop on the street. Then the driver and his passenger got out and began to unload wounded soldiers and take them upstairs to the second floor of the building opposite me, where the Malag Clinic operated. The two men lifted the almost lifeless bodies from bloodsoaked mattresses padding the back of the pickup truck. Some of the soldiers were already unconscious from massive loss of blood, and those who were still conscious were moaning and screaming as the assistants in the clinic roughly dragged the bodies out. In a few minutes, the assistants brought back down those soldiers who expired and asked the driver of the pickup to take the corpses to the military morgue. A crowd gathered, and we all watched in horror. The government sent the troops to crush Mr. Taylor and his rebels, but, it seemed, the rebels had ambushed and slaughtered them.

Sometime in early April 1990, a neighbor and a former schoolmate knocked on the door to my home at around eight o'clock at night. I was a bit surprised by the visit, considering that he only waved from his car as we drove past each other. We never seemed to have the time to visit. But tonight, he was at the door waiting for me to let him in. He sat down and said that the purpose of his visit was to advise me to leave the country for my safety and that he and his wife had already decided to leave. He reminded me that Charles Taylor had once attended the same high school with us and knew us well. He also reminded me when Thomas Quiwonkpa, the former commanding general under President Doe, returned in 1985 to overthrow the Doe government, he prematurely named his cabinet on the radio. When the coup was foiled, the Doe government targeted and arrested all of those whose names were on Quiwonkpa's list of officials, notwithstanding that they may not have even known of Quiwonkpa's adventure. My neighbor was worried that Charles Taylor was audacious enough to do the same thing, and in that case, he feared that we might be named by Taylor as some of his prospective officials, exposing us to certain danger. I agreed with his deductions, and after he left my house, I decided to discuss my plans to leave with my husband when he got home from work.

At the end of April 1990, I bought two round-trip tickets for my minor daughter and myself. My husband decided that he would remain to help with medical problems related to injuries arising from the civil war but also to pursue his private project of repairing the torn bladders of young women. The condition is called fistula. He told me a lot of the untrained midwives in the rural areas used crude methods of delivering babies, such as a mortar (a large, vertical, wooden vessel used to pound food) to press from the chest toward the uterus to force the baby out. In the process, the uterus would sometimes rupture or the bladder of the pregnant woman at times tore; at worst, the mother could bleed to death, or, at best, she could become incontinent from a torn bladder. He felt the project was worth the risk, and I agreed.

On May 25, 1990, I dressed and went to work like any other day. I met with clients and discussed with them what we needed to do to move forward on their respective matters. I recall conducting separate meetings involving two Europeans, a Chinese, and a Nigerian. Strangely, during each meeting, my client offered me refuge of some sort in the event the civil war escalated and hit the capital while I was still in the country. I thought the whole discussion about refuge was weird. I did tell them at the end of each meeting that I was traveling but for a short time, and they all appeared to be relieved that I was leaving.

By two o'clock in the afternoon of May 25, 1990, I took a last look at my office and walked out, leaving the five-room suite undisturbed, with the intention of returning in less than a month to a law firm that had been in existence for barely a year. There was a fleeting trepidation that the civil war might not end quickly and that I would lose my investment in no time to looting, but I walked away anyway. Then I stopped by the house to pick up my family on my way to the airport, and, as I did at the office, I walked through the house looking around as though for one last time. While standing in the bedroom, it occurred to me to collect all my land deeds and pack them in my carry-on bag, which I did. Interestingly, I kept the deeds and my jewelry together, but I did not pick up my jewelry, and I don't know why.

On the way to the airport, soldiers posted in front of the military barracks, midway between the capital and the airport, stopped us and asked a few questions. They did not pose any problems since my husband was not traveling. We also went through the military checkpoint at the airport without much ado.

As we sat on the tarmac waiting for takeoff, I thought about how much I had invested in Liberia in such a short time. I established an elaborate five-room office suite, including a library/conference room combo, and hired staff. Beyan Howard, a smart young man with a very promising future, had just graduated from law school and had agreed to join as a junior associate. I had also taken quite a bit of the money I earned from a foreign client and commenced the construction of a four-bedroom split-level house in Sinkor near the beach. But now, like in 1980, I was again facing an uncertain future.

The plan was to leave the country for only three to four weeks, as the fall of the Doe government seemed imminent. This time, I was determined not to get caught up in another coup d'état and all the attending violence and looting. We did not discuss our plans with anyone; in fact, it was not usual, under the circumstances, to publicly broadcast that you were planning to flee the country. The government was giving the public the impression that everything was under control and that Taylor would fail in his endeavor like Quiwonkpa. The public had a different perception though; to the public, security was weak. Officials paid very little attention to security and spent more time plundering the country. The people had become disillusioned and disgruntled and no longer saw President Doe as the redeemer who had emerged from the 1980 coup d'état. The president had his corps of advisers, but I do not know what advice they were giving; all I know is that the security of the country was spiraling downward, almost like a malfunctioning roller coaster headed for an abyss.

My husband (a.k.a Doc) left our home on Duport Road on the outskirts of the city on the morning of July 2, 1990, to go to work at the JFK Memorial Hospital close to Central Monrovia. He did not return home at the end of that day because the Taylor-led rebels had entered our neighborhood and taken over the homes of residents who had fled the area. They marked their names on the entry and exit doors and shared among themselves all the personal property they found, including money, food, furniture, wigs, and lingerie.

We did not hear from Doc between July and September and kept receiving conflicting messages about his well-being. Some said he was dead, while others insisted that he was still alive but somewhere held up in one of the rebel camps. We continued to pray and be hopeful. Suddenly one day in September 1990, Doc called to inform us that he was still alive but had not had access to a telephone. He explained that he had lived at the JFK Medical Center, the government hospital, for a couple of months, and later, he was evacuated to an area of the city controlled by Prince Y. Johnson, head of the Independent National Patriotic Front of Liberia (INPFL), a breakaway faction from Charles Taylor's National Patriotic Front of Liberia. He recounted government soldiers would come to the hospital at night, unannounced, in huge trucks and order all the men to come out and line up; apparently, the government received reports that some suspicious characters were hiding in the hospital. They would pick out of the lineup anyone whom they believed was from Nimba County, particularly young men from the Gio and Mano tribes. The soldiers would then take them away. The government alleged that the two tribes from Nimba County were supporters and sympathizers of Charles Taylor, perhaps because Charles Taylor invaded the country through Nimba County.

When Doc returned home after three months, there was no place for him to sleep; thirty-three individuals had taken up residence in our home. Even the bathrooms had been used provisionally as bedrooms. A few of the occupants were relatives, but a vast majority were complete strangers. He discovered that they had plundered through our personal effects and were even wearing some of our clothes.

CHAPTER 18

Temporary Protected
Status (TPS) in the
United States

By August 1990, my three-week visit to the United States had become three months, and I did not see any light at the end of the tunnel. Instead of abating over time, the civil war had not only reached Monrovia, the capital, but it had intensified.

Around this time, the ECOMOG, a peace-monitoring group deployed to Liberia by the ECOWAS (Economic Community of West African States), had somewhat established itself firmly on the ground with the approbation of the Liberian government. Although it was called a "monitoring group", I believe that the ECOMOG was a peacekeeping military force that became a de facto participant in the fight against National Patriotic Front of Liberia (NPFL), a warring faction opposed to the Doe government. Apparently, the newly appointed ECOMOG leader, a Ghanaian national named General Arnold Quainoo, arrived at the Freeport of Monrovia by ship, and someone advised or encouraged President Doe to go to the Freeport to meet the general. I do not know who advised the president to leave the secure environment of the Executive Mansion to go to the port to greet the general. There is a common expression in Liberia: when a monkey is ready to die, it does not hear the whistle of the hunter.

According to news reports, when President Doe arrived at the Freeport, his security officers were advised to leave their weapons outside, and they complied. Shortly after that, shots rang out from guns other than those carried by President Doe's security. Onlookers believed that the shooters were men led by Prince Y. Johnson, a member of the Gio ethnic group hostile to President Doe and his Krahn ethnic group. Some of the men who accompanied President Doe to the port were killed during the shoot out. The shooters captured President Doe and led him to the base of the Independent National Patriotic Front of Liberia (INPFL). Prince Y. Johnson was then the leader of the INPFL, a breakaway faction from Charles Taylor's National Patriotic Force of Liberia (NPFL). The captors taunted and tortured President Doe. He eventually died from injuries to his body.

In the meantime, the number of Liberians fleeing Liberia and seeking refuge in several West African countries and the United States began to grow exponentially. The increase in the refugee population, the emergence of splinter warring factions, the widespread violence throughout the country, and the breakdown in major institutions were all signs that peace was eluding Liberia. The realization hit most Liberians that there was no end in sight to this war. For some of us who had relocated to the United States temporarily due to the war, our lives now appeared to be in limbo; we did not know whether we should plan to return home or start planning to live in the United States for an indefinite period. Just when we thought we might finally start recovering from the lingering effects of the 1980 coup, we found ourselves in a situation even more uncertain and unsettling. How do you ever establish yourself when almost every decade you have to start life all over, either at home or in a strange land?

One morning toward the end of August 1990, Joyce Mends-Cole a Liberian attorney, and also a human rights advocate, called and said Ellen Johnson Sirleaf had informed her that a bill was being presented on the floor of the US Senate within forty-eight hours to provide temporary protection for nationals of Somalia, Lebanon, and Kuwait. We also learned that Senators Edward Kennedy of Massachusetts and Paul Martin Simon of Illinois had expressed willingness to support the inclusion of Liberia in the bill but that the Liberians would have to petition on their own volition. Joyce was tied up with work in a major human rights organization and could not prepare the petition on such short turnaround. Therefore, she asked Vivian Sayeh-Weeks and me to draft the petition and obtain at least five hundred signatures within forty-eight hours since it had begun to appear more and more that both of us might ultimately become beneficiaries of the program. We agreed, and that same day, we met at the Silver Spring apartment of Vivian Sayeh-Weeks and her husband, Vittorio Weeks. George Williams and Wendell Addy were also present. The five of us, ordinary Liberian citizens, drafted the document and quickly obtained the required number of signatures and submitted the document promptly.

The bill for temporary protected status (TPS), when passed, would provide temporary refuge for aliens fleeing from natural disasters or ongoing civil conflicts in their home country. In the meantime, Liberians were benefitting from a six-month Safe Haven program (September 1990 to March 1991). This program would protect Liberians in the interim while the TPS bill was being enacted. It meant those Liberians who had fled the civil war and did not qualify for refugee status or other US Immigration programs, such as family or employer sponsorship, could now obtain a work permit and get a job, as well as enroll their children in public schools, under the temporary program. Unlike the refugee program, an applicant did not have to be a specific target of violence because of social, religious, or political beliefs or affiliation. All you had to show was that you had fled from a country where violence was widespread, indiscriminate, and ongoing.

Before the end of 1990, the TPS bill passed, and Liberians became eligible to remain in the United States temporarily. It meant that once the Safe Haven program expired on March 31, 1991, the TPS, a one-year renewable program, would kick in. However, there was a proviso that only Liberians who entered the US on or before March 31, 1991, would be eligible; this cut-off date could have been lifted administratively to accommodate those who came after March 31, 1991, but it wasn't. We suspected that the US government did not want to remove the cut-off date for fear of opening a floodgate, which was understandable. Some non-governmental organizations convened a meeting with a few Liberians to explain what the TPS program was all about and how the Liberians could avail themselves of the opportunity. Subsequently, a few of us convened a mass meeting in a church basement to share the information with the Liberian community.

Yvette Chesson (later Yvette Chesson-Wureh), a lawyer and an immigration advocate, chaired the meeting. Yvette's father, Joseph J. F. Chesson, was the attorney general of Liberia at the time of the military coup d'etat in 1980. He was one of the thirteen officials executed by the new military government on April 22, 1980. The execution of the thirteen was an event that left a lot of Liberians, especially family members, devastated, distraught, bitter, and angry. Yvette left Liberia immediately after the execution of her father and had been living in the United States legally since and, therefore, did not need the benefits of the TPS program; however, she wanted to help her fellow Liberians who might otherwise lose the opportunity because they did not know what to do.

Those who lost loved ones violently during the April 1980 coup reacted to the experience in many different ways. A few people immediately became withdrawn after all the horrific events of April 1980. Some left Liberia in 1980 and vowed never to return. Some continued to live in Liberia but avoided a relationship with anyone they felt was responsible for the death of their loved ones. Some have continued to live in Liberia but use all of their energy and skills to develop themselves personally in complete disregard for the development of the country as a whole. Others, like Yvette Chesson, have become more energized to work to promote unity, peace, and social justice among Liberian communities in Liberia and abroad.

Over the years, many Liberians worked to ensure that Liberian citizens who sought refuge in the US receive the requisite protection under the law. Some advocates stayed aboard on a sustained basis, while others dropped out along the way, but in all, the contribution, no matter how little, made a positive impact on the Liberian community living in the United States. Some of those whose contribution has remained in my memory, and with whom I had the privilege to work with directly are: Mohammedu Jones, John Lloyd, Christine Hoff-Williams, Moses Saygbe, Zachary Sharpe, Saah En'Tow, Michael Wreh, Anthony Kesselley, George Fahnbulleh, Dugpeny Cooper, Joseph Korto, Ayele Ajavon, Marbue Richards, Mary Broh, George Kieh, Saah Joseph, Saah Johnny, Calvin Bropleh, Michael Wotorson as chairman of United Liberia Association of the Americas (ULAA), the late Norman Leslie Cole, the late Rev. Justus Reeves, Isaac Vah Tukpah, and Amos Sirleaf. Their commitment was more than just sporadic, notwithstanding their full-time jobs, family responsibilities, and other obligations.

The Rhode Island Liberian community lobbied their politicians and local philanthropic organizations on a sustained basis. Reverend Phil West of Rhode Island Common Cause and the Rhode Island International Institute provided technical and advisory support for the Rhode Island Liberian community, which became our strongest base outside of the Washington, D.C. metropolitan area.

I am sure that there are many who worked just as hard in their respective communities across the United States, sometimes as members of other advocacy organizations; to them, we are also very grateful. It is the collective and persistent efforts of the entire Liberian community that made everything possible.

There were some Liberians who desired to retain a private lawyer to handle their immigration matter. In those instances, we provided services for a fee or referred them to other Liberian lawyers like Carlos B.Z. Smith, Tilman Dunbar, Jr., Patricia Minikon, Edward Neufville, or American immigration lawyers. Some of the lawyers handled immigration matters exclusively and others, as in the case of Yvette and me, simply added immigration to their existing portfolios.

For some strange reason, Yvette Chesson and I became the unofficial legal representatives on the Liberian immigration matter. Perhaps it was because we had, on various occasions, written letters to seek clarification on one issue or the other on behalf of the Liberian community. The renewal of the TPS was not automatic; every year, Yvette and I received citations to a TPS reassessment meeting at the Adjudication Office at the US Department of Justice. At that time, the Bureau of Immigration and Naturalization Services (INS) was a part of the U.S. Department of Justice. All we had to do was justify that the conflict was ongoing and that our fellow citizens could not return to Liberia in the midst of a vicious civil war. Should the US government, during any year, determine that the war had abated and that it was safe for Liberians to return home, the meeting would involve multiple US government agencies. Those agencies would consist of the US Department of State, the US Justice Department (now the Department of Homeland Security), and sometimes the Office of National Security at the White House.

In the meantime, by mid-1990, and continuing into 1991, the war intensified. It seemed as though there was no end in sight. Therefore, by the end of 1991, my family decided to exercise another option available to us for adjustment of immigration status. In 1992, I became an adjunct professor at the American University in Washington, DC; subsequently, I left that position to take up a full-time position at Morgan State University in Baltimore. Teaching was the best option at the time.

The toughest challenge we had to keep Liberians in legal residency in the US was between 1996 and 1999. In 1996, there was a fresh outbreak of conflict in the capital. I planned a three-week visit to Liberia, starting March 17, 1996, but had to cut my trip short and get out on March 23rd because of all the wrangling among the various political factions. I told my hostess, Mrs. Theresa Leigh-Sherman, that the capital city was a time bomb waiting to explode. It was easy to reach that conclusion when you read the newspaper or listened to the radio. On April 6, 1996, exactly two weeks after I left, a new conflict broke out in the capital. Mrs. Sherman called me and said, "You eat witch." It is an expression we use in Liberia when a person makes a prediction and it comes to pass. She managed to escape Liberia on a fishing boat traveling to neighboring Sierra Leone.

Just after the April 6, 1996, outbreak of violence in Liberia, the US Department of Justice conducted a review hearing on Liberia. Yvette and I were in attendance, and we requested that the cut-off date of March 31, 1991, be lifted and extended to cover the Liberians who had arrived in the United States between March 1991 and July 1996. It was a big request from us, considering that the TPS legislation was only meant to provide temporary refuge. Here, we already had more than twenty-thousand Liberians who had been on the program for more than five years, due to intermittent skirmishes in Liberia, and now we were asking to increase the number by lifting the cut-off date. In spite of the challenges, the US government eventually renewed the program and extended the cut-off date to include Liberians who fled the outbreak of violence that began on April 6, 1996.

The 1997 TPS assessment hearing was even more challenging because Charles Taylor, a former rebel leader, had won a democratic election for the office of president of Liberia by a landslide over Ellen Johnson Sirleaf, a seasoned politician. The US Department of State in its assessment of the TPS program that year recommended discontinuing the program because the war had abated, and the people of Liberia now had a democratically elected leader. The State Department wanted us to explain why we thought it was still unsafe for Liberians to return home when Liberians on the ground had overwhelmingly elected Charles Taylor as president. Young people had run through the streets, just before the election, chanting, "He killed my ma and killed my pa, but I will vote for him."

Making an argument for remaining on the TPS just after the people of Liberia had installed a democratically elected government was tough. However, we countered by maintaining notwithstanding the country had just experienced a democratic election, there was no guarantee that a former warlord could maintain peace in a country that had become so polarized by the very same leader. We argued that this new turn of events certainly required a wait-and-see attitude; they agreed and renewed the TPS for another year.

CHAPTER 19

Charles Taylor's Intervention Required for Liberian Immigrants in the U.S.

The yearly meeting to justify a renewal of TPS was becoming onerous. We needed to find a more permanent solution going forward; that would require the application for permanent residency, or green card, for the twenty thousand some odd people on the TPS program. Eventually, the green card would lead to US citizenship. We learned from the Haitian and El Salvadoran experiences that it is not likely for a community to transition from the TPS program to permanent residency since the purpose of the TPS was to provide temporary refuge.

For the US Congress to consider a bill for permanent residency for a community of foreign nationals residing in the US, the community would have to be on another temporary program called Deferred Enforced Departure (DED) instead of TPS. Essentially, the TPS program was specifically enacted to provide temporary residency for foreign nationals who meet the eligibility requirements; therefore, the U.S. Congress cannot grant permanent residency to holders of TPS in violation of its own law. The DED is very similar to TPS in its benefits, except that DED is not granted by an act of Congress but, rather, by the discretionary power of the president of the United States under the US Constitution to conduct foreign affairs.

Obtaining the Deferred Enforced Departure (DED) for the Liberian community was not as easy as we had thought. We discovered that we were required to get a letter from President Charles Taylor stating that a mass deportation of Liberians from the United States would destabilize Liberia. Charles Taylor had just been democratically elected in 1997 as president of Liberia; therefore, it was a tall order to ask him to state in writing that the country was still politically unstable. Coincidentally, I received an invitation from the government of President Taylor to participate in a national conference on the future of Liberia scheduled for July 1998, at the Unity Conference Center in Liberia. At first, I was not sure that I was interested in taking a trip to Liberia at that time, but I determined that traveling to Liberia and meeting with President Taylor face-to-face might be the only way to convince him to provide this letter.

Charles Taylor and I attended the same boarding school (Ricks Institute) when we were children. He was my senior. He left after two years in attendance, and I did not see him again until 1980 when we were adults. In March 1980, he stopped by my office to say hello after he left a meeting with the minister of justice, Joseph J. F. Chesson; then in April 1980, he stopped by our house to ask my husband to provide medical care for a relative. I did not see or hear from him again until I received the letter to participate in the July 1998 national conference in Liberia. I did not think all of this gave me sufficient clout to ask President Taylor to admit in a letter that Liberia was somewhat unstable just to accommodate Liberians seeking legal immigration status in the United States, but I decided to give it a try; otherwise, the US government would deport a significant number of the twenty thousand Liberians on temporary status in the US.

President Taylor and I, surrounded by protocol and security officers, sat in an office at the Unity Conference Center during a short break from the conference. Before I requested the letter, the president immediately began to chitchat about the days we were all teenagers at Ricks. Since we were not classmates, the only memory I had of him was when he and four other teenage boys chased me from the mess hall to the girls' dormitory. There was a strict rule against girls and boys being seen together on campus, except in the classes and general assembly. I was so terrified; I ran for my dear life so that this student and his buddies would not get me in trouble with the authorities.

After I recounted the incident to him, I told him that I could only remember the names of four of them; I just could not remember who the fifth person was.

First, he laughed raucously as I recounted the incident; now, it is funny to me, but it was not funny then. Second, when he finally stopped laughing, he said, "The fifth boy was Alfred Budy. He has died, you know, but he did not die in my war." I was stunned that this man, now president, had such a vivid memory of the incident. For some reason, I expected him to either be dismissive of my recollection or just smile politely. But to my amazement, his memory of the incident was more vivid than mine.

President Taylor wanted to know if members of my family would come to Liberia to help his government. I promised to think about it and convey his desire to my family. My brother John is an architect who specialized in urban planning; my sister, Lucelia, specialized in banking & finance, as well as budgeting on the graduate level; Henri, the agricultural economist, is also an insurance specialist. Another brother, Albert, studied computer science. Certainly, my family would have loved to serve Liberia but that was just not the right time.

I believe President Taylor already knew what my response would be, but he felt it was worth giving a try. I don't think I would have lasted one month in the Taylor government. I had too many concerns with how the country was being governed: the arms deals, the mismanagement of natural resources, the conscription on child soldiers, and the abuse of human rights were top on my list of issues. I figured that if I really wanted the letter for the U.S. immigration advocacy program, then I needed to press for that and deal with the other matters of concern later.

President Taylor did not want to write the letter at all, stating that he would be helping the very Liberians in the United States opposing his government. He said, "Christiana, you are tying my hands behind my back." I reminded him that he was now president and represented all Liberians. Therefore, he had to live above the provocations. After fifteen minutes of back and forth, he agreed to write the letter. He called in the minister of state and gave the instructions on the spot. I had to leave Liberia the following day, but Yvette Chesson, who was also in attendance at the conference, worked with Mr. Wisseh McClain, an official in the president's office, to conclude the letter. The formal request from President Charles Taylor to President Bill Clinton was finalized to form part of the package for our petition to United States government to transfer the Liberian community members from the TPS to the DED program.

With the letter from President Taylor in hand, we sought the assistance of our ambassador to the United States, Madam Rachel Diggs, to have the letter properly delivered to the President of the United States. Not only did we want Liberians removed from TPS and placed on DED, but we also wanted the DED granted for at least two years so that we would have enough turnaround time to process the petition for green cards for the Liberian community through the US Congress.

This process would require support at the highest levels of the United States Congress. As a result, we began to make contacts with members of the US Senate and the US House of Representatives. The Liberian community in the state of Rhode Island used its strong political influence to win the support of Senator Jack Reed to sponsor the bill in the Senate and Congressman Patrick Kennedy, who was known to have participated in many immigration marches and rallies with Liberians in Washington, to sponsor the bill in the House. But first we needed the DED approved by President Clinton; for this, we turned to the Congressional Black Caucus. The late Eugenia Wadsworth Stevenson, a former Liberian ambassador to the United States, and the late Leslie Norman Cole (a Liberian criminal justice expert) helped connect us with key members of the Congressional Black Caucus (CBC).

Eventually, the following CBC members came aboard to support our cause: the late Honorable Donald Payne of New Jersey, Honorable Elijah Cummings of Maryland, Honorable John Conyers of Michigan, Honorable Corinne Brown of Florida, Honorable Sheila Jackson Lee of Texas, Honorable Maxine Waters of California, Honorable Eleanor Holmes Norton, delegate from the District of Columbia. There were others who did not actively participate but gave their blessings. True to their word, the members of the CBC worked with us until the DED was approved.

We received mixed reactions from the Liberian community. Some called and thanked us and wanted to know more about DED and what they should do to avail themselves of benefits under this new program. Others called and insulted us, saying that we did not know what we were doing since we had taken them from one temporary program and transferred them to another. Instead, we should have taken them from TPS to green card status. We began communicating with as many people as possible by telephone and the internet to explain what was going on. We called consultative meetings several times, before taking any action, to explain why it was necessary to switch from one program to the other, but, as always, only a few people showed up. We learned that Liberians were of the impression that we were trying to entrap them and set them up for deportation. The rumor was not only untrue but crazy. Nonetheless, we continued to work.

What a lot of the Liberians did not know was that I had my own personal challenges I had to deal with. In 1991, on my birthday in December, my mother was rushed to the emergency room only to find out that she needed a ten-hour brain surgery to clip a vessel in the brain due to a ruptured aneurysm, a condition I had never heard of before. In hindsight, we realized that she often complained of frequent headaches after she received news from Liberia that her brother, a diabetic and double amputee, had been evacuated from his home to an unknown area by rebels; he died shortly after the evacuation due to lack of medical attention. When my mother recovered from surgery, we discovered that she was experiencing severe memory loss and would, therefore, require nursing care for the rest of her life. My husband and I decided to take her in our home, for to do otherwise would be out of step with the Liberian culture, especially in the case of a mother who had devoted her life to educating and caring for us when we were children.

In 1993, the doctors diagnosed our one-year-old son with autism and told us he was at the lower end of the spectrum. This diagnosis meant his mental development would be severely delayed and, as in the case of my mother, he would require tremendous commitment and dedication for the numerous trips to doctors, hospitals, and therapists. Additionally, I had to drive about ninety miles, an hour and a half, one way, three times a week, to conduct lectures at Morgan State University in Baltimore and, from time to time, appear in immigration court either in Baltimore, Maryland, or Arlington, Virginia, to prevent the deportation of private clients.

In the late 1990s, I added yet another activity to my plate. Phillip Banks informed me that he had received a grant from the US Department of Justice to review and edit the Liberian Supreme Court opinions spanning twenty years (1979–1999), as well as revise the civil and criminal procedure laws. The US government was essentially paying us to preserve documents critical to rebuilding the legal system when the war ended. Banks asked if I could join him and the Monrovia team consisting of Varney Sherman, as head, David A. B. Jallah, and Benedict Sannoh. We spent nearly three years working intermittently in the basement of Varney and Joyce Sherman's house in the United States. Joyce provided lunch from time to time without asking for reimbursement from the project. The late Emmanuel Wureh, a lawyer and later an associate justice, assisted our project team with proofreading. Pearline Johnson was the computer specialist, and Sampson Itoka was our secretary. Others who helped with proofreading were Lucelia Harmon, Gertrude Horace, Michen Tah, Edward Dillon, and Sam Russ. Rose Marie

Banks-James and Emmanuel James, both counsellors at law, assisted Phillip Banks with the revision of civil and criminal codes.

In spite of all the other things we had to do, the immigration team gave immigration advocacy its best efforts, as though that was the only task we had to do.

Shortly after President Clinton honored President Taylor's letter and granted the DED, Congresswoman Corinne Brown, who had worked above and beyond the call of duty to assist our community, called us into her office on Capitol Hill and introduced us to the aides of Senator Reed and Congressman Kennedy. She told us they had begun working on the bill for permanent residency for Liberians and that if they had any questions while preparing the document, she had asked them to call us since we were lawyers. She did not want any group in the Liberian community to get lost in the drafting of the documents. We thanked the congresswoman and excused ourselves.

A couple of weeks after the meeting in Congresswoman Brown's office, Yvette Chesson called around eight o'clock one evening, asking me to come to the Rayburn Building on Capitol Hill for a meeting with Congresswoman Brown. It was cold and wet, and I had been wheezing all day and did not want to go out again. But Yvette insisted that the congresswoman wanted to see us urgently, although she had no idea why the Honorable Brown was calling for a meeting. I drove to the train station, parked my car, and hopped on the Red Line subway to Washington, DC. I met Yvette in the waiting area of the congresswoman's office with two other people in a mood of solemnity. Upon my arrival, the congresswoman asked us to come to her office. We sat there anxiously as she began to speak; she said that she would no longer be able to continue to work with the Liberian community on its immigration matters. She told us that during the months that she had been assisting us, she had been receiving numerous calls, regularly, from people purporting to represent various Liberian organizations in the United States, accusing her of being biased in favor of Liberians who were "descendants of our oppressors."

I can imagine how mixed emotions of disappointment and confusion must have enveloped the congresswoman. Her only intention, she told us, was to assist the Liberian community within the confines of the laws of the United States irrespective of ethnic background or sociopolitical orientation. As we sat there looking quizzically at one another, she wrote the name of the last such caller on a pad and handed it to us so that we would know where to go to follow up. My lips spontaneously dropped open, and Yvette and I looked at each other and then looked at the congresswoman. *This cannot be real,* I thought. *All of this is a dream that we will soon wake up from, or, better still, the congresswoman might tell us this is early April Fool's Day.* I sat there thinking, *What are we going to do without the congresswoman who has taken time to guide us through this very complicated process?*

When we left the congresswoman's office, we stood outside talking for a long time before we headed to our respective homes. Why would Liberians in the community go out of their way to undermine their fellow Liberians who so desperately needed to have their immigration status regularized? We gleaned from the conversation with the congresswoman that these individuals in the Liberian community who had been calling her office just wanted equal time with her. They could have just told us that. I would have been happy to step aside and let them do the job. The congresswoman's request to us was simple: "Since your community says that you have not been authorized to speak on its behalf, I suggest that you go back to the community and let them designate who they want to represent the Liberian community. If they designate the both of you, I will be more than glad to continue to work with you. I just don't want to be unnecessarily dragged into your national conflict."

The congresswoman was merely trying to help us understand how the US government works on matters like immigration.

Almost in unison, Yvette and I said, "What is wrong with these people? Do they have any idea what they have done to the Liberian community?"

I was thankful we had refused to accept funding from the Liberian community. There were some out-of-pocket expenses for paper, transportation, and meals, but we managed with personal funds.

"What do we do now?" Yvette said. I told her the most difficult tasks were over. We had gotten President Charles Taylor to write the letter that was crucial to our petition for DED. We had received the approbation and support of the United States president, Bill Clinton, by his granting of the DED for two years, giving us adequate time to petition Congress for amnesty. No community in the past had received more than a one-year approval for DED. All that was left was for the Liberian community to follow the bills until they were approved by the US Congress.

The next day Yvette and I met with a couple of people who claimed to be the community leaders. They wanted us to continue and complete the process for the petition to the U.S. Congress, but demanded that we work under their direction and prepare all documents for their signature and on the letterhead of their organization. We disagreed, handed over to them the pertinent documents to facilitate their work, and offered to assist in an advisory capacity on a pro bono basis going forward.

The whole green card process in Congress fell through. Neither Yvette nor I had the spunk to follow up after the congresswoman's decision to become disengaged. I don't think the "community leaders" ever submitted the name of the representative for the Liberian community as she had asked us to do. I don't know whether the new representatives of the Liberian community ever followed up with the bills that were being drafted in the House and the Senate. When DED ended after the two-year period granted by President Clinton, the Liberians went back on the TPS. In subsequent years, various organizations in the Liberian community led the process. The erstwhile lengthy but intermittent character of the Liberian civil war would keep Liberians under one temporary immigration program or the other longer than expected.

The permanent residency we sought more than twenty years ago for the Liberian community is now being pursued by a new generation of Liberians. Many of the original beneficiaries have since left the program and have attained residency and citizenship through marriage, sponsorship by a family member, sponsorship by an employer, or some other legal means.

CHAPTER 20

The Decision to Remain
in the United States

By 1995, most Liberians were exhausted and frustrated over the prolonged war. Each time we thought that there was some hope for peace, there was an unexpected civil disruption between or among two or more warring factions, or rumors and news of extrajudicial killings by both government and nongovernment actors. Our hope that the war would soon end and we could return home to grow old and die in our native land was constantly being dashed.

Notwithstanding the challenges with regularizing the immigration status of the general community, most Liberians by the mid-1990s realized they would be in the United States for longer than they had planned and should, therefore, make concrete plans to establish roots so that their children would have a less tumultuous future than theirs. Some professionals, such as doctors, engineers, accountants, lawyers, nurses, and social workers, were fortunate to land jobs in their specific area of training early on, especially those previously trained in the United States. Others decided to retrain to find suitable placement in the system. Others, who did not have the luxury of obtaining training, as they had to go to work immediately to take care of family needs, accepted jobs that required far less than the training and experience they had, and, of course, the pay was low.

A lawyer who accepted employment as a night security guard wrote on his application that he was only a high school graduate so that he would not be rejected for being "overqualified." One day when he wrote and submitted an incident report, he was summoned to the office of his boss and forced to confess that he was more qualified than he had admitted. The true identity of a former ambassador's wife was discovered by her employers when she polished their old silverware they were planning to toss out and set the table for a dinner party. Many Liberians went into the health care industry working as caregivers for the sick and disabled. Others conducted a catering business out of their homes or worked as salespersons for large companies on a commission.

The biggest disadvantage for Liberians who continued to be under the TPS program was that their children were given free education only up to high school. They would have to pay for college tuition and other expenses as though they were foreign or out-of-state students. The costs could run anywhere from $20,000 to $60,000 per year, depending on whether it was a state school or a private school. Young Liberians who were awarded US government scholarships because of stellar academic performance in high school had to turn down the scholarships since they did not have permanent resident status (green card) or US citizenship.

Liberians spent hours on the telephone talking about the war and reassuring one another the war would end soon so that we could return to Liberia and get on with our lives. Some of the Liberians who came to the United States after the 1980 coup, and a few who had fled the civil war in 1990, had already decided to write off Liberia and move on with their lives. To them, the uncertainty was too painful and the readjustment too stressful. For me, by the end of 1993, I decided that returning home was not an immediate option due to the medical conditions of both my mother and my son.

The question was, How do I utilize my two graduate degrees, one in law and the other in sociology / criminal justice, and balance that with my role as caregiver for both my mother and my son? An African American friend, Dr. Glenda Hodges, also a lawyer, suggested that I work in academia full-time and then practice law on my terms by designing my practice to comport with my circumstances. She was right. I did not have to give up teaching to practice law or give up the practice of law for academia. That way, I could work in both disciplines, take care of my family, and do advocacy work, all at the same time. The schedule of a college professor seemed very attractive; it would provide the flexibility I needed to do a zillion things at one time.

The demographics of the student population was always a major consideration in deciding where I wanted to conduct lectures. The position at the state university in Baltimore was interesting because the population was urban, but it did not provide the balance I desired. The ideal post that I felt would meet all my requirements of diversity of the student population, commute time, salary scale, and so on was at Montgomery College. It was a twenty-minute drive from my house, as opposed to an hour and a half to Baltimore one way. It was seven minutes away from the shared space where I had established my law practice. The salary was attractive, and the schedule was flexible. The student body was ethnically and racially balanced, with students representing 170 different countries (including Liberia), and the resources needed were available for both students and faculty.

In 2005, I accepted the position of full professor at Montgomery College. Essentially, the job allowed me to be all things to all people. By then, my mother had passed away; she died in January 2001 after a ten-year protracted illness. She was the last survivor of the four children of her mother, so we knew with her passing, a chapter in the lives of members of my immediate family had closed. Her passing was a challenging and painful period for me. She would not be around when the war ended to decide whether she wanted to see Liberia just one more time, as some of her contemporaries had had the opportunity to do. It is always my prayer that her soul is in a good place.

CHAPTER 21

Promises of the Millennium

In early 2003, another one of many peace conferences was planned for Accra, Ghana. Like always, Liberians were hopeful but not holding their breath. Peace, it appears to me, is always so difficult to broker, but garnering external assistance to buy weapons and kill one another seemed so easy to effect, most especially when discussions on ending a war focused more on pecuniary interests than humanitarian considerations. The only victims of a civil war are always the ordinary people, no matter whether you're physically present in the war zone or living in exile in another country. Even those who reap the spoils of war will eventually have to live with their conscience and the victims.

The peace conference brought together an array of Liberians, including the usual: the Progressives; leaders of the various warring factions; religious leaders; politicians; and civil society organizations. I recall speaking on the phone with two individuals in Ghana, on separate occasions, and I was told that the international community would only support an inclusive interim government, as that was the only way Liberia would be able to achieve peace. I also recall saying that it made sense to have all Liberians, including key members of warring factions, in governance as we moved to rebuild the country; however, I had a germane concern. My concern was that it would be difficult to prosecute high-level government officials who actively participated in the war. "I agree," one of my contacts said on the other end of the phone, "but what can we do? We are tired of this war and just want it to end."

President Charles Taylor, who was also in attendance at the Accra Peace Conference, left abruptly to return to Liberia after he received information that the Special Court for Sierra Leone had indicted him. The eleven-count indictment consisted of war crimes against humanity (including rape, murder, and mayhem) and other serious violations of international humanitarian law. It is noteworthy that President Taylor was indicted by the Special Court for Sierra Leone because the allegations in the indictment were levied against him by the people of Sierra Leone for his role in the civil war in that country.

A couple of months later, specifically August 2003, a deal was struck with Liberian politicians and the international community to remove President Taylor from Liberia to Calabar, Nigeria. He remained in exile in Nigeria for two and a half years, until allegations surfaced that he had attempted to escape from the custody of Nigerian authorities sometime in 2006. According to news reports, the Nigerian security forces recaptured him at Nigeria's border with Chad and transported him by air back to Liberia, where his indictment was read to him on the tarmac of the Roberts International Airport by the then solicitor general, Tiawon Gongloe. Security officials escorted Mr. Taylor to Sierra Leone and turned him over to the Special Court, which subsequently transported him to the Hague for his trial.

On the one hand, the fact that Charles Taylor said, "God willing, I'll be back," as he left Liberia in 2003, left a lot of his supporters with hope that their charismatic leader would return. On the other hand, his statement left anti-Taylor activists and the newly elected Sirleaf government very anxious, perhaps precipitating the move to commence the trial outside of Africa as quickly as possible. The Dutch government agreed for the Special Court for Sierra Leone to hold the trials in the Hague, provided that a third country committed in advance to accept Taylor as a prisoner if he was found guilty of the charges. The trial commenced in 2008, and President Taylor was convicted on all charges in 2012 and sentenced to fifty years in prison. He is now serving his sentence in England.[17, 18]

There are serious allegations by the government and people of Liberia that Charles Taylor committed war crimes and human rights violations in Liberia while amassing wealth in the illicit trade in guns, diamonds, and timber, but, to date, the government and the people of Liberia have not brought charges against him.

Although President Taylor had to leave the Accra Peace Conference unceremoniously, the conference progressed, and all parties in attendance signed a comprehensive peace agreement. It is noteworthy that women and civil society organizations played a pivotal role to ensure that the conference would achieve a positive outcome.

The Mano River Women Network (MAWOPNET), led by Theresa Leigh-Sherman at the time, is a regional women organization with membership from Guinea, La Cote D'Ivoire, Sierra Leone, and Liberia. Its members participated in the peace talks.

Then, there was another group of women, led by Leymah Gbowee, Asatu Bah-Kenneth, Vaiba Flomo, Grace Jarso, Etty Weah, Edweda Gbenyon Cooper, and others, focused on galvanizing women from the grassroots; bringing together all women irrespective of age, religion, ethnicity, education, or socioeconomic status. This group, operating under the aegis of Women in Peace Building Network (WIPNET), called itself the Liberian Women Mass Action for Peace. They requested that the warlords be locked up in the conference hall until an agreement was reached to end the war. The women also threatened to strip off all their clothing if the warlords did not cooperate and heed their request for peace. It is not a good thing in the Liberian tribal culture for a woman to have to remove her clothing publicly to attain an outcome that benefits all of the society. It is a sign of desperation that forces the opponent (especially if the opponent is a man) to rethink his behavior.

Many things came out of the Accra Peace Conference. However, there were two things significant enough to mention here: (1) the parties agreed that an interim government of inclusion would be formed to lead the country to democratic elections; and (2) the parties agreed to the establishment of a Truth and Reconciliation Commission with specific terms of reference, including the mandate to determine the root causes of the civil war in Liberia and make recommendations for moving forward. The participating groups and organizations elected Mr. Charles Gyude Bryant, a Liberian businessman, to head a two-year interim government. Although his administration was somewhat uneventful, towards the end, he would be pressured to sign a little over a hundred agreements on one day, and at the end of his administration, he would be asked to answer charges of corruption during the time he ruled as interim head of government. But one of the agreements he was asked to sign would be remembered by a few Liberians in the diaspora. It was called the Economic Governance Assistance Program (EGAP).

Sometime in 2005, Counsellor Philip Banks called to say that he had emailed a document he wanted me to read and provide my comments, but he was concerned that I had not bothered to acknowledge the email. I asked what the document was about; he said, "Please just read it, and then we can talk."

I called Yvette Chesson-Wureh (by now Yvette and Counsellor Emmanuel Wureh had married) and asked whether she had seen the document and discovered that she had also received it but had not gotten around to reading it. I begged her to read it and tell me what it was about, as I was overwhelmed with other matters at the time.

Within less than an hour, Yvette called back sounding very agitated. "You have to read this document yourself; I hope Chairman Bryant is not planning to sign it as is. It is recommending that a steering committee consisting of international stakeholders be established to manage Liberia as it rebuilds." One of the recommendations etched in our minds was that a group of lawyers from a country in the African subregion would take complete control of the affairs of the Liberian judicial system, including the Supreme Court. Also, the steering committee would manage the natural resources, public corporations, and financial institutions, with Liberia playing a minority role. There was no limit to how long this committee would be in existence.

We convened an emergency meeting consisting of Yvette Chesson-Wureh, Patrick Burrowes, Ayele Ajavon-Cox, Philip A.Z. Banks III, and me. We drew up some initial comments on the document and sent them to Chairman Bryant through Marie Leigh Parker. Many other Liberians called by telephone to express their concerns and asked that we articulate their position in the draft comments to the chairman. We gathered from Mrs. Parker that Chairman Bryant was elated and relieved when he received our comments. We had provided him with the resources and confidence he needed to counter many points in the document. For instance, we made it clear that to have any other nationality from the subregion appointed to take over the Supreme Court of Liberia or any subordinate court in the country would be in contravention of the Liberian Constitution.

After a couple of weeks, when we did not get a response from Chairman Bryant on our final set of comments, we called Mrs. Parker, who told us that the chairman had already signed the document. I recall gasping on the phone. Mrs. Parker paused and then said, "He signed but not without modifications. You will be glad to know that he deleted the part suggesting that foreigners take over the judiciary, and the proposed steering committee will provide oversight in a much more limited capacity over a period of only three years, rather than for an unlimited time. Most interestingly, the document has been labeled Governance & Economic Management Assistance Program (GEMAP)." We were very relieved to receive this report from Mrs. Parker.

In 2013, I heard a top government official say that GEMAP was the big elephant in the room. I sat there with a smirk on my face thinking, *If you only knew that this elephant is an ant compared to its forerunner (the EGAP).*

On a Saturday morning in February 2006, I saw a missed call from Mr. Willis Knuckles, the minister of state for presidential affairs. When I returned his call, he said that President Sirleaf had asked him to call and offer me the post of deputy minister of justice for administration. I told him that it was regrettable that I had to decline, as I had no immediate plans to relocate to Monrovia at the time. He then said, "I believe she will be calling you herself." I was not sure what he meant, but I said, "Okay, it would be an honor," and I ended the conversation.

A few days after our conversation, I received a call from the Mansion informing me that President Sirleaf would be traveling to Washington, DC, in March 2006 and would like to meet with me. I immediately called Counsellor Philip Banks and told him frankly that I was not ready to go to Liberia but suggested that since his international consultancy had recently expired, it might be a good thing for him to join Mrs. Sirleaf, who needed all the help she could muster. He was reluctant to attend the appointment, stating that the president had not extended him a personal invitation. "It doesn't matter," I said. "She has just won an election and is probably still too overwhelmed to remember all her friends. I do not know her, but I think someone must have mentioned my name," I said. "She needs help," I repeated.

In the end, Banks, as I usually referred to him, agreed to attend the appointment, and the president seemed happy that he had come to meet with her. We both decided that before the appointment, we would draft an abbreviated proposal each for the establishment of a Law Reform Commission and a Land Commission; he would draft the former, and I would draft the latter. Banks and I met with the president separately, and at the end of my meeting, she asked me to give the proposal for the Land Commission to her sister, Jennie Johnson Bernard. During our meeting, she, again, asked if I would accept the post of deputy minister of justice for administration, and again, I respectfully declined. Then she said that there might be an opening for an associate justice on the Supreme Court; she intimated that she nominated a man whose confirmation seemed unlikely. I declined that as well. We parted company with the understanding that I would keep an open mind going forward. A couple of months after the meeting with the president, Banks left for Liberia to join the Governance Commission.

Also, in late 2006, I received another call from the president; again, she offered the opportunity to join the Supreme Court of Liberia as an associate justice. This time the position was truly vacant; it was not the same seat shrouded in political controversy. I traveled to Liberia toward the end of 2006 to meet with President Sirleaf; Banks and his fiancé hosted me. I was still very ambivalent about going to Liberia at a time when my legal practice had picked up, and I had started my ideal position in academia that fitted perfectly into my plans, but the president was very persuasive. I called my family, and they agreed to support my decision, as I stated in Chapter One. I remained in Liberia for three weeks, long enough to have my Senate Committee hearing conducted before my return to the United States in early January 2007. The plan was for me to return to Liberia in time for the opening of the Supreme Court on the second Monday of March 2007, by which time the Senate would have completed the confirmation of my nomination.

In the meantime, there was pressure from the college to commit for the fall semester by March 1, and then I had to decide what to do with files of my clients, especially those who had upcoming assignments and settlement negotiations. Therefore, on March 1, 2007, at about 8:50 a.m. eastern standard time in the United States, I made a call to President Sirleaf and expressed my concern that the matter of my appointment had not been finalized by the Senate, considering the Supreme Court was expected to open in two weeks. She simply said, "The Senate just heard and rejected your nomination this morning." I asked if there was a reason for the rejection; she said something to the effect that the lawmakers did not know me.

Right after my conversation with the president, I telephoned a friend in the Liberian Senate, and repeated what she had told me, and he said, "Actually, the plenary is still discussing your matter on the floor. We have not reached a decision yet." I was silent for what seemed like an eternity when he asked, "Are you still there?"

"Yes, I am here. I am just thinking about what you just said." I knew then that it was the President who had decided to withdraw the nomination but did not know why. We would meet again several months later, and she would tell me, simply, "it was all politics."

By evening that same day, my phone began to ring off the hook; the Senate had finally and formally rejected the nomination to the Supreme Court. Most of the callers very upset with the president and her female stooge in the Senate who reportedly orchestrated the outcome in the Senate. Others told me stories of their experiences with many of the people who now governed the country and why they would never go to Liberia at this time. I said very little, but listened intently, as I needed to process all that had happened that day.

A few weeks into the debacle, Yvette Chesson returned to the States from Liberia and said that she, along with Olubanke King-Akerele, the then minister of commerce, would come to spend an afternoon with me. They wanted to discuss my continued involvement in the upcoming International Women Colloquium that was being hosted by Liberia;they also wanted to know from my end what had gone wrong with the Supreme Court nomination. I did not have an answer; neither did they. We were all astounded and concluded that this was a side of the president that none of us knew and understood. They, however, were of the strong opinion that I should return to Liberia to help the country, even if it meant working in the private sector.

Olubanke and Yvette were concerned that I might not want to continue to work with the organizing committee for the colloquium, but they did not know that I had learned a long time ago to stay above the fray. I learned to distinguish service to humanity from service to an individual.

CHAPTER 22

Liberian Women See
Hope on the Horizon

Electing the first female head of state in Africa was a big deal not only
for Liberia but for all people of goodwill, especially women, all over the
world. The Liberian women saw this as an opportunity to rekindle the fire
that ignited the feminist movement in the 1960s and 1970s. The war had
taken us off course, but it had not broken the spirit that inspired us to follow
our dreams. After all, the determination, perseverance, tenacity, sacrifice,
and prayers of ordinary Liberian women had helped to bring the fourteen-
year war to an end. Perhaps, conducting a presidential election shortly after
the victory of these women may have been a blessing in disguise for Ellen
Johnson Sirleaf's ascendency to power. Who knows? But Yvette Chesson and
the women she brought together to organize the colloquium felt that this
convention should set the stage for mapping the future of the ordinary women
who had done this extraordinary thing.

Sometime in 2006, Yvette Chesson contacted me to join her and a
few others to mobilize men and women around the globe to assist with the
planning and convening of an international colloquium for women in Liberia
in 2009. The convener would be President Ellen Johnson Sirleaf of Liberia,
and the co-convener, Her Excellency Tarja Halonen, the then head of state

of Finland. Both leaders would use their influence to attract the participation of other prominent women from around the world.

I was not sure that I wanted to add any more on my plate at the time, but after working well with Yvette in the 1990s on matters pertaining to immigration advocacy, I felt that this just might be another interesting experience.

I recall the first meeting was in the conference room of the Legal Aid Clinic, on Kenilworth Avenue in Prince George's County, Maryland, where Yvette worked as one of its senior lawyers. There were a few people in attendance: Carole Tyson, John Wulu, the late Beverly Bruce (an African American who had worked with the Peace Corps in Liberia in the seventies), Laurinda Dennis, Veda Simpson, and me. There may have been a couple of others whom I cannot now recall. We spent the first meeting trying to grasp the plan that Yvette had developed in her mind. The one thing we all agreed on was that we had to find a way to harness the resources of women and empower them to participate in every facet of society. We should no longer settle for tokenism in our participation in public service but strive to ensure that the involvement of women in the development and growth of society will be significant and sustainable. One of our objectives was to promote the implementation of Resolution 1325 passed by the United Nations Security Council in October 2000 so that women, among other things, would be encouraged to become more involved in conflict prevention, conflict management, and conflict resolution.

Eventually, the group of organizers and advocates expanded to include several hundred people around the world. A few of the women were Mary Robinson (former president of Ireland); Helen Clark (former president of New Zealand and currently the administrator of UNDP); Elizabeth Rhen (former minister of defense of Finland); Lalla Ben Barka (deputy executive secretary-general of UN Economic Commission for Africa); and Rachel Manyanga (assistant secretary-general and special adviser to the secretary-general on gender issues). The advocates and organizers also included Thelma Awori (assistant secretary-general for UNIFEM, now UN Women); Binta Diop (executive director for Femme Africa Solidarite); Natalie Fisher-Spalton (executive director of World YWCA); Sabine Meitzel (head of African Division of the World Trade Center in Switzerland); Bisi Adeleye-Fayemi (African Women Development Fund); Diane McCoy (Association of Black Charities); Elizabeth Lwanga (former UNDP resident representative and head of UN Mission, Sierra Leone); the Council of World Women Leaders; Ciata

Victor (TLC Africa); Ndioro Ndiaye (head of International Organization for Migration); and the list goes on.

We formed various committees and met from time to time in different cities around the world to ensure that this herculean project we had embarked upon would succeed.

Olubanke King-Akerele, the then Liberian minister of commerce, and Vabah Gayflor, the Liberian minister of gender and social protection, would become the contact people for the colloquium on the ground in Liberia. Amelia Ward, Theresa Leigh Sherman, Marie Leigh Parker, Ruth Gibson Caesar, and many others joined in to assist them, and by 2008, the entire organizing and planning activities were transferred to Liberia.

In 2008, we decided to implement several pre-colloquium activities, one of which would be a workshop on the "Implication of the New Inheritance Law for Indigenous Liberian Women." I volunteered to go to Liberia in January 2009 to conduct the workshop. This issue had concerned me for a long time. In brief, for more than a century, there was a dichotomy in the law when it came to the inheritance rights of women in Liberia. The Liberian customary law viewed women as chattels, and, therefore, when the husband died, a male relative (most likely a brother) of the husband would inherit all the property of the deceased person, including the wife. Women who married under the civil statute could own real property and inherit from the husband if he predeceased her. It is important to note that there was a time in Liberia (during the nineteenth century and part of the twentieth century) when even the "civilized" women were not allowed to own property or institute a lawsuit in their own name, but that later changed. It is also important to note that the indigenous women, especially those with little or no education, were the ones most affected by the discriminatory inheritance law.

Fortunately, in 1986, a new constitution was written, which provided equal protection for the inheritance rights of all Liberian women irrespective of the form marriage. But then it became a challenge to enact an enabling statute in a legislature dominated by indigenous men, as they stood to lose the special privilege conferred by our African tradition upon the passing of the law. The enabling statute facilitates the implementation of the constitutional provision. Notwithstanding the stumbling block, the legislature passed the enabling statute in 2003. Therefore, the workshop was designed to educate the indigenous women about their rights under the new law.

I recall that about a hundred indigenous women living in the urban area participated in the workshop. At the end of part one of a two-part workshop, I asked the women how many of them owned land in their name. About fifteen women raised their hands. Of the fifteen, I wanted to know how many of them had a deed for the property; twelve persons raised their hands. When I showed them what a deed looks like, only three people in the group admitted to having a real deed. Some of the women showed me what looked like receipts or promissory notes. I knew then that the colloquium was just the beginning of our work; we had to find a way to guide these women on a sustained basis.

Historically, educated women also experienced other forms of discrimination, such as lower wages than their male counterpart; limitation in choice of profession in terms of steering women toward nursing, education, home economics, and library science; limited access to the legal system in that a male relative had to represent the legal interest of a female complainant, and so on.

Then in the late sixties, we began to hear of women occupying political positions when Angie Brooks, a trained lawyer, became Liberia's permanent representative to the United Nations and, to this date, the only African woman to become president of the UN General Assembly. Also in the sixties, Mai Wiles Padmore became minister of health and social welfare. Catherine Harmon-Cummings and Elizabeth Collins were members of the legislature. Eugenia Wadsworth Stevenson headed the Liberian consulate in New York and later became the Liberian ambassador to the Federal Republic of West Germany in the seventies. Leona Tucker-Chesson, the first female to graduate from the Louis Arthur Grimes School of Law, University of Liberia, later became the assistant minister of justice for taxation. Then there were the university professors like Fatima Massaquoi-Fahnbulleh, Agnes Cooper Dennis, Wede Jones, Agnes Nebo-Von Ballmoos, Tidi Bryant, Mary Antoinette Grimes Sherman (later, president of the University of Liberia), and many others who blazed the trail and provided the inspiration for young women to dream of a better life.

By the mid nineteen seventies, more women were in the government, and more young women were attaining degrees in medicine, law, engineering, and accounting. Christine Phillips and Alpha Brownell returned to Liberia as architectural engineers. Florence Chenoweth, the first female to graduate from the University of Liberia in the field of agriculture in 1968, had returned to Liberia with a graduate degree and was appointed in a mid-level position at the Ministry of Planning. She later served as minister of agriculture from 1977 to 1979. Also, in mid to late nineteen seventies, Dr. Kate Bryant, a pediatrician, became the minister of health and social welfare, and Ellen Johnson Sirleaf became minister of finance. Angie Brooks returned to Liberia from the United Nations and became the first female associate justice of the

Supreme Court of Liberia. Counselor Emma Shannon Walser was appointed a circuit court judge, Counselor Gladys Johnson was probate judge, Luvenia Ash-Thompson was deputy minister of labor, Linnie Kesselley was the first female head of the Civil Service Authority, and Counselor Henrietta Koenig was commissioner of internal revenues.

When we were children, the doctors used to be men, and the nurses used to be women. Don't get me wrong; the nurses, a few of whom were Maggie Dennis, Jemima Wheaton Graff, and Ayo Cummings, were very competent, but somehow one got the feeling that society expected girls to become nurses and not doctors. Other than two female dentists, Marie Johnson and Yeda Baker Dennis, in the sixties, I had never heard of a female Liberian doctor before the mid-seventies. By then, there were quite a few of them. In addition to Dr. Kate Bryant, others were Rhoda Peal (internist); Ayele Ajavon Cox (dentist); Roseda Marshall (pediatrician); June Kamara Butscher (pediatrician); Eleanor Neal Ehanire (ear, nose, and throat specialist); and Juliette Phelps Maxwell (internist); and more came later.

Moreover, the First Lady and wife of President William V. S. Tubman, Antoinette Padmore Tubman, led the way for many social services institutions in the country to provide homes for adults and children in need of assistance. Under the Tubman administration, a refuge home was established for elderly indigent citizens and was served by volunteers like Florence Tolbert McClain. Ellen Mills Scarborough donated about 150 acres of land in the fifties, near the ELWA Hospital, to establish a home for the mentally ill; the government named the rehabilitation center after Scarborough's mother, Catherine Mills. Other institutions included the Antoinette Tubman Children Welfare Foundation, established in the sixties to provide care for children with all types of disabilities, and the School for the Deaf, operated by its founder, Rev. S. N. Dixon, in partnership with the government of Liberia. Maima Fahnbulleh, as assistant minister for social welfare in the mid-seventies, introduced the first program for the blind to ensure that blind citizens receive comparable formal education as other citizens.

The government also established and operated separate facilities for citizens stricken with tuberculosis and leprosy. In all the facilities established to provide care, women played a very important role. Theresa Leigh-Sherman was appointed in the seventies to coordinate all nongovernmental social services, which she did until she left in the late seventies to establish the Leigh-Sherman Secretarial School.

Unfortunately, after the unsettling events of the military coup in 1980 and the fourteen-year civil war that erupted in 1990, there was a breakdown in the social institutions built over so many decades. While a few remained in Liberia, the growing population of business and professional women of the sixties and seventies went into exile. Most of the highly educated and highly placed Liberian women, whom the younger women saw as role models, were no longer around. Their children and grandchildren were being born and raised in exile, in another country and another culture. The setback was devastating not only for the country as a whole, but also for women in particular. This experience was analogous to a situation where a two-year-old suddenly stops walking and talking, and no one knows what to do.

Therefore, the convening of the colloquium in Liberia, under the gavel of the first female head of state, brought a lot of hope that the women of Liberia would have a point of reference and would be able to dream again.

The colloquium, held in March 2009, was well attended by women from around the world. In short, it was very successful. As a follow-up on the goals and objectives of the colloquium, the Colloquium Committee established, in Liberia in 2009, the International Center for the Empowerment of Women and named it after the late Angie Brooks. The committee also agreed to construct its headquarters in Suacoco, Bong County, Liberia, and name it after Suah KoKo, a prominent female Liberian chief from the Kpelle tribe who was very influential in uniting the various ethnic groups in Liberia during the late nineteenth century and early twentieth century.

Today, the Angie Brooks International Center (ABIC) is fully operational and funded by many international organizations, including the United Nations. The center provides adult literacy programs for women; conducts workshops to help women understand their rights and responsibilities as members of society; and provides mentoring programs for young men and women in planning for their future. The center also operates the Women Situation Room (WSR), a multinational initiative designed to assist African governments with the prevention of elections violence. The center provides mentoring for women in various types of businesses, conducts training in conflict prevention and conflict resolution, and the list goes on. The ABIC also intervenes during a national crisis by providing public education to reduce the adverse impact on the population.

III

Full Circle

CHAPTER 23

The Return to the Ministry of Justice—An Overview of the Job

I began my assignment as attorney general of the Republic of Liberia in July 2009, in a post-conflict environment emerging from fourteen years of chaos, atrocities, and destruction. Major government buildings and installations, such as the water and sewer plant, the telecommunications system, and the hydroelectric power plant, had been destroyed. There was a total breakdown of social institutions, such as the family, the school system, the court system, and the health system, leaving members of the society confused about the acceptable values and norms.

I compared my new job to that of a monkey bridge; it is a bridge built of bamboo sticks and ropes by the locals and very often built more than a dozen feet high above gushing waters and huge boulders. When you first see a monkey bridge, you get the impression that this is shoddy handiwork by unskilled villagers; as you walk on it, it tends to sway from side to side (or wobbles), but somehow it works. You eventually end up across the river safely; but until you reach the other side, there is this lingering fear of impending danger.

Six weeks had gone by since my arrival in the country; the Senate had confirmed the president's nomination of me as attorney general/minister of justice, and I needed to start work right away. I sat with three of my deputies poring over the organogram for the ministry of justice and thinking of how much bigger the ministry had grown since I was last there more than two decades prior as assistant minister of justice for rehabilitation, now referred to as Bureau of Corrections and Rehabilitation.

I wanted to know the names and qualifications of all those who held top and middle-level positions, how long they had been with the ministry, what they had accomplished, and what they were currently working on. Together, we needed to review the strategic plan for each institution, as well as the three-year national plan then referred to as the Poverty Reduction Strategy (PRS).

I sat across the table from three of the people who would comprise my senior staff in the Ministry of Justice. Micah Wright, the nominee for solicitor general, had been a circuit court judge and an associate justice of the Supreme Court of Liberia. He was an experienced lawyer and a team player. He was the one I had known for the longest. Then there was Sam Russ, whom I had met during the previous ten years. His friends call him the most educated Liberian. He has a law degree, a Master of Science degree in mathematics, a Master of Science degree in geophysics, and an MBA from Columbia University. I felt he was the right person to head the Department of Economic Affairs, where agreements pertaining to natural resources are reviewed and negotiated. Then there was Eva-Mae Mappy-Morgan, a lawyer who had been recruited to return to Liberia on a special program as a consultant to my predecessor. I had also known her for a while, since the nineteen eighties; we were one class apart in law school at the University of Liberia. She was now the deputy minister of justice for administration, and the president wanted her to remain in the position. I posed no objection to the wishes of the president, as Ms. Mappy-Morgan had done a good job in the position.

The other key deputy, whom I had met in a separate meeting, was Marc Amblard. He had been nominated as the director of police to replace Mona Sieh. He had a Bachelor of Science degree in agriculture and had just recently returned from a nine-month training in the United States in police science. Prior to his recruitment to the Liberia National Police (LNP), he served for three years as deputy director at the National Security Agency. He seemed very enthusiastic about coming on board. It was my hope that he would bring professionalism back to the police, as Edwin Luzon Harmon did in the seventies when he recruited trained officers like Charles Ebue King, Robert

Budy, Wongbeh Sonkarly, Gabriel Scott, Joseph Flomo, Varfee Kieta, Lemuel Reeves, Gerald Richards, Charles DeShield, and so on.

There were now more than a dozen justice and security institutions supervised by the minister, including the Police, Bureau of Corrections & Rehabilitation, Bureau of Immigration & Naturalization Services, the Drug Enforcement Agency, Department of Codification, Department of Economic Affairs, Prosecution, National Fire Service, Administration, and the list goes on. The first time I met the justice minister from another West African country and described my terms of reference, he laughed and said, "Madam, you are running two ministries: a justice ministry and a ministry of security." It was then that I realized how daunting the task ahead would be.

I am result-oriented and therefore decided to focus, among other things, on where I wanted the country to be regarding security and the rule of law in readiness for the exit of the United Nations Mission in Liberia by 2015. We would need to build a holistic criminal justice system to foster interdependence rather than independence of the components that make up the system. To achieve that goal, we would have to build capacity, develop infrastructure, enhance the structural framework of the system, improve coordination and collaboration, and decentralize management so that delivery of justice and security services would be accessible across the country. It appeared to be ambitious but not insurmountable.

First, Liberia has a wealth of natural resources; second, the president had been able to marshal financial and moral support from the international community, such as the United Nations, the African Union, the World Bank, the International Monetary Fund (IMF), the European Union, the United States, the Economic Community of West African States (ECOWAS), and the African Development Bank. Others included in the rebuilding process were Nigeria, the United Kingdom, Japan, Ghana, Norway, Sweden, Australia, China, India, Russia, Ukraine, Egypt, France, Germany, Botswana, South Africa, Australia, Ireland, Poland, Spain, Switzerland, and Belgium. I engaged most of our partners on the rule of law and security issues, but most of these same partners (plus others, not necessarily engaged in justice and security matters) were equally involved with energy, agriculture, infrastructural development, health, education, and governance.

As much as the international community was willing to assist, I felt that the government of Liberia should be our primary source of funding. Foreign aid is meagre and sporadic and should therefore be considered supplemental and not the primary source of funding for running the justice and security systems of the country.

After a meeting with the general staff and after having obtained information on the qualifications of employees, it was clear that *capacity building* would have to be the priority among priorities. City solicitors were either illiterate or had less than a high school education and earned around fifty US dollars per month. Prosecutors were very few, with sometimes one prosecutor serving almost five hundred thousand people (as in Nimba County) and earning less than US$1,250 per month. They lacked specialized training in certain transnational crimes, such as money laundering, drug trafficking, maritime piracy, and human trafficking, which were now becoming so prevalent.

For a population of four million people, the number of police officers, immigration officers, and corrections officers combined was far from adequate to manage the border and internal security; most officers earned less than US$200 per month. The police often complained of not having vehicles, uniforms, and communications equipment. Moreover, I figured that I could only count on about 20 or 25 percent of the staff to perform at an acceptable level.

My priority was to develop the capacity of employees at the Ministry. In addition to competent deputies, I needed well trained middle level managers who were on the same page regarding our goals and objectives. But I worried that the salaries offered by the government were low, understandably so, since the country had just emerged from the war. Ministers earned US$3,000 per month before taxes. Deputies earned $1,800, and assistant ministers, $1,250. Some of us who were recruited under special programs enjoyed a salary augmentation but only for a few months.

We had to do something better to attract competent lawyers because we had a lot of work to do. I believe in delegating authority not only to relieve the pressure on me but also to provide the opportunities for my staff to acquire experience. The minister of justice was a statutory member of several boards of public corporations, which paid an extra $10,000 or $12,000 per year, payable in quarterly installments. I decided that I would sit on only two boards and share the other board assignments among the deputy and assistant ministers, and each would collect the fees from the meetings they attended. They would only be required to brief me on what transpired at their respective meetings so that I could effectively articulate legal issues affecting the corporations in cabinet meetings.

The entire annual budget for the Ministry of Justice Central Office was around $5 million, most of which went to salaries. The amount covered the following departments: administration, codification, corrections, prosecution, economic affairs, and public safety. The police, the National Fire Service, the Drug Enforcement Administration, and the Bureau of Immigration had their respective budgets. The budget for the prosecution of cases was negligible; it was worrisome when one considers that the cost to prosecute a high-profile case sometimes exceeds $100,000. Prosecution cost sometimes involves contracting the services of private lawyers to strengthen the prosecution team;, sequestration of jurors; relocation and financial support of witnesses; and the list goes on.

The budget for security services was also negligible, specifically for special operations and intelligence gathering around the country. "Special operations" refers to a planned or random mission conducted in any part of the country to avert or remove a problem. Sometimes it involved deployment of a number of officers (the numbers depended on the magnitude of the problem) to a remote area to intercept suspected human trafficking operations; raid a mineral-rich area to drive out illegal miners (some of whom might be foreigners); convene a town hall meeting with workers and management in a concession area to avert a riot; and so forth. Residual funds would be used to gather intelligence information from across the country to aid our decisions on security matters. The National Security Agency shared intelligence information from time to time, but we could not rely on another agency to run the day-to-day activities in the ministry.

During the first Poverty Reduction Strategy (PRS) retreat I attended, I discovered that there were two rule-of-law pillars under the PRS: one under the Ministry of Justice and the other under the judiciary. I prevailed upon the then chief justice, His Honor Johnnie N. Lewis, in the presence of the president, who presided over the meeting, that it was more prudent to merge the two pillars into one as we strived to reform the criminal justice system. Chief Justice Lewis, himself from a long line of jurists and a former dean of Louis Arthur Grimes School of Law, University of Liberia, readily agreed to the collaboration. He would turn out to be one of my strongest supporters of criminal justice reform, along with Associate Justice Kabina Ja'neh.

The stance I took at the retreat would be my first attempt to convince the government and international partners that it is imperative to develop the system holistically. The criminal justice system consists of the police, the prosecution, the courts, and corrections; therefore, to extract one component and rebuild it separately would misalign the system. We needed to create linkages among the various components to avoid duplicity, conserve resources, and yet ensure that the independence of the judiciary was respected. It took about a year and many meetings with all stakeholders to get the idea to stick, but it eventually did. It was important for the institutions to collaborate to make critical reforms, such as finding a way to reduce the number of inmates in pretrial detention status from the high rate of nearly 80 percent.

Other than building capacity and strengthening the criminal justice system, the third goal was to *decentralize the management of justice and security services* so that citizens all over the country would have better access to justice. With funding from the government and the international partners, especially the United Nations, we decided to construct five regional justice and security hubs in strategic locations across the country; that way, the services to citizens, especially in rural areas, would be greatly enhanced. To accomplish these objectives would require funding, a change in the structural and legal frameworks of the criminal justice system, and the activation of good laws on the books that had been dormant for decades, such as the laws governing probation and parole programs that provide alternatives to incarceration. It would also require many trips to the countryside to consult with the local communities and assess the needs in the various parts of the country.

After introductory meetings with heads of missions and international organizations, I discovered that I had just seen the tip of the iceberg. I recall thinking that as daunting as the task of running the Ministry of Justice might be, I was fortunate to have a senior staff with the requisite education and experience to move the ministry in the right direction. I took a notepad and started to jot down all the items that my staff and I needed to prioritize:

- follow up on the recommendations in the report of the Truth and Reconciliation Commission;
- develop a plan for transition after the United Nations Mission in Liberia (UNMIL) ended;
- convene a national conference to address the harmonization of the formal and informal justice systems;
- review the numerous auditing reports on corruption from the General Auditing Commission and determine which cases presented sufficient probable cause for prosecution;
- investigate the illegal mining of our natural resources by foreign nationals, especially in the Sapo National Park, and take appropriate action(s);
- review and develop implementation plan for security protocols of the sub-regional organizations, such as ECOWAS and the Mano River Union;
- assess the increase in transnational crimes and establish a transnational crimes unit to address the emerging problem;

- coordinate with the Land Commission, as land disputes were the root causes of many security disturbances;
- coordinate with other agencies of government, especially the Ministry of Gender and Social Protection, to combat the high rate of sexual gender–based violence;
- work with the National Investment Commission on the upcoming negotiations of major concession agreements in 2010;
- determine how to properly coordinate and utilize the professional assistance from abroad to lessen the stress on ourselves;
- develop a strategy to combat the resurgence of ritualistic killings around the country, especially in Maryland County; and
- review various international treaties with the view to determining how best to domesticate them to address the Liberian realities, and so forth.

The problem was that everything was a priority.

CHAPTER 24

Orientation to the Politics of My New Job

A s I sat down behind the desk in the office of the attorney general, it was like déjà vu. It seemed like it was not so long ago that I was assistant minister of justice and stood in front of the desk of Minister Oliver Bright Jr., trying to justify why I needed funding for corrections. I recall that he once said, as I stood before his desk waiting for his approval on a project, "One day you will sit in this chair." *How fortuitous*, I thought.

Within a week of taking office, I had to meet formally with the president, my new boss, to get a sense of where she stood on many critical issues and to ascertain what kind of funding was available for all that the Ministry of Justice was expected to do. Our first meeting was on the sixth floor of the Ministry of Foreign Affairs, in the office officially designated as the Office of the President while the real Executive Mansion office was under renovation. We talked about many things, and she expressed how delighted she was that I had come to Liberia to work with the government. The three observations I made from our first meeting were that the president had a retentive memory; that she was a good listener, even if she did not agree with you; and that she preferred to micromanage the affairs of government.

But there was a fourth observation: it was difficult for the president to

148

change her position on an issue if the advice or first impression came from a relative or confidante. Case in point: a couple of years before my appointment as minister of justice, a visitor from another West African country arrived at the Roberts International Airport with US$508,000 taped to his body, intending to conceal the money from the Liberian airport authority. Someone tipped off the security officers, who then searched for and seized the money and informed the visitor that the security authorities would take custody of the money pending a thorough investigation.

The airport security suspected that the money was from criminal activities, but there was no proof of that. When investigators could not link the money to any specific crime, the visitor asked, some weeks later, to have his money returned to him; not only did the government refuse to return the money, it also could not account for the money. I informed the president during our first meeting that she was ill advised by security officials who kept insisting that the money was the fruit of criminal activities without providing any proof. My advice was that the security authorities should return the money to its owner, less 25 percent for concealment in violation of a Central Bank of Liberia regulation. Apparently, someone had convinced the president that the man had a history of involvement in criminal activities. Therefore, it was more likely than not that the US$508,000 were proceeds derived from crime(s) of some sort. I tried to convince her that it did not matter what crimes this man may have committed in the past, so long as there was no evidence that the money in question was derived from criminal activities, it would be unjust to retain the funds.

I wondered, as I drove home, who had given the president this advice. If there were others out there whose opinion she was likely to adopt as her official position, then I would spend a lot of time, figuratively, jumping hurdles. I had the choice of quitting the job just after one week in office or riding the storm and hoping that a case of that type would be few and far in between.

Just as I took office, the government completed the legislation on the reform of the security sector, but the president held onto the document until I took office because she wanted my comments before submission to the legislature. After meeting with relevant stakeholders, I prepared a five-page reaction to the proposed law and forwarded it to the Office of the President through the usual mail channel. The document did not reach her desk. She kept asking me to release the document, until finally I hand-delivered to her a filed copy of what I had transmitted since a month previous. In the end, we discovered that the document had been in the Mansion all the while, in the drawer of one of the officials. It meant that going forward, I would have to personally deliver to the president any document that was considered important and highly sensitive.

I remembered that I had been on the job for several weeks and had not paid the customary courtesy call on the chief justice of the Supreme Court of Liberia, so I made an appointment as quickly as I could and went to see him. Before leaving his office, I asked the chief justice what advice he would give me in this new position. He said, "I have three things to tell you: (1) Never sign a document when you are tired, in a hurry, or leaving the office to go home at the end of the day. The individual giving you the document to sign does not think about what would be the consequences to you if anything goes wrong; rather, he thinks more of his pecuniary interest. (2) Do not do anything in your capacity as attorney general that the law does not give you the power to do. And (3), last but not least, please ask the president to commission you as soon as possible so that no one will question the validity of your authority."

My commissioning ceremony was delayed for a couple of months for no specific reason, and that seemed to bother Chief Justice Lewis. The process of becoming an attorney general is straightforward. First, the president nominates you to the Senate; the Senate confirms the nomination if it is pleased with your credentials and the report submitted by the Senate Judiciary Committee after the conduct of a hearing with the nominee. Then the president officially appoints the confirmed nominee. The final step is the commissioning by the president.

I followed the chief justice's advice and discussed the delay of the commissioning with the president, and she immediately set a date for the ceremony.

On the day of the ceremony, I prepared a three-page speech since I had been selected to speak on behalf of all the honorees. When I arrived at the hall for the program, one of my deputies approached me and asked if she could take my original speech to make copies to share with the media. I agreed. Within a few minutes, she returned with the original and kept the copies with her in a separate folder. Ten minutes before I was scheduled to speak, I decided to read over the speech. To my astonishment, page three of the speech was missing. When I contacted the deputy, sitting in the back of the hall, she said all the copies were only two pages each and that she had not seen a third page. She suggested that the secretary must have forgotten to print the third page. That was not possible because I stood over the secretary as she printed the final copy of the speech and I knew that she had printed three pages. I sat down and hurriedly wrote a new page three to spare myself from what would have been a major embarrassment. As disconcerting as the incident was, I could not afford to allow it to distract me. Therefore I chose to accept her explanation and moved on with my work. We eventually parted company on another issue. I would not have included the foregoing anecdotes in the book but for the fact that in the few weeks I had spent on the job, I had seen a lot of behavior that seemed innocuous but bordered on treachery. This type of deviance appeared to be pervasive in the general society, and most people did not think it was such a big deal. I was concerned that if we continued to condone this type of behavior on the senior level in government, the process of restoring the rule of law would be very difficult.

Within the first few months, the Ministry of Justice had to deal with certain matters that just came out of nowhere.

First, there was a major human trafficking case spanning Asia, Europe, Africa (Liberia), and North America. One of the senior immigration officials, a close relative of the president's best friend, was at the center of the investigation. Of course, the president's friend told me that her cousin was innocent and wanted to know if I could just let it go. In Liberia, no one is ever guilty. "There is no way my cousin could have done such a thing," she said. I am more inclined to be forgiving if the crime is minor and the suspect is remorseful, but it was not the case here. The man had credible evidence against him but felt that I could be bullied by his relative because of the connections with the president. I passed on the matter to the solicitor general because the barrage of phone calls on this man's behalf was distracting me from my job. The case bounced around for a while and even reached the courts; just when I thought it would finally be concluded, it bounced off the radar, and the guy was walking around free, accusing the ministry of witch-hunting. It was the first lesson I learned on how to stay on top of a case, especially when it has social and political dimensions.

The other case involved the sexual abuse of young girls, under twelve years of age, by an expatriate employed with an international organization. We placed the suspect under house arrest pending the preliminary investigation. First, he escaped from custody with the assistance of police officers assigned to guard the house; we jailed the officers responsible for his escape, put out an all-points bulletin, and the suspect was recaptured and placed back under house arrest with a new set of officers assigned. The officers were instructed to monitor him at thirty-minute intervals. Notwithstanding, the suspect committed suicide less than twenty-four hours after his capture.

There was a case of the ritualistic killing of a Fulah businessman. Two individuals were vying for a seat in the Senate. The one who prevailed in the elections accused the losing candidate and his wife of engaging in witchcraft.

The complainant claimed that the couple had paid their driver to murder the businessman and extract parts from the corpse to be used by a witch doctor for rituals. I instructed the police to investigate and provide more concrete evidence; otherwise we would have to close the file.

By the time the case of the former director of police, Mona Sieh Brown, was submitted to the ministry, we had learned from previous cases that it was important to take a careful look at both the political and legal dimensions of each case but that, in the end, the rule of law should prevail.

Mona Sieh, who was relieved of her post as director of police one month after I arrived at the ministry, was referred to us for prosecution by the General Auditing Commission (GAC). The report alleged that Ms. Sieh could not account for $199,000 given to the Liberia National Police in 2008 to purchase uniforms for the police. We investigated this case off and on between 2009 and 2011—off and on because we kept requesting more documents and needed to speak to more witnesses.

A case from the GAC is never ready for prosecution unless and until the ministry has examined the evidence to determine whether probable cause exists for prosecution; sometimes, the investigation involves talking to witnesses and suspects, who may not have been contacted during the auditing exercise, to ensure that due process rights are not violated. I returned this case more than twice to the Office of the Solicitor General (SG) to request additional information. The last piece of evidence needed was from the United Nations Development Program (UNDP), where the SG's request to ascertain certain information remained unanswered. The records from the logistics officer at the Liberia National Police showed that she took delivery of uniforms for the police valued at around $200,000 in 2008. We also learned that the UNDP supplied the police with uniforms valued at a little under $200,000 around the same time in 2008. We needed the UNDP to confirm this, but the agency had been unresponsive.

Sometime in 2011, I decided I would write to UNDP myself, and this time the agency responded. The UNDP informed me that it did supply the LNP with items valued at nearly $200,000 around the same time in 2008 the police director was given government funds to purchase uniforms, but the consignment from the UNDP consisted mainly of officers' shirts (white in color) and accessories. The question then was, who supplied the standard blue uniforms valued around $200,000 that the logistics officer claimed to have received? Under the circumstances, we could not commit the Ministry of Justice resources to prosecute this case. The Liberia Anti-Corruption Commission (LACC), then headed by a former minister of justice and former boss of Mona Sieh, insisted that it would go ahead with the prosecution of Ms. Sieh. Unless there was some other evidence that the LACC possessed that the ministry was not privy to, I did not see how it could prosecute without any evidence to prove the allegation. What the public did not understand was that at this point our position had very little to do with guilt or innocence; it had to do with whether we had sufficient evidence to proceed with prosecution, no matter how we felt personally.

The job was always more difficult when the accused was one of our colleagues, meaning a fellow official of government. It was especially challenging if the colleague was also well connected with key players in one or all three branches of government. I would receive phone calls or visits all hours of the day and night from folks prevailing upon me to either do nothing about a matter or take a lesser course of action than the law required. At times, the request was a humble plea for mercy; other times, it came in the form of a subtle threat that I could lose my job if I took any action contrary to the request. I am not easily intimidated by threats, especially when I believe that my action is just and fair. A few weeks into the job, I began to feel like a short-order vendor for jungle justice where citizens on a revenge binge could call in and demand whose head they wanted on a platter.

In addition to the sporadic uncovering of crimes not on the radar, there were the everyday crimes of murder, rape, armed robbery, assault, and bank fraud pending before us. By the time I shut down my office at 9:00 p.m., my brain would be too tired to remind me to eat. Sometimes I would wake up at three in the morning and find myself in the den, fully dressed in my work clothes from the day before, television on, and the plate of food (untouched) on the coffee table.

At times, phone calls from the police director or immigration commissioner would awaken me to alert me to some disruption in the city or in the interior that had occurred overnight. Or perhaps, I would receive a call from the person in charge of the prison system, informing me of the latest prison break involving some of the most dangerous inmates. If the matter was already under control, I would simply go back to bed. But if the situation was ongoing, I would have to be fully briefed by key security figures (principally, the chief of police) so that I could decide to do one or more of the following:

1) Contact the president immediately;
2) Contact other members of the Joint Security Committee immediately;
3) Ask the UNMIL for backup;
4) Wait until morning to brief the president;

5) Plan to convene a joint security meeting first thing in the morning to get input from other members; or, perhaps,

6) Implement numbers 1, 2, and 3 if the situation was determined to be serious.

Most often, the police and immigration authorities and I would do our best to bring a situation under control so that we would not have to disturb the president or others needlessly.

One of the highlights of my job within the first year was the visit of Honorable Hillary Rodham Clinton, the then Secretary of State of the United States of America, to the Liberia Police Training Academy (LPTA). I received a message from President Sirleaf's office to join Mrs. Clinton and her at the LPTA one afternoon. The US government had financed the training of an elite unit of police officers of the Liberian National Police (LNP), called the Emergency Response Unit (ERU). The young men had just graduated, and Mrs. Clinton had decided that she wanted a visit to the academy placed on her itinerary. I was truly impressed that the U.S. secretary of State took time to visit a project funded by her government. She asked a lot of questions and was truly interested in ensuring the training of the special unit would improve the service delivery of the LNP to the people. The ERU was indeed a blessing. Because of their special skills, a lot of would-be catastrophic consequences were averted.

Notwithstanding all the political challenges I faced in the first few months, I did not regret accepting the job. Before my arrival, President Sirleaf and her financial team had succeeded in negotiating a US$4.7 billion debt relief for Liberia. Civil servants had received a salary raise. For example, law enforcement officers who earned ten US dollars per month prior to the election of Ellen Johnson Sirleaf now earned one hundred dollars or more per month. Road construction projects were in progress all over the country. Investors were presenting proposals for multimillion-dollar investments in iron ore, oil palm, gold, and so forth. Government buildings were being constructed or renovated, and plans were underway to restore water and electricity to most parts of the capital. International organizations such as the United Nations, the European Union, the African Union, ECOWAS, and many foreign governments, including the United States, were investing in capacity building.

It was a daunting task for a group of Liberians diverse in age, education, and experience to come together and try to rebuild the nation. But it was worth the try.

CHAPTER 25

The Truth and Reconciliation Commission's Report

The peace agreement to finally end the fourteen-year Liberian civil war was signed in Accra, Ghana, in 2003. No one was surprised that the agreement would provide for the establishment of a Truth and Reconciliation Commission (TRC). The Liberian public wanted the government to address deep-rooted grievances of the many Liberians who had personally experienced pain and suffering at the hands of their fellow Liberians or witnessed their loved ones suffer as a result of the prolonged civil war.

Under the act establishing the TRC, article IV, section 4, provides, inter alia, for the commissioners "to foster truth, justice, and reconciliation by identifying the root-causes of the conflict, and determining those who are responsible for committing domestic and international crimes against the Liberian people ..." and "make recommendations to the Government of Liberia for prosecution, reparation, amnesty, reconciliation and institutional reforms where appropriate to promote the rule of law and combat impunity."[19] To carry out its mandate, the commission conducted interviews and collected statements from victims and witnesses in each of the fifteen counties in

Liberia and the diaspora (including the United States, the United Kingdom, and most countries in West Africa). A total of 20,460 statements were taken compared to twenty-one thousand statements during the Truth Commission's investigation in South Africa, a country with a population approximately eight times the size of Liberia. The commission (a.k.a. TRC) placed seventeen thousand statements in its database for analysis. The investigation lasted three years, from 2006 to 2009.

The commissioners of the TRC were Jerome J. Verdier, Sr. (chairman), a lawyer with background training in business administration; Dede A. Dolopei (vice chair), a social worker and peace activist who holds a bachelor's degree in business administration and accounting; Massa Washington, member, a journalist with a bachelor's degree in mass communications; and Oumu Syllah (treasurer), a social worker and HIV/Aids counselor who holds a bachelor's degree in nursing. Others on the commission were: John H. T. Stewart, member, a journalist and human rights activist; Gerald B. Coleman, member, an electrical engineer and spiritual leader; Pearl Brown Bull, member, a lawyer with a background in political science and experience in politics and social activism; and the late Sheikh Kafumba Konneh, member, a leader in the Muslim community, with experience in conflict-resolution matters. The advisers to the commission included Bishop Arthur F. Kulah, a prominent United Methodist prelate in Liberia; Professor Henrietta Mensa-Bonsu, an internationally known legal scholar of Ghanaian nationality; Dr. Kenneth Attafouah, also a lawyer from Ghana with a background in sociology and criminology; and Dr. Jeremy I. Levitt, an American professor of international law at Florida A&M College of Law.[20]

Because Liberia was in a transitional period, emerging from a civil war, the drafters of the TRC Act adopted aspects of the South African Truth Commission's model that included a reconciliatory component, as opposed to the Nuremberg model that seemed more focused on retributive justice. However, unlike the South African Commission, the Liberian TRC operated under a more limited scope and did not have the mandate to conduct prosecutions or grant amnesty. Some victims viewed this move on the part of the government as a sign of weakness and the lack of political will to bring perpetrators to justice.

Apart from the subject of the fight against corruption, the TRC report brought more visitors to my office during the first few months on the job than any other topic. The visitors consisted of Liberians, foreigners, men, women, old, and young. They all wanted to know whether the government would implement the recommendations of the commission. In fact, that was the most frequently asked question. The public also wanted to know whether the list of perpetrators was exhaustive. The implication was that there were names that had been excluded that should have been on the list. My response was always simple: "Only the Truth and Reconciliation Commission can give you an answer."

Some Liberians expressed disappointment in the way the commission conducted the hearings. They felt that the perpetrators were treated with kids' glove and allowed to brag about their pursuits in complete disregard for the emotions of victims and survivors who expected that the activities of the commission would have brought closure.

I was appalled when I read that Dr. H. Boima Fahnbulleh testified before the Truth and Reconciliation Commission that he "owes no apology" for his role in history. During his testimony, he went on to say, "We owe no one apologies for our role in fighting this oligarchy. Why should we apologize for what we proudly did? They imprisoned our fathers; we went to jail at the tender age of 18."[21]

Yvette Chesson, whose father was among the officials executed on April 22, 1980 following the military coup, called me immediately after Dr. Fahnbulleh's testimony and exclaimed: "my father was killed for the second time today." "What do you mean?", I asked. She replied, "Dr. Fahnbulleh's testimony was arrogant and insensitive. He showed no remorse."

I could not resist the thought that Dr. Fahnbulleh had mesmerized the crowd and perhaps the Commission with his usual eloquent rhetorical discourse or tirade against the fallen True Whig Party government controlled by Americo-Liberians. No doubt his performance may have, regrettably, overshadowed the true reason he had been summoned before the commission in the first place.

When I became attorney general, I was aware that part of the responsibility the Ministry of Justice was to assist with the implementation of the TRC recommendations, specifically the recommendation pertaining to prosecution. Nevertheless, there were practical reasons why I felt that it would be difficult to carry out the recommendations of the TRC at that time:

1. Many citizens had concerns that the neutrality and objectivity of some commissioners may have been compromised. The allegations against certain commissioners who were said to have been influenced by officials of government were never investigated by the Ministry of Justice because we did not receive a formal complaint with supporting evidence.

2. The fact that a lot of those listed in the TRC report also held high positions in all three branches of the Liberian government meant the likelihood that the government would support the implementation of the recommendations in the report, especially the call for prosecution, was almost next to nil. The Ministry of Justice was not involved, during my tenure in office, with the preparation and submission of the periodic report to the legislature on the status of the implementation of the TRC recommendations.

3. Many of our citizens who visited my office to discuss the status of implementation of the TRC report left me with the impression that they viewed the process by which the commission conducted the hearing as a platform for perpetrators to defend themselves. They witnessed perpetrators perform as though the hearing was an opportunity to erase public scorn and engender sympathy and understanding for their past bad deeds, effectively neutralizing the victims' desire for justice.

In sum, there was no pressure on the Ministry of Justice from the government to implement the TRC report in whole or in part, other than the move to strengthen the justice and security sectors, which would have been done with or without the TRC recommendations. The prosecutor of the International Criminal Court, Madame Fatou Bensouda, visited my office briefly in 2010 following our participation in a workshop at the Liberian legislature, to find out what plans the Liberian government had to implement the TRC report. I told her quite frankly the report should be implemented, but I was not optimistic that it would happen during the Sirleaf administration. A couple of our international partners offered to help develop a model for prosecution and even offered to help raise funding if we wanted to set up a prosecution mechanism, but the government did not pursue those offers.

It appears that the government may have been reluctant to pursue prosecution of Charles Taylor because the Special Court for Sierra Leone sitting in the Hague had essentially accomplished the same results a Special Court of Liberia would have sought. Furthermore, the financial resources that would be used to prosecute Mr. Taylor could be used elsewhere in the rebuilding efforts of the government.

To compensate for the lack of political will to prosecute for war crimes, the government shifted its focus to the recommendation in the TRC report calling for reconciliation. The citizens waited anxiously to see where this would lead us. The international community (particularly the United Nations) and civil society joined the government's team, led by the Ministry of Internal Affairs, to develop and launch a road map for reconciliation, an exercise comparable to a national action plan. The focus of the road map appeared to be the establishment of palava huts; "palava" is a local term for dispute. The palava hut would be a place where citizens could come and discuss and, hopefully, resolve issues that related to past injustices. This strategy was good for a few people who were not seriously affected by the experiences of the war but not for those who saw their innocent loved ones killed indiscriminately or their property confiscated unjustly. Victims wanted real justice, not an avenue to vent and let the perpetrator off the hook with ease.

Before the minister of internal affairs was asked to take the lead in the reconciliation process, the president had appointed her political rival in the 2011 general elections, George Weah, and her co-winner of the Nobel Peace Prize, Leymah Gbowee, consecutively, to lead the reconciliation process. Both soon realized that the appointment was political rather than a serious commitment to unify the country, so they each eventually declined. In a country that has been so devastated by war and laden with a lot of psychological scars, reconciliation is much more than a political game.

Most victims who visited my office to seek redress told me that they had no closure because the perpetrators held high government positions. This is the paradox of what we call justice in Liberia. Usually, perpetrators are ostracized by isolation or exclusion from society, bringing pressure to bear so that they are forced to think about the wrong they have done to others and make amends. Even if a perpetrator makes an apology under false pretext, it serves the purpose if the victim believes that the apology is sincere. Instead, most perpetrators walk around and interact with everyone in society, including the victim(s), as though there had never been a war.

Interestingly, some victims complained that those who had been identified by the TRC report as perpetrators wanted to be regarded as heroes and expected the victims and other members of society to show gratitude for their deliverance from the oppression of past governments. Other victims noted that perpetrators who occupied high-level government posts did not seem to understand that their unwillingness to accept responsibility for past wrong against their people posed a real obstacle to reconciliation.

The other recommendations of the TRC report that I felt deserved very serious attention were those that pertained to disarmament, demobilization, rehabilitation, and reintegration (DDRR). According to a UN Secretary-General Report, a total of 101,449 ex-combatants had been disarmed and demobilized between December 2003 and December 2004.[22] This number included 22,313 women, 8,547 boys, 2, 477 girls, and 612 foreigner nationals

(308 from Guinea, fifty from Cote D'Ivoire, 242 from Sierra Leone, seven from Nigeria, four from Mali, and one from Ghana). These figures only represent the initial group of ex-combatants enlisted in the DDRR program. Between 2004 and the end of the program in 2009, there would be many others identified and registered in the program. The ex-combatants received vocational training, stipend, and psychosocial counseling.

By the time the program ended in 2009, due to lack of funding, only a fraction of the tens of thousands of combatants in the West African subregion had been reached.

The wars in Liberia and Sierra Leone had involved not only young people from these two countries but also many other countries in the subregion, as mentioned previously. For instance, in 2010, I visited a town called Kenlay in Nimba County, Liberia, near the Ivorian border and met with armed young men of four different nationalities. They were living in the forest, subsisting on foraging and illegal mining of minerals. They told me since the war ended, they had been abandoned by their respective countries, so they were surviving the best way they could. The war did not just affect Liberia and Sierra Leone. It affected the entire subregion. For instance, those countries that were not directly involved in combat either had their youth moving into conflict areas for hire, or they had to accept an unending stream of refugees. Therefore, I had hoped that after the United Nations had done its part and left, our government and the sub-regional organizations would have developed and adopted a multi-national approach to rehabilitation of the youth in the region. But it did not happen.

At the end of the TRC exercise, the country continued to be weighed down with thousands of young people scarred by war, yearning to become part of mainstream society, yearning for the opportunity to acquire formal education, vocational training, and regular jobs. Quite a number of them found their way to the newly formed military and police. The young people whose values and norms had been shaped by years of war and disorder were being trained to enforce conventional rules in the name of re-establishing the rule of law. This decision became a challenge for the government and ended up contributing to the high attrition rate among police officers.

Also, at the end of the TRC exercise, the direct victims and survivors of atrocities received no justice from the government. The children of the thirteen government officials who were executed by the PRC government on April 22, 1980, formed an organization called the April 22nd Memorial Group." Almost every year since 1980, they have commemorated the unwarranted and untimely deaths of their loved ones. In the statement for the commemoration program for April 2015, they wrote:

> We have forgiven but cannot forget. We will always remember our loved ones. In their memories, as we forge ahead to re-establish Liberia's prominence in the comity of nations, we must look within and heal ourselves and Liberia. We take the peace and reconciliation proposal for Liberia seriously and call on the Government of Liberia to treat it with the respect and seriousness it deserves.

From the foregoing statement, it is difficult to conclude that the country has reconciled, or is even close to reconciliation, when citizens continue to remind the government that the dark past is more than just a lingering thought. Those sentiments expressed by family members who lost their loved ones are indicative of the almost indelible consequence of our failure as a society to address unresolved issues that have left many of our citizens with gaping emotional wounds. These sentiments are just as relevant for those who suffered irreparable losses as a result of the prolonged civil war.

As though she sensed the controlled fervor of the Liberian public as her second and final term of office began to wind down, President Sirleaf released her updated status report to the legislature on the TRC report on September 22, 2015. She mentioned, among other things, that of the 207 recommendations from the TRC report, eighteen were essentially general principles that did not lend themselves to practical implementation or actualization; and that forty-two recommendations were implementable in the short to medium time frame. Most interestingly, in the letter addressed to the House of Representatives, she asked the honorable body to use its power to "set up an extraordinary criminal court through the joint effort of the executive and legislative branches of government." Of course, the Liberian public questioned the sincerity of this request. Was the timing set so that the burden of responding to the quest for justice from the Liberian public would shift to the new leader? I guess it will all unravel as we move into the future.

It would have been so easy for the perpetrators to stand before the TRC and say, "Surely, we should be held accountable for what has occurred in this country in the last thirty years. It was our sincere commitment to transform the country so that the majority of our people would enjoy the resources of this land; unfortunately, we did not expect the level of atrocities that accompanied the transformation we sought. We were in error in our calculation of the reaction of the public. We are therefore truly sorry and pledge to use the opportunity given us to restore Liberia in a way that our young people will have a more stable and more promising future. We ask you to forgive us and forgive all of those who may have acted under our influence or authority." The Liberian public is very understanding and forgiving; a statement like this from those named in the TRC report as perpetrators would have helped to begin the healing process. But, unfortunately, some perpetrators bragged about what they did before and during the war, while others denied that they were involved in the commission of crimes against humanity.

In 2012, the government launched its Vision 2030 plan for Liberia. In the plan, the government promised "to reduce poverty and grow the largest middle class the country had ever known by putting the country on a sustainable, equitable, and inclusive growth path".[23] The Vision 2030 plan includes an indispensable component for a road map for national healing, peacebuilding, and reconciliation, an area we have not devoted much time to heretofore, in spite of persistent urging from the United Nations for Liberia to make reconciliation a priority.

Among the recommendations in its report, the TRC barred all those who were named in the report "from holding public office, elected or appointed, for thirty years." It meant that if the recommendation were enforced, a lot of officials in all three branches of the government would be affected. In an appearance before the Senate Foreign Relations Committee in October 2010, Counselor Varney Sherman, chairman of the ruling Unity Party, argued that the recommendation was in violation of Article 21(a) of the Liberian Constitution that prohibits ex-post facto laws and that President Sirleaf had broken no law for which she should be penalized simply because she had financially supported Charles Taylor during his incursion in Liberia.

A few months later, in January 2011, the Liberian Supreme Court ruled in *Williams v. Tah*, a case brought by one of the individuals banned from politics by the TRC for thirty years, that the TRC recommendation was a violation of the procedural due process of the individual and therefore unconstitutional. Although the foregoing opinion of the Court may have diminished the significance of one of the TRC's recommendations, on the bright side it helped the country to move forward.

In any case, when one considers the contextual political environment in which the Truth and Reconciliation Commission conducted and concluded its inquiry, it is only fair to conclude that the Commission did its best.

CHAPTER 26

Post-Traumatic Stress Syndrome (PTSD)

In November 2010, I was one of several guest speakers, including the then chief justice of Afghanistan, at the Rule of Law Week program sponsored by the World Bank and held at its headquarters in Washington, DC. At the luncheon, later that day, a woman across the table asked if I had seen the report from a survey on PTSD in Liberia conducted by Kirsten Johnson, MD, MPH, and others, published in the *Journal of the American Medical Association* (JAMA) sometime in 2008. I admitted I had not seen the study but was very curious about its findings. She went on to say that the results of the survey revealed that at least 44 percent of the population in Liberia showed symptoms of PTSD emanating from its prolonged civil war.

Of course, as soon as I returned to the hotel, I went on the internet to find the article, which I felt would buttress my concerns since my return to Liberia to take up the assignment as minister of justice. I observed that mental health might be a bigger problem for the country than we wanted to acknowledge. There was no way a whole generation of young people could experience the most horrific actions of human against human over a long period and come out unscathed. Even the older generation, as well as Liberians who lived abroad during the war, had been affected in some way or another. I do not know of one citizen, including the perpetrators themselves, who did not lose a loved one as a result of the civil war.

The researchers interviewed a cross section of 1,666 adults eighteen years and older over a three-week period and discovered that 40 percent of the households that participated exhibited symptoms of depressive disorder, 44 percent showed symptoms of post-traumatic stress syndrome (PTSD), and 8 percent met the criteria for social dysfunction.[24] PTSD manifests itself in many ways, such as having difficulty sleeping, inability to concentrate, easily startled, nightmares, always guarded, lack of interest in things that matter, inability to manage anger, and so on. But the symptom of most concern to me as the attorney general was the constant irritation and angry outbursts among the youth, which often resulted in mob violence and violent personal crimes of various types.

Those of us who lived abroad as Liberian refugees, or in other such legal or illegal statuses during the war, saw many video reports on CNN (Cable News Network), YouTube, and ABC Nightline of the atrocities. Boys, as young as eleven years old, executed their contemporaries or bragged about executing other young children and eating their organs or drinking their blood to become powerful and fearless warriors. Dogs ate human carcasses, and the humans, in turn, ate the dogs to stay alive. It was difficult to watch the evening news in Europe or the United States and eat dinner at the same time. There was always some news that was grotesque and emotionally unsettling about the ongoing war. The reports were often graphic.

As attorney general/minister of justice, I spoke to quite a few young men who confirmed that many terrible things happened during the war, including murder, rape, cannibalism, armed robbery, kidnapping, and human trafficking, but denied that they were directly involved. I did not expect them to implicate themselves, knowing what the consequences might be if they confessed to me. Many of these young people (boys and girls) had now come of age and were raising families of their own. Some of them worked in various unskilled jobs in the public and private sectors, but a large number of them were unemployed and lived in ghettos, surviving on panhandling, prostitution, peddling drugs, illegal mining of minerals, or selling stolen goods.

Many other children did not participate in killing and maiming of others but became negatively impacted by all the human suffering they witnessed or had to endure themselves. A case in point: One Saturday morning, Saah En'Tow, the head of a mentorship program, President's Young Professionals (PYP), asked members of the cabinet to spend some time with young people enrolled in the PYP program. The young people were mainly in their twenties.

He wanted cabinet members to share their work experiences with the young people so that they would have insight into what we do in our respective posts in government. The cabinet members and the students formed an inner and an outer circle so that each student faced a cabinet minister; then the facilitator would suggest a question that either the student would ask the minister or vice versa. At one point, the facilitator asked each of the ministers to look the student in the eye and ask, "What did you miss the most during the war?" The twenty-two-year-old young man, standing in front of me, looked me in the eye and said, "Toys, I missed having toys." I just stood there looking at him in amazement, not knowing what to say or do.

Then I asked, "What do you mean?"

He went on to explain that he was only four years old when the war broke out in Liberia in 1989, and by 1990, his family became externally displaced in a refugee camp in a neighboring West African country. Even in the refugee camp, there was no refuge, as families had to constantly worry about where to get the next meal and how to stay safe. Some refugees in the camps were predators and survived off the misery of others. As children, they went out during the day to fend for food. There was no regular income to take care of basic needs, let alone buy toys. Either they begged on the streets, stood in line for rations from international organizations, or prayed and hoped that a relative abroad would send some money through the Western Union. At night, he would lie on the floor, and before falling asleep, he would daydream about having beautiful toys. I just stood there with tears streaming down my face as he said softly, "Don't cry, ma'am. I am all right now." *Here is a young man,* I thought, *who is not mentally ill; he is not a criminal, yet he has been affected in such a profound way.*

Then, there was this well-known woman who owned and operated a popular restaurant in the 1970s. She recounted that during the war, she woke up every morning and went to the streets to search the pockets of dead bodies to see if there was money or other valuables on them; this was her principal means of survival.

The incident most mind-boggling and often talked about in the international community is the 1997 presidential elections when Charles Taylor ran against Ellen Johnson Sirleaf. Charles Taylor won by a landslide due to the overwhelming support of the youth between ages eighteen to thirty-five years who took to the streets in the thousands chanting, "He killed my ma and killed my pa, but I will vote for him." No one even tried to understand the logic here because there was none. One Liberian man living in the United

States at the time said to me, "We are in deep trouble, not because Taylor has won the presidency but because we have lost our children."

"I think all of us have lost our way, my friend, not only the children," I said. I went on to tell this man that a prominent figure from one of the countries in the West African subregion told me that he would never forget the impression he formed of Liberians when he was asked to join others to try to bring the Liberian warlords together and broker peace. He said that when the warlords entered the room, they were so elated to see one another. The room was filled with handshakes, hugs, laughter, and exchange of information on friends and family. He said, "My dear sister, when we go to broker peace with warlords from other countries, we cannot even get some of them to sit in the same room, let alone shake hands. But when the Liberian warlords entered the room, it was like a long-awaited family reunion."

Today, in post-conflict Liberia, violent personal crimes have become rampant. In 1978, only thirty-three persons out of 1,500 prisoners around the country were incarcerated for murder. The majority of the murders that year had occurred in Maryland, Montserrado, and Lofa Counties. Today, the number is much higher, and the incidents of murder are occurring all over the country. One day in 2010, the police were called to a residence near downtown Monrovia where a young man had killed his wife, chopped her body into pieces, and buried it under the area rug in their bedroom. The suspect eluded the police and managed to escape the country. Within a few weeks, some Liberian businesswomen spotted the suspect in the hotel where they were staying in Togo (another West African country) and called the local police, who then called Interpol to assist in bringing the suspect back to Liberia.

In another unrelated case, a nineteen-year-old killed his father, who tried to stop him from raping his nine-year-old sister. In 2010, the Annual Report for the Sexual Gender-Based Violence Unit (SGBV) revealed that nearly half of the rape victims were under twelve years of age, some as young as two years old.

Not only has the number of violent personal crimes increased over the years since the war began, but also the age of the perpetrator is now much younger. In 2013, we had a case of an eleven-year-old who killed his four-year-old brother and mutilated the corpse because, as he claimed, the father paid more attention to the younger brother. It was the first time in the history of the country that we had in custody a murderer so young, and, therefore, it took us several weeks to decide how and where to place him. We did not want to place him among adults, and all the boarding facilities for children in need of assistance turned him away.

And then there were the thousands out there who did terrible things daily, but no one ever bothered to report to the authorities, either because they were afraid of the perpetrators, or perhaps the incident occurred in an area so remote from civilization that the inhabitants had probably never seen a police officer or a courthouse and did not know what to do.

To compound the problem, some of our youngsters who used drugs during the war to masque the pain still used illicit drugs as the panacea for marginalization by a society that was oblivious to the ails of lost souls. Against this background, how does society draw the line between punishment and treatment?

It was not uncommon to find a dead body near your fence early in the morning; it was not uncommon for a thief or a reckless driver who ran over a motorcyclist or a pedestrian to be lynched by a mob. All of this anger appears to result from the distrust of the government and the formal justice system, from many years of witnessing and experiencing the most horrific injustice, and the lack of closure due to the government's inability to address the unlimited number of grievances.

Moreover, there were many people with titles (eg. General) during the war (both in government and on the battlefield) who operated under unconventional rules that prioritized personal survival. Those rules, internalized over a protracted period, became the new normal and continued to underpin the basic understanding of governance and power generally, leaving the general society with a misguided understanding of power. To some, power is money, or a gun, or a high-level government position, or control of illegal mining operations, or control of an illicit drug business, or all of the above.

During the war, people did not generally go to jail for such crimes as murder, rape, and robbery, unless the action of the perpetrator specifically offended someone with power. The question, then, is, How do we transition from this general mind-set to law and order? How do we replace the new normal internalized during the war with the rule of law now being promoted by civil society and the international community? What is the acceptable option for the vast majority of those whom we have asked to conform to the new order we call the rule of law? How do you transition a young person, who wielded a lot of power during the war by carrying a gun, from the violence to civility?

Most disappointingly, instead of providing a viable option for survival, we showed extreme tolerance to those who continued to play by the rules of war by often compromising core values in the name of politics and peace. In one instance, the police, the parent of a rape victim (a minor), and the perpetrator struck a deal, whereby the perpetrator paid some money to the mother and the police and walked away to his freedom. The resolution did not consider the physical and psychological damage to the young and helpless victim. The Ministry of Justice intervened and ordered the police to rearrest the perpetrator for proper investigation and, possibly, prosecution. The ministry's intervention effectively canceled what the parties considered to be a resolution of the problem.

I observed that, generally, we have become a society where people lie about everything. No doubt, lying is a vestige of the prolonged war where people had to lie about their ethnicity, their religion, their possessions, their relationships, their occupation, and everything else just to remain alive. There were so many warring factions, each with its own idiosyncratic beliefs and demands. You just did not know who you were dealing with, what they wanted, or what you might say that could cause you your life. Unfortunately, the falsehood has continued to pervade the society to the extent that we lie even when it is not necessary to do so.

But then, the bad habit of lying is not just a problem with the general society, or among the poor and the uneducated, or among those who physically witnessed the war. This behavior, unfortunately, is exhibited by highly educated individuals in positions of power both in the private and public sectors. What is even more appalling is that quite a few people who lived abroad during the war, and who had been expected to return to Liberia to rebuild and help our traumatized brothers and sisters to readjust to life in a civil society, exhibited the same deviant behavior. In other words, some of the supposedly model citizens from the diaspora joined the beat on the ground and became fully acculturated by their traumatized brothers for whom they should have been role models.

When we tolerate behavior that undermines law and order and tramples over the rights of others, we give the impression to the general society that it is the acceptable way to live with one another. Citizens become confused when one group of officials condemn certain kinds of behavior, while other officials embrace and display that same behavior. This unquestionable tolerance for dysfunctional behavior by the rich and the powerful blurs the line that we ought to draw between good and evil and, consequently, emboldens the ordinary citizens to view bad behavior as normal. For instance, the government puts ordinary citizens in jail who commit theft, while some officials steal money entrusted to them for the citizens and continue to occupy the public office without any consequences.

There is only one mental health facility with a capacity of less than two hundred. Others who exhibit harmful and aggressive behavior are processed through the courts under a criminal charge of some sort, such as assault and battery, and remanded to prison. Of the approximate prison population of two thousand in the country, we suspect that nearly 50 percent suffer from some behavioral disorder. Unlike the 1970s, when it was easy to attach some motive to a crime, most of the violent personal crimes today are senseless. It takes very little for a person to get angry, and if others do not calm the angry person down within minutes, someone might lose his or her life before it is all over.

During the first few weeks I was in office as minister, I retained the services of a mental health social worker, in person of Fatu Daramy Mensah, as a consultant to the Bureau of Corrections. Some of my colleagues in the legal profession kept saying to me that we need to employ more lawyers and not social workers. "You cannot run a criminal justice system with just lawyers," was my response. We tried assiduously to raise funds to provide rehabilitation and mental health services in the prison system, but it just never gained traction. Mental health did not seem to be a priority at the time, except for the Carter Center, where a small mental health project was being developed in collaboration with the Liberian Ministry of Health.

The UN Women (formerly UNIFEM) provided a small grant of $300,000 to the Ministry of Justice, which we decided to use to introduce rehabilitation programs in the two largest prisons in the country, one in Monrovia and the other in Zwedru. The programs consisted of sewing school uniforms to sell at an affordable price to underprivileged students, baking, graphic arts, tie-dying, gardening, soap making, adult literacy, and psychosocial counseling. Ms. Mensah contracted the services of the Liberian Association of Psychosocial Services (LAPS) to assist with the group counseling services. The proceeds raised by the inmates were used to defray the cost of operating the prison. Due to limited funding, the psychosocial program was designed to provide a one-hour group counseling session twice a week for each group enrolled; we could not afford the much-needed individual counseling services.

Interestingly, the first group counseling session with inmates, which should have run for an hour, lasted for four hours. The inmates could not stop talking. Amid the pleas from the inmates for the counselor to keep running the session, she was compelled to discontinue due to exhaustion. During our discussion of the outcome of the first session with the inmates, we realized that most of them had pent-up anger from unresolved issues for so long that they just simply needed the opportunity to vent if nothing else.

The funds and, hence, the program would last for only a year, and that was the end. We expected that the government would assess the program and realize how important it was to continue; the government did assess the program and was impressed, but nothing happened after that.

One small consolation is that a number of these young people who were at risk have pulled themselves up by the bootstrap, realizing that they cannot count on the government alone to provide a place in mainstream society. With assistance from local and international nongovernmental agencies, some have opened small businesses, moved into the rural areas to do farming, or have sought employment with large concessions operating in the country.

CHAPTER 27

Fighting Corruption

The Liberian society, like many other places around the world, has historically been plagued with the problem of corruption, both in the public and private sectors. But for obvious reasons, corruption became much more institutionalized during the years of civil war when social institutions hardly functioned.

Usually the values of a society are reflected in the laws and policies promulgated by its people; but when the moral compass that undergirds a society malfunctions and remains out of commission for a protracted period of time, social disorder becomes the "new normal" and re-establishing the rule of law becomes a colossal challenge. For instance, young people who held others at gunpoint during wartime and collected huge sums of money on a regular basis found it difficult to wait for thirty days to collect a meager paycheck from a regular job in a civil society. Therefore, they resorted to illegal mining, sale of illegal drugs, or other such activities to earn fast money. Those who were fortunate to land white collar jobs in government or in the private sector were also haunted by the war vestige of instant gratification.

In my third year at the Ministry of Justice, I recall thinking how futile it seemed our fight against corruption had been over the years, merely moving in circles. The few cases we had won did not seem to have served as a deterrence. Corruption continued to be prevalent in both the private and public sectors, among the young and old, among the educated and uneducated, and among the rich and poor.

Some of the cases we received for investigation were very alarming. For instance, young people working in the banks had organized shadow lending services within the banking system. They would use bank funds to give out loans to people in the business community on a short-term basis at very high interest rates (e.g., 20 percent), pocket the interest payment, and put the principal funds back into the system before their portfolios were audited. Then there were government officials, as well as low-level employees in government, opening up procurement companies and doing business with the government, often paying themselves for services never rendered. In other cases, employees of government were padding payrolls; people in the private sector were offering bribes, and officials and employees were accepting the bribes to do work they were already getting paid by the government to do. Investors were experiencing shakedowns by some government employees on a regular basis but were afraid to complain because of fear they might lose their investment.

Even the ordinary man on the streets stole metal pipes used as protective railings on the highways to make pots and other aluminum wares. Others made underground electrical connections to the property of unsuspecting homeowners, and the list goes on.

There was tension among the transparency agencies of government, especially the Ministry of Justice and the Office of the Auditor General of Liberia. The General Auditing Commission (GAC) would conduct audits of government ministries and agencies and send the reports to the Ministry of Justice for what it termed "prosecution." As much as we applauded the GAC for its diligence and determination in going after corrupt public officials, it was our duty as a justice institution to ensure that due process was respected by conducting a thorough criminal investigation before proceeding to prosecute. Most of the accused complained that they had not been questioned or asked to provide evidence in their defense before the GAC concluded and submitted its reports to us. Therefore, the ministry set up a team, which included Jim Dube, an International Senior Legal Partner (ISLP) lawyer from Toronto, Canada, to review and analyze the reports and make recommendations. In most cases, the team called in witnesses, including the accused, to answer questions and provide additional documentation for clarification. We found that only a few cases required prosecution; some cases were civil in nature, and others either required some administrative action or a simple final step to complete a project.

Besides, the Ministry of Justice just did not have the funding to run a robust prosecution program. The annual budget was $250,000, and sometimes a high-profile case would cost more than $100,000, and if you had to conduct a retrial, the one case could wipe out the entire budget.

There are also other reasons, in my point of view, why the fight against corruption in Liberia is difficult:

1) *Lack of commitment*: The funding allocated by the government to fight corruption was far too inadequate. There was one corruption court (criminal court C), always with an overcrowded docket. If there were a dozen cases on the docket for a specific term of court, chances were only two or three might be tried due to lack of resources, while the rest would become part of the existing backlog. The discussion to set up a second corruption court remained only a topic for discussion. Nearly all transparency agencies, such as the Ministry of Justice, the Public Procurement Concession Commission, the Liberian Anti-Corruption Commission, and the Office of the Auditor General, operated with a very low budget.

2) *Lack of collaboration*: The government's divide-and-control strategy impeded coordination and collaboration among transparency agencies. Instead of collaboration, most of the agencies armed with authority to fight corruption were competing against and undermining one another.

3) *Political connection*: A substantial number of individuals charged with corruption had ties to the president, and, therefore, they exploited those connections to frustrate the prosecution, even though the president may not necessarily have been aware of, or have been involved in, the targeted corrupt practice. For instance, I recall where a certain municipal official, charged with embezzling development funds, tried to beat the charges not in court but in the Executive Mansion. The solicitor general, Micah Wright, and I found ourselves in the Office of the Minister of State, with the president and the defendant present, around ten o'clock at night, struggling to explain that we had not indicted this man without probable cause. We also explained that the municipal official's allegation that the solicitor general had solicited US$30,000 from him to drop the charges was unfounded.

In yet another matter, the president went on the radio a few days after the chairman of the Board of the Liberian Airport Authority was indicted for economic sabotage and announced that she had the "highest confidence in his integrity."

4) *Effects of the civil war*: After fourteen years of civil war and a little more than two decades of political and social upheaval, resulting in death and destruction and internal and external displacements, the values of our people were transformed drastically. Conventional norms defining right and wrong no longer made sense to a lot of people, especially the youth. For example, theft and physical aggression are not necessarily viewed as crimes in wartime but rather as enviable survivor skills. After repeatedly exhibiting or witnessing this type of behavior over a prolonged period, it becomes the norm, a new normal that is not automatically reversed when the war ends.

5) *Vertical collusion*: When I was in government in the seventies, I do believe that some high-level officials (e.g., cabinet ministers) were engaged in corruption, but I do not know of instances where these officials were regularly in collusion with lower-level officials or employees. Because we were unaware of what they were doing in the privacy of their offices or homes, we were of the impression that, except for a few indiscreet individuals who got caught, they were upstanding individuals, committed to serving the public. In other words, the type of corruption, then, could aptly be described as horizontal corruption because of its general confinement among people on the same level of stratification. Whereas, corruption in Liberia today is more or less vertical and intergenerational, meaning that officials engage in corrupt activities with people on all levels of the stratification ladder, irrespective of age or social status. For instance, it is not unusual for a cabinet minister to form a criminal alliance with a secretary. The problem with this latter characterization is that young people tend to think that the behavior is acceptable because those who should be serving as role models, or mentors, are equal participants, and therefore the call for re-establishing the rule of law appears to be a mere political gimmick.

CHAPTER 28

Negotiating Government Contracts

Of the many functions the Ministry of Justice has to perform, one is its responsibility to participate in the review, negotiation, and execution of government contracts, most often in collaboration with other government institutions, such as the National Investment Commission, the Ministry of Finance, and a sector ministry or agency. The major contracts included the concession agreements, covering natural resources such as iron ore, gold, timber, and hydrocarbon; and other concessions agreements relating to rubber and oil palm. Concession agreements usually run for a term of twenty-five years, except for oil palm, which has a life cycle of thirty-three years. Between 1960 and 1980, mining alone constituted around 60 percent of the country's export earnings. (Source: Poverty Reduction Strategy, 2008, page 65.)

Other major contracts consisted of construction contracts involving mainly road and building construction. Lease agreements include the lease by the government of private real estate for government use, or, in other cases, the lease of real property by government as lessor to individuals or businesses. Then there are also procurement contracts involving the procurement of goods and services, such as the purchase of vehicles, fuel oil, office equipment, office furniture, stationery and supplies, and the painting of public buildings, landscaping and so on.

The Ministry of Justice also reviews bilateral/multilateral agreements, grants, and loan agreements. The Department of Economic Affairs is the arm of the Ministry of Justice responsible for ensuring that contracts have been reviewed and cleared with the minister to be returned to a sector ministry or agency for correction or implementation. Other times, the Ministry of Justice sends the agreement to the office of the president (in the case of a concession agreement) as part of the process for ratification by the legislature.

It is not as easy as some might think to attract traditional investors to a developing country, even if the country is rich in natural resources. It is especially difficult when the developing country, as in the case of Liberia, has just emerged from a lengthy and brutal civil war, that resulted in the destruction of almost all social institutions and infrastructure. On the one hand, as much as the foreign investor needs the natural resource, it must consider the financial and security risks of investing in a place with weak institutions. The country, on the other hand, desperately needs the revenues to get back on its feet and provide the requisite services that underpin stability. So it seems both parties need each other. But somehow, I felt that we always gave our citizens the impression that the investors need us more than we need them. Against this background, it is important to recount a few of the challenges encountered during my experience with negotiating foreign and domestic contracts:

A. Multitasking

For those Justice Ministry employees who are mainly concerned with economic affairs, they might not be aware that at all times the ministry is involved with a crisis of some sort in other areas of responsibility, especially law enforcement and national security. For instance, the solicitor general might receive information that a state witness in a major case is threatening to back out of the case and the witness protection program unless we provide US$5,000 within the next hour for him to take care of his personal needs. Or a judge has awarded US$15 million to an undeserving private investor whose case against the government is unfounded and is unsupported by facts or the law. Or the police have received news that an accused thief has just been beaten to death by an angry mob in the community, and someone needs to bring the crowd under control to keep the violence from escalating. Or the director of the National Fire Service has called to say that a major fire is occurring in the largest slum near the city center, but the fire truck cannot get to the burning structure because shacks are obstructing the alleyway closest to the house on fire. Or immigration officers have discovered dozens of children in a truck near a border town about to be trafficked. Or in the early morning, more than a dozen of some of the most notorious criminals in the country have broken out of jail and escaped.

The point is, as minister of justice, I had to constantly engage in multitudinous tasks and, therefore, had to be able to switch the thought process from one area of engagement to the other when the situation required. The key is to determine whether to take on the task yourself; delegate the task and the authority that comes with it to a deputy; delegate but superintend the activity; or multitask, by assuming the responsibility to be all things to all people at all times. I often delegated because I believe that doing so provides the opportunity for others to learn and to grow in the organization; it provides for efficiency as well, as I did not expect the office to stop running in my absence.

B. Low Capacity

I cannot stop reminding myself, and others, of the brain drain Liberia experienced due to the war. On the one hand, the few highly competent lawyers on the ground during the war wanted to remain in private practice. On the other hand, very few lawyers practicing abroad were interested in returning to Liberia without being offered a reasonable salary with benefits.

Faced with a depleted practicing bar due to the long civil war, President Sirleaf sought help from an international nongovernmental organization in the United States called the International Senior Lawyers Project (ISLP). ISLP, under its Board Chairman, Joseph Bell, and the Executive Director, Jean Berman, then recruited skilled and experienced lawyers in North America to volunteer their time and energy to assist post conflict states in resurrecting the rule of law. For Liberia, it was a perfect fit: skilled lawyers with the capacity to provide legal expertise on a pro bono basis. Over the succeeding years, many ISLP volunteers worked with the Ministry of Justice, both onsite (short term) and on a remote basis, to review/advise on resource agreements, provide legal education programs for prosecutors, and assist the government in defending cases brought against it both in Liberia and elsewhere.

ISLP volunteers, in turn, had the support of their respective law firms, mostly large, internationally known law firms that were prepared to underwrite expenses of volunteers and contribute to ISLP's work. To these law firms, lawyer volunteers, and other philanthropists, we owe a great debt of gratitude. They saved the government millions of dollars needed to fund other pressing expenses of a government emerging from the devastation of a war. Numerous ISLP volunteers came to Liberia between 2006 to 2015 to assist the government of Liberia on various legal matters. If I were to attempt to name these generous, spirited individuals, I would run the risk that I might inadvertently omit someone. But they know who they are and what they have done to help us in our efforts to recover from our national disaster.

We were also fortunate to benefit from the services of young foreign advisers, sponsored by international philanthropic organizations, who fulfilled a similar role as the ISLP. It would be remiss on my part not to mention the few young advisers with whom I came into contact during my tenure at the ministry and whose contribution to Liberia was remarkable. They are Jared Schott, Amanda Rawls, Chelsea Payne, Peter Chapman, Belinda Richards, Stefan Rusche, Susan Maples, Lara Eldridge, and Susan Altman; also, Samuel Agyakwa-Opoku, Paola Barragan, and Catherine Barley from the UNMIL office.

I am very grateful for the strong support of Jared Schott, who was assigned to me as an adviser for a couple of years. He was especially helpful to the government of Liberia in reviewing, drafting, and advising on natural resource agreements. I was also able to avail myself of the services of Belinda Richards, who was then the adviser assigned to the minister of finance, Augustine Ngafuan. The minister permitted Belinda to share her services with the Ministry of Justice in the early days of my appointment as attorney general before the arrival of Jared Schott. She regularly provided oral and written briefs on the status of natural resource agreements to bring me up to speed on what had transpired before my appointment.

As a result of the partnership mentioned above, a lot of our local staff were able to acquire meaningful skills on the job to augment what they already had. Moreover, the government provided scholarships for young Liberians to attain academic training both locally and internationally. The Ministry of Justice, itself, conducted many workshops and training programs for its staff.

C. Resistance to Change on Both Sides

The template for a lot of the concession agreements we negotiate today was developed in the 1960s, right after several African countries gained independence from colonial powers. Although Liberia had been independent since 1847 and had entered into concession agreements before the nineteen sixties, it had not necessarily enjoyed the benefits of arm's length negotiations of resource contracts. During the post nineteen sixty period, often referred to as the period of neocolonialism, Africans were inexperienced in such matters and still gave deference to former colonial masters; therefore, agreements negotiated and concluded at the time tended to be asymmetrical and paternalistic in content. However, this trend began to gradually change over the last three decades with collaboration from some of the international organizations, such as the United Nations, the Office of Economic Cooperation and Development (OECD), the World Bank, and others. They have provided resources to developing countries with natural resources to develop model Mineral Development Agreements (MDA) reflective of the current realities in transnational investments.

Another contextual example, specific to Liberia, is the Firestone Rubber Plantations Agreement executed in 1926. Almost every new Administration in Liberia, since the 1930s, has called for the review and renegotiation of the Firestone agreement, signifying the frequent requirement by the Liberian government to make current this hundred-year term agreement. In an interview with Gerald Padmore, a former deputy minister of finance during the Tolbert Administration and currently one of the lawyers for Firestone/Bridgestone, the "Firestone" agreement was renegotiated about fifteen times between 1926 (when it was first signed) and 1976. It is important to recall the historical context of the Firestone agreement. In the nineteen twenties, Liberia was still struggling with debts it had incurred since 1871. "By 1912, repeated defaults on loan repayments culminated with the establishment of an international receivership over all Liberian revenues. Only European rivalries and shrewd Liberian diplomacy prevented outright annexation of the country by England, France, and Germany."[25] Consequently, the Liberian government signed an agreement with Firestone who needed a home for its rubber plantation to compete with the British rubber plantations in Asia. Accordingly, the Liberian government entered into an agreement with Firestone and received a five million dollar-loan in exchange for a hundred-year lease to one million acres of land.[26]

Mr. Padmore further explained that the Firestone agreement was totally revised in 1976 and the Company thereafter became subjected to all tax laws of Liberia without exception. In 1980, Firestone wanted to get out of the rubber farming business and turn over the entire plantation to the government, but President Doe asked them to stay which they did on condition that export taxes were removed; otherwise, the 1976 agreement remained in effect. After the civil war, Firestone requested a review of the terms with the view to determining how best it could recover some of its losses from the war and restore production. Therefore, in 2005, under the Transitional Government, the Firestone agreement was reviewed, the Cavalla part of its plantations in

Cape Palmas was returned to the government, and stability of some of the fiscal terms of the agreement was granted. In 2008, the Firestone agreement was again reviewed but only marginal improvements were made over the 2005 agreement.

Quite frankly, it is unfair to the investor to have a concession agreement come under review with every change of government. While review of an agreement may be necessary, it should not be arbitrary. Investors often asked to include a "stabilization clause" in the agreement, whereby certain terms, specifically the fiscal regime, are frozen over the life of the agreement. That way, the investor feels that it is operating under a document that is certain and predictable. A stabilization clause is not acceptable to the government's side because we cannot predict what will occur over the life of the agreement from both economic and political standpoints. Therefore, it does not make sense to freeze a law such as this for a long period. As a compromise, we spend a lot of time developing other provisions that will provide some economic equilibrium satisfactory to both sides, such as providing for renegotiation when there is profound change of circumstances and/or including a definitive periodic review clause.

As a member of the negotiating team for Liberia, I saw our role not only as developing a model investment agreement similar to those in other countries of the subregion but also to examine and revise, as we went along, individual provisions in each agreement that take into consideration our unique circumstances as a country. One of such provisions was the arbitration clause. Historically, in every commercial agreement between our government and another party, we had agreed that if the investor prevailed in a dispute with the government, the investor would be allowed to enforce the arbitral award against any and all assets of the country. It means that if an oil palm investor wants to enforce an award against the government, it could attach assets of the Liberian Maritime Authority, the National Port Authority, the Liberian Petroleum Refining Corporation, or any other available asset of government. My suggestion was that if a concessionaire was awarded judgment against a state-owned corporation, then the judgment should be enforced against the assets of the state-owned enterprise that is party to the dispute in arbitration, rather than pursue enforcement against another government agency that was not a party to the agreement. This was one of the many lessons I learned in the International Commercial Arbitration course taught by Professor Michael Reisman in graduate law school. My colleagues on the negotiating team were in full agreement, and as a result, the arbitration clause was modified to reflect our requirement.

Additionally, the negotiating team focused on ensuring that new concession agreements include plans for infrastructural development, especially construction and maintenance of roads used regularly by the concessionaire to facilitate their business operations; contribution to social and economic development in the concession area; local content considerations for Liberian entrepreneurs, and so forth.

D. Investors' Access to High-Level Officials of Government

Relatives and friends of high-level government officials have always seen, and still see, investment contracts as an opportunity to peddle influence and, perhaps, a means of acquiring financial security for the future. Therefore, to circumvent a difficult negotiating team, an individual with connections would introduce the investor to a senior-level official. Once this happened, and the official intervened on behalf of the investor, the effectiveness of the negotiation team was weakened. If the investor had promised a well-connected local or foreign lobbyist some money, then there was pressure to speed up the process so that the lobbyist/influence peddler would collect on the deal. There was usually no concern, on the part of the influence peddler that his actions might undermine the integrity of the process or cause the country to lose millions of dollars in the long run.

E. The Problem of Investors' Perception of Officials

In one of my first meetings with an international partner working with the government on public sector reform projects, I got the sense that the foreigners across the table were conducting a mental assessment of the officials sitting on the opposite side of the table. Irrespective of the fact that some background inquiry may have already been conducted to ascertain the capability of the officials involved in the negotiating process, it was easy to sense a general concern that government officials were incompetent and corrupt.

This perception may have been well founded in 2004 when the war had just ended and spillover values from a lawless era permeated every nook and cranny of the society. But the quality of public servants improved significantly between 2006 and 2010 due to persistent capacity-building programs and diligent recruitment and vetting of professionals. For instance, George Soros, the well-known philanthropist, provided the Sirleaf administration with a lot of financial support for the recruitment of qualified Liberians in and out of the country. Unfortunately, the integrity index showed that integrity lagged behind competence. In other words, the competence of an individual did not necessarily guarantee honesty. Corruption has continued to be a major problem in Liberia. The few who dared to try to change the negative perception were often castigated and referred to as a non-team player or plain stupid. Consequently, professionals who were committed to service soon became disappointed and disillusioned and began to look for a way to get out of the government. All the excitement to promote an agenda for transformation just simply waned.

F. Land Issues

One of our biggest challenges had to do with the land awarded to concessionaires who wanted large parcels of land for multimillion-dollar mining and agricultural projects. Some lands are owned communally by tribal communities, some are owned by the government, and some are owned by individuals as private property. Because of the fourteen-year-old civil war, there had been a lot of encroachment on land by folks who thought the owners who fled the war might not come back. Additionally, previous governments had awarded concessions without consulting the communities concerned. The Sirleaf administration established a Land Commission in 2009 to address the multitudinous land issues, and one of the terms of reference of the commission would be to engage the local communities.

The land issue continues to be an unresolved post war problem in Liberia. Other than the land grab involving some major foreign direct investment projects, there are numerous cases of land dispute between two private parties, between businessmen and citizens, or among family members. For instance, the military coup d'etat of 1980 and the fourteen-year civil war, that began in 1989, caught a lot of our people off guard. Some of those who met their untimely death did not have time to disclose to family members what they owned, nor prepare a *will* to ameliorate the likelihood of intrafamily disputes. Moreover, in the nineteen fifties and sixties, some families entered into long term real estate leases for prime properties and provided for payment in what they believed would always be United States dollars. In mid nineteen eighties, the Doe administration introduced the Liberian dollars which they said was on par with the U.S. dollar. As I write today, one United States dollar is equivalent to 200 Liberian dollars. This means, those who signed leases prior to the change in currency might not be receiving payment for what their property is really worth.

G. Dealing with Domestic Contractors

I had always wondered why Liberians have not formed a consortium to buy an oil block or invest in iron ore mining and the like, but after I became minister, it was easy to understand. Those in power would rather give a concession agreement to a foreigner than a Liberian. The reason was that "Liberians don't pay debt" or "they are not good business managers." It is true that there are a few who do not repay a loan or squander the profits rather than reinvest in the business, but there are a lot of good Liberian entrepreneurs who are simply not given a chance.

Among the first cases on my desk when I took over as minister of justice was that of a Liberian businessman who owned a hotel/restaurant business overlooking the Atlantic Ocean. The government claimed that he owed US$8 million in back taxes. I discovered later that the actual tax bill was US$1.7 million, but the $8 million included interest and penalty. The value of the business at the time was less than US$2 million. Therefore, I suggested that we waive the interest and penalty and negotiate a payment plan with the business owner. After all, the government was partly to blame for allowing the tax bill of a taxpayer to remain delinquent long enough to spiral out of control. For instance, why did the government not act when the bill was just $300,000 in arrears? Instead of working with the business owner, the government continued to put pressure on him to pay the US$8 million bill, which continued to increase until the business finally closed.

A few Liberian engineers did sometimes receive lofty contracts from government, but the majority were encouraged to bid for uncomplicated building and road construction contracts, such as the construction of farm-to-market laterite roads, construction of one-level or two-level concrete buildings, and the like. Sometimes, the contract was worth several thousand dollars, and sometimes it ran in the millions. For years, these contracts flowed out of the Ministry of Public Works as though on a production line, since such contracts did not have to endure the rigors of a concession agreement that involved the president and the legislature. One evening when my workload was not too hectic, I sat down to review some of the construction contracts pending for my signature, a task usually assigned to the deputy minister of justice for economic affairs. After I read through the first four contracts, I discovered that each contract was not more than three or four pages and had no evidence of compliance or eligibility documentation attached, although each contract was worth between US$4 million and US$11 million. I decided to put the entire batch of fourteen contracts on hold and proceeded to write to the acting minister of public works, informing him that the Ministry of Justice would no longer execute construction contracts unless and until they meet the following minimum requirements:

- evidence of a certificate of review and approval by the Public Procurement Concession Commission;
- evidence of an approved performance bond;
- evidence of financial wherewithal of the company; and
- evidence of the technical capability of the company.

My staff informed me that the acting minister hit the ceiling when he received my letter. To him, I was violating the norm. Those who opposed my position made it appear as though I was working against the interest of the "poor" Liberian contractors who were struggling to stay in the game. The acting minister wanted the roads built, but I had to worry about what would happen if the contractors did not perform. As much as I understood how anxious the minister was to go ahead with some of these projects, I was not prepared to back down. I had given leeway to a lot of officials with the understanding that they would be more diligent the next time around. The more I tried to be understanding, the more relaxed officials tended to become. In the end, the acting minister agreed to comply.

H. Members of Negotiation Team Need to Be on the Same Page

The negotiation team nowadays tends to be diverse in composition in terms of age, education, experience, and purpose. Therefore, team members may not always agree on what constitutes conflict of interest, when to draw the line between business and personal friendship with the investors, or when to pursue firm or flexible negotiation tactics. Investors receive mixed messages when they are presented with one set of requirements at the negotiation table and later receive assurances, in private, from one or more team members that strict adherence to the team's requirements is not necessary.

Every official who is expected to append his or her signature to an agreement should be involved in the process from its inception. For instance, a partially executed petroleum contract surfaced in April 2011. Apparently, the contract had been signed by all the relevant officials of government in November 2009, except the minister of justice and the president. Now the investor was requesting that I append my signature to the agreement, and I refused on the grounds I was minister of justice in November 2009 and did not understand how and why the contract was executed without my involvement. Furthermore, I was not inclined to sign a document we had not properly negotiated with the investor. The new CEO of NOCAL, Christopher Neyor, agreed with me, and the contract was set aside.

Do I regret signing any agreement? Of course, I do. There are a few agreements I did not like but at times you have to reach concessions with your colleagues. You cannot be a team player and disagree all the time. But there was this mining agreement I did not like at all as we all knew from the beginning that the deal was going to be flipped. This was a project I had completely delegated to a deputy, as I did often, so that the deputies would be empowered and feel included in what the Ministry was doing. Unfortunately, the deputy abused the opportunity and misguided me. Had I retained control or adequately superintended the process, it is very likely that the agreement may never have been executed.

Collective responsibility:

If an agreement turns out to be unfavorable, it is a reflection on each member of the team, not just the chairman of the National Investment Commission (usually the head of the negotiation team) or any other individual member of the team. For instance, the minister of justice never signs any contract alone. All contracts go through a vetting process that includes a transparency agency like the Public Procurement Concession Commission (PPCC). A concession agreement could take months or years to negotiate and is usually signed by at least four cabinet members (Justice, Finance, National Investment Commission, and the sector ministry or agency). The legal advisor to the president participates in negotiations but does not sign agreements. When the negotiation team completes its work on the agreement, it is forwarded to the office of the president for signature, following which, it is submitted to the legislature for ratification.

The process of negotiating and concluding a concession agreement is not always as easy and straightforward as it seems. When there is disagreement between the legislative and executive branches on certains terms in the agreement, the ensuing back and forth between the two branches of government is likely to persist for weeks or months until the disagreement is resolved.

I. Closing Notes

Most Liberians who negotiate mining and agricultural concessions would rather see the Liberian rain forest remain intact and the ownership rights of citizens in land undisturbed. But the reality is that the revenues from other sources, such as real estate taxes, port fees, and maritime fees, are just not enough to run the country. Therefore, the government engages foreign investors who have the capital to invest in the natural resources. This does not mean that we should give out natural resources for free, or accept less than what our resources are worth, or allow a few officials to put their pecuniary interest above that of the country.

Moreover, the destruction of infrastructures during the war weakened the bargaining position of the country. Most investors want to invest in places that have public water and sewer services, electricity, good roads, reliable internet service, a strong judiciary, and so on. When a country lacks these services, it has to make a lot of concessions, especially when it comes to taxes, in order to convince an investor that the investment is worth the risks.

CHAPTER 29

Serving A Female
Head of State

The election of Ellen Johnson Sirleaf as the first female president of Liberia ushered in a new era for women around the world, but especially in Liberia. Most Liberian women, both in the private and public sectors, had high expectations that their lives would be affected positively. They believed that women would play more prominent roles in public service. They believed that the female entrepreneur would flourish, and fewer women would suffer physical, verbal, and mental abuse at home.

They also believed that parents would be encouraged to send young girls to school, and social institutions, especially the family, would be reintegrated. All of these things appeared to be achievable when, during her first term in office, President Sirleaf introduced many programs that focused on females. For example, the establishment of a special court for gender-based sexual offenses was a signal that her administration would not tolerate sexual violence against women. The appointment of a cabinet with at least 25 percent females, the appointment of a female associate justice to the Supreme Court, and the appointment of a few female superintendents to head government subdivisions gave additional signs that women were moving in the right direction.

In fact, the coming into power of a female president was one of my major considerations in deciding to return to Liberia and join the government in 2009. I felt that we needed more than taxes and foreign aid to rebuild the country. We needed compassion and sincere commitment, something in great demand after nearly three decades of ruthlessness and callous disregard for human life that permeated the society. Who else, I thought, could promote compassion, empathy, and reconciliation more than a female leader?

But collective gender elevation is merely wishful thinking; it is as ludicrous as assuming that the socioeconomic status of every black citizen in the United States would automatically improve simply because a black man, Barack Obama, became president of the United States of America in 2008. In the first place, if there is any substantive change at all to celebrate the race or gender of a new leader, it will not happen overnight. The first black or first female leader of a country does not ascend to power with his or her governance frameworks but, rather, steps into structures and systems that have been built over time and occupied by the very people who have been criticized and dethroned.

Therefore, the first pitfall faced by the Sirleaf administration was that she tried to reintroduce the system condemned and discarded with the overthrow of the Tolbert government in 1980. Essentially, the old order of the Americo-Liberian system was her point of reference because this was what was most familiar to her. She had grown up under the administration of President Tubman and had worked in both the Tubman and Tolbert governments, becoming more prominent when she was appointed by President Tolbert in the late 1970s as minister of finance. We soon realized that old habits die hard and that any attempt at change is a gradual process. Besides, how does one effect change in a situation where human resources are extremely limited due to the mass killing of talented people, massive brain drain, and a dysfunctional educational system occasioned by the civil war? Effecting constructive change entails well-prepared agents of change not only to reintroduce aspects of a governance framework that once worked but also human capacity prepared to introduce innovations that will properly address the current realities.

Interestingly, the most visible change was the dress code; the president, by example, encouraged women to wear the African attire in formal and informal gatherings so that the public did not continue to associate the native dress with being illiterate, as had been done historically.

The second challenge I observed as a woman in the Sirleaf administration was the fact that most of President Sirleaf's closest associates were men, some of whom had been with her since their days of activism in the 1970s. Surely, a few other women were involved in activism, but they always seemed to have been on the fringes, lending support in fundraising, recruiting members, disseminating information, and providing hospitality for meetings. This left the public with the impression that Ellen Sirleaf was the only female of prominence among the Progressives.

The female activists of the progressive movement are not meant to be confused with President Sirleaf's female associates who comprised the so-called kitchen cabinet. The kitchen cabinet consisted of a few women who were relatives or personal friends of the president. They were often perceived as peddling influence and seeking to advance their pecuniary interests, but they appeared to be fiercely loyal to the president. They played their role in the realm of policy decisions, but it did not always rise to the level of significance comparable to their male counterparts.

For very important decisions affecting the economy or security of the country, the president seemed more inclined to defer to one of her sons, her brother-in-law, highly placed male progressives, and certain members of the opposition groups (especially those who were most vocal in the media and antagonistic toward the Sirleaf government). The professional women did not wield as much power and influence as the public assumed. To the discerning, it was plausible that the professional women were recruited mainly to bring apparent credibility to the government, especially in the international arena.

In any case, it is important to specifically mention some of the women in the cabinet who contributed to the success of the first term of the Sirleaf administration: women like Olubanke King-Akerele who served as minister of commerce (2006-2007) and minister of foreign affairs (2007-2010); Antoinette Monsio Sayeh, minister of finance (2006-2008); Vabah Gayflor served as minister of commerce, minister of gender & development, and minister of labor between 2006 to 2012; Miata Beysolow minister of commerce 2008-2013; Florence Chenoweth, minister of agriculture (2009-2015); Etmonia David Tarpeh, minister of youth & sports (2007-2012), minister of education (2012-2014) and chairperson, national investment commission (2012-2016. All of these women have advanced degrees and experience in supervisory positions in numerous international organizations including the United Nations, the International Monetary Fund, the World Bank, and so forth. By the end of the first term most of these women, who had once served as cabinet ministers, had either resigned or had been relieved of their respective posts.

These women worked hard and left individual legacies for posterity. The impact of their accomplishments was paradoxically captured by the assertion of a gentleman who said to me at the end of 2011, "You ladies were deliberately recruited for the first term of the Sirleaf administration so that your performance would make a second term for her possible."

In early 2012, just after the president's inauguration for her second term, another gentleman said, "Now that you are in the second term of this administration, you will see big changes in the makeup of the government. The five prominent groups that will wield power will be: (1) A handful of women that we know as the kitchen cabinet. They will keep the president happy with small talk and make sure they tell her what she wants to hear. (2) A lot of small-small children (local expression for young adults) will be appointed to high offices because they are inexperienced and can be easily controlled. (3) The Progressives and their protégés, especially those who share a history of activism with the president, will continue to hang on. (4) A few members of the opposition who are not necessarily loyal to anyone but seek to get ahead at any cost;. (5) Lastly, but most importantly, the family of the president."

If there is any truth to what these guys are saying, I thought, *then the change in the direction of the Sirleaf government would effectively erode the foundation for the future we all had tried to build during the first term. It just did not make sense.*

Coincidentally, by the end of 2015, all the women listed above had been replaced by men who did not necessarily have better education and experience. Robtel Neajai Pailey, a Liberian scholar, in her article entitled "Patriarchy, Power Distance, and Female Presidency in Liberia," wrote:

> Despite efforts to transform the office of the President while empowering Liberian women and girls, Johnson Sirleaf's presidency has in some way entrenched the patriarchal norms. Study challenges the assumption that a positive correlation exists between women occupying positions of leadership and fundamental changes in structures limiting gender equity; "Women can replace men in economic and political positions without necessarily transforming structural inequalities embedded in society" (2006, 2). During her campaigning, Johnson Sirleaf vowed to meaningfully incorporate women in Liberia's postwar recovery (Johnson Sirleaf 2009, 277-278), yet her record on appointing women in positions of leadership does not represent a shattering of the glass ceiling. For instance, Johnson Sirleaf has attempted to decentralize fiscal authority through Liberia's decentralization policy, but much of that process has been administered by men at the Ministry of Finance. In addition to selecting five female superintendents,

the President also appointed only five women at a time to head cabinet-level ministries and agencies in her first and second administrations. The representation of women in county and cabinet posts is a mild form of tokenism and does not indicate a fundamental break from the past. Furthermore, Johnson Sirleaf has appointed middle-aged women in these positions, while carving out lucrative positions in her cabinet particularly for younger men in their late thirties and early forties.[27]

In her 1997 essay entitled, "Why Equal Protection No Longer Protects: The Evolving Forms of Status-Enforcing State Action," Reva Siegel introduced the concept "preservation through transformation." My understanding of the concept is that we sometimes introduce new rules and rhetoric to effect change without dismantling the structure that is the basis for change. In the end, we produce the same results. In applying this concept to the Liberian situation, the appointment of women during the first term of the Sirleaf administration merely restructured the sociopolitical hierarchy affecting gender status but did not destroy it. Therefore, the eventual replacement of professional women in their fifties and sixties by men in their thirties and forties was justified as an opportunity to include the youth in the governance structure of the country.

The third pitfall I observed in the Sirleaf government was that her leadership style characteristically consisted of micromanagement, and to do so, she maintained contact with one or two deputies (and sometimes lower-level employees) in each agency of government. In other words, the individual selected in an agency or ministry as the contact person made regular visits to the Executive Mansion, or to the home of the president, and reported on what was going on, in addition to the information the president received directly from the head of the agency or ministry. At times, the deputy was instructed to act on major policy issues without the knowledge or involvement of the head of the agency or ministry. Because the deputy was not always knowledgeable about everything that was going on in the agency or ministry, he or she was likely to misinform the president simply to maintain her confidence. This type of leadership style easily creates rifts among officials in the respective institutions, encourages deputies to be disrespectful, and tends to ultimately undermine the efficient management of the agency or ministry by its head.

Fourth, and most importantly, the president appeared to be very tolerant of men who were verbally disrespectful toward women, including herself. I did not understand why she even engaged the company of such men. I did not know whether she was afraid of them or if she just did not know where to draw the line between verbal abuse and free speech. I grew up in Liberia and completed high school before I left to go abroad for further studies. I returned after my studies in the mid-seventies and worked for the government, but never did I ever see or hear men abusing women publicly, on the radio, in the newspaper, or in person. The tolerance of this sort of behavior on the highest level tended to undermine the rule of law in the country. Because this was commonplace in the society, it tended to give the impression to young people that it was acceptable behavior. Several men who went on the radio regularly to insult President Sirleaf (one of whom publicly proclaimed that the President had "desecrated" the Executive Mansion by her presence there) were eventually appointed to government positions, including cabinet-level positions, or given some financial opportunity.

Opposition leaders went on the radio and threatened to put young people on the streets and make the country "ungovernable." The public soon learned that this was a ploy to extort money from the president or other government officials. Some officials, including some cabinet ministers, often paid local journalists to write disparaging stories about people both in the public and private sectors that they did not like.

Lastly, it appeared often that either some of my colleagues were confused about their role in the security sector or they saw the need to change the leadership dynamics. The minister of justice is the head of the security sector in Liberia, but the structure is quite different in most other countries in the West African subregion. Most other countries have placed security agencies under the ministry of interior or internal affairs. In a couple of countries, the Ministry of Defense takes the lead in security. Therefore, communication on security matters from the various African countries were likely to end up in another agency of government instead of the Ministry of Justice. Rather than consult with the Ministry of Justice, the official would act on the information without any reference to the Ministry of Justice. This is always a challenge when one is dealing with very sensitive matters.

As the 2011 elections approached, the president had to make a quick one-day security trip to Cote D'Ivoire to meet with the Ivorian president on border issues. The day before the trip, and right after a cabinet meeting, she called me aside and asked whether I was aware of the meeting. When I answered in the negative, she said she wanted me to attend.

During the meeting in Cote D'Ivoire, the Ivorian officials kept referring to the minister of defense as chief of Liberian security. President Sirleaf briefly interrupted the meeting and explained that unlike other West African countries, the minister of justice is the head of the Joint Security in Liberia. I knew what had been going on all along but was unsuccessful in trying to get the president to understand that my colleagues had found a way to override the status quo. I realized then that I must have conveniently been left out of many important security meetings. Therefore, I was relieved that the president had witnessed the misperception that permeated the security community in the subregion and had corrected it herself.

For the security meetings in the subregion I did attend, the Liberian delegation was the only delegation headed by a female, and I do not think that went down too well with my colleagues.

Understandably, it is a slow psychological transition to acceptance of a female leader in a culture where male leadership has traditionally been predominant.

---·◆·◆·◆·---

CHAPTER 30

---·◆·◆·◆·---

A Taste of Rural
Hospitality

Traveling in the interior was an important part of my job. There were many times when I had to travel to the rural areas accompanied by staff or other cabinet ministers. The trip was always a mix of work and relaxation riding through the countryside. I read papers as we traveled on parts of the road that were not in such serious disrepair, listened to the radio, talked on the telephone, stopped to buy fresh fruits from roadside markets, and lectured to the security officers on the history of Liberia before we arrived at our destination.

Some days we left the capital around six in the morning and traveled three hours north to Bong County, or an hour westward to Tubmanburg. During most out-of-town trips, we would meet with the local officials and people in the community, inspect projects, settle disputes, and then return to the city by mid or late afternoon and go to the office and work until nine o'clock at night.

Good accommodations and food were always difficult to find. The food from county to county has always varied, and still does, with the widest variety found in Montserrado County due to the diverse immigrant population and its urban flare. The people on the seacoast eat a lot of fish, as well as chicken and beef; additionally, the population on the seacoast, especially in Montserrado

194

County, bake a variety of bread and pastries. Certain dishes are popular all over the country, even though we tend to associate them with specific groups. For instance, many of us consider fufu (a starchy ball made from cassava) and pepper soup a dish from the Bassa tribe. Palm butter (a sauce prepared from the nuts of the palm tree and eaten with plain rice) is associated with the Greboes. Cassava leaf (called *Kpassa jama* in the Vai dialect) is associated with the Vai ethnic group. Jollof rice, beans, cabbage, and collard greens are foods associated with descendants of black Americans and West Indian immigrants. In the north and northeast, you find a lot of goat meat, chicken, bush meat, snails, and bamboo worms in the diet. The list is not exhaustive.

For minimum comfort, it is advisable to travel with bottled water, disinfectant, mosquito repellant, toiletries, a blanket, notepad, pens, and nonperishable food (such as crackers and sardines). Other than Monrovia (the capital city), Nimba County ranks the best in the country when it comes to accommodations. The county has many guest facilities, some ranking 2.5 to three stars on a five-star stratum. However, if you travel with the president and live in the Presidential Palace in Lofa or Bong, then you will be looking at four or four and a half stars. In many other places, if you travel on your own, you will certainly find half a star.

I recall that Rose Stryker, the then deputy director of police for administration, and I once declined a half-star government accommodation and slept in our respective vehicles out in the front yard, while our security officers took turns patrolling all night. The bathtub in this facility had several paint coats of various colors, clearly indicating that it had had its share of paintover. In the dim light, one could see that the bed sheets were soiled. The ceiling had stains in various places due to damage from heavy rain and the failure to conduct repairs.

Sometime in 2012, some officials were traveling with the president to Lofa, in northern Liberia. It must have been for the Independence Day celebration, July 26. The then minister of commerce (Miata Beysolow), the then minister of agriculture (Florence Chenoweth) and I obtained permission from the president to leave her convoy and drive ahead to do some work before it got dark. Driving in the president's convoy sometimes took six hours to arrive at a destination that would normally take two or three hours because the president stopped in every village and hamlet to give out gifts to villagers, especially children.

The good thing about traveling with the president is you don't have to worry about sleeping in poorly managed accommodations or risk drinking contaminated water. The deputy minister of state, Pearine Garnett Parkinson, who was often in charge of logistics, made sure that everyone who accompanied the president had clean, comfortable accommodations and good food.

The county attorney (chief prosecutor for Lofa County) came to see me at the president's residence as soon as he heard I had arrived in Voinjama, the capital of Lofa County. He was elated to show me the two gallons of palm wine he had brought for me. The lightly alcoholic drink with a tart/sweet taste is called palm wine because the drink is derived from the heart of the palm tree. Some call it African champagne.

It is customary for inhabitants of a village or town to welcome guests with a white chicken, kola nuts, white rice, a goat, or even a cow. But we observed that in this part of the country, inhabitants sometimes offer guests palm wine.

As the county attorney placed the two plastic jugs on the sixteen-foot rectangular dining table, he said, "This is for you and the American Ambassador; I hear she is coming with the President and she likes palm wine too." Then he lifted one of the jugs, opened it, and poured some of the palm wine in the bottle cap. As he drank it, he said, "Minister, you know in Africa, the person who gives you food has to taste it to take the witch (meaning *poison*) out." He then resealed the jug and started to leave.

I said, "Not so fast; you have to do this ritual to my satisfaction." The forever smiling, hardworking county attorney, Luther Sumo, just stood there like an obedient schoolboy, looking at me quizzically.

I said, "You need first to shake each jug vigorously and drink a gulp or at least a half of cup of each jug; remember, the US ambassador will drink this, and perhaps the President too. Do you know what it would mean if anything happens to either one of those women?" I heard one of the two ministers (commerce and agriculture), whom I thought were too busy on their personal computer to pay attention, say, "What if the guy does not drink alcohol?" At that point, even Luther, the king of palm wine, and I had to laugh. He drank a half of a cup from each jug and turned toward the door to leave. As he left, I yelled after him, "We expect the president and her party to be here within two hours. If you are still alive, then I will offer them the palm wine." He laughed and said, "Okay, Minister," and disappeared.

The then US Ambassador to Liberia, Linda Thomas Greenfield, is an African American originally from Louisiana, USA, but she recounted that back in 1978, she came to Liberia to do her dissertation and went up to Lofa to conduct her research. While in Lofa, she was adopted by the Kissi tribe and was named Sia (pronounced See-yah, which means "first daughter"). So, for her, this trip to Lofa was a homecoming. Therefore, the show of hospitality by the county attorney was not only thoughtful but also appropriate.

As the president and her entourage entered the hallway of the presidential palace and headed in our direction, the two ministers and I rushed to the door to greet them as they strolled by en route to their respective sleeping quarters. When they arrived at where we stood, they stopped long enough for the agriculture minister to tell the US ambassador that we had palm wine for her. The ambassador was excited and told us to ask the butler to bring the palm wine with glasses. After they went on to their respective rooms to settle in, I turned to the agriculture minister and said, "I did not want to mention the palm wine until I hear from the county attorney."

She looked at me in horror and asked, "Do you think he's dead?" I choked on laughter as I began to dial the number of the county attorney, but there was no response. The phone seemed to have been turned off. I immediately went into a panic mode and called one of my security officers to go and find the county attorney, who lived only two minutes away. When the ambassador came out and asked for the palm wine, we told her that we needed five minutes to chill the drink. It would give us time to get the much-needed update on the condition of the county attorney.

Then I called my security officer to find out what was going on. The county attorney was asleep and had turned off his phone; that's why he didn't answer. I wanted to know about his general condition. "He's fine, Minister," the officer said. "He looks a little drowsy."

I felt a knot in my stomach. "What do you mean?" I asked.

The security officer responded reassuringly, "He only looks the way normal people look when they just get up from sleeping." I relaxed. By then, the ambassador and the president had each had the first sip of the palm.

I poured myself a glass of palm wine and quietly thought, *If this is what I have to go through just to give someone a palm wine treat, then the next time I will just simply decline the offer of palm wine.*

CHAPTER 31

Focusing on the Exit of UNMIL

After the inauguration in 2012, the Ministry of Justice and other security agencies began to focus on the future of security in Liberia post United Nations Mission in Liberia (UNMIL). At that time, the government of Liberia was aware that the UN Mission in Liberia would substantially reduce its operations in Liberia by 2015.

The mandate of the UNMIL, which began in 2004, was to support the ceasefire agreement signed in Accra, Ghana, in 2003 between warring factions and civil society; disarm, demobilize, reintegrate, and repatriate combatants from the civil war; support humanitarian and human rights activities; support security sector reform; and support the peace process.

This is a broad mandate but, remember, when the United Nations deployed peacekeepers on the ground in Liberia, the situation was still somewhat chaotic. An interim government was installed under the leadership of a businessman, Charles Gyude Bryant. The peace agreement had required warlords and civilians to come together and figure out how to run the country peacefully. This was harder than it appeared to observers. ECOWAS had deployed troops in Liberia since the early nineties, and had it not been for those officers from the subregion, Liberia would have collapsed completely.

Back in 2010, the UNMIL sponsored a security retreat in Monrovia, primarily to begin to work with the Liberian government to develop plans for the inevitable drawdown of UN security personnel in Liberia. The fundamental question was, How do we replace the UNMIL? We did not have the manpower to replace fifteen thousand personnel; neither did we have the resources to perform all the tasks the UN had performed theretofore.

The thought of replacing the UNMIL was overwhelming, as the tasks they performed were so numerous. They provided security for the president and vice president; they investigated serious crimes; they intervened to quell riots and mob violence; they kept all airstrips clear of debris; they transported government funds between banks and between political subdivisions; they provided security for some of the prisons, and they conducted workshops; they drafted legal documents; they helped to man the borders; they manned checkpoints in the capital city and on the highways throughout the country; they engaged in major institutional reforms, such as collaborating to conduct a national conference to discuss the harmonization of the informal and formal justice systems; and the list goes on.

Also, in February 2010 (before the retreat), there was a major clash between the Muslim and Christians in Lofa County, one of the country's largest political subdivisions. A couple of people were killed, and several people suffered severe physical injuries. As the violence raged, the citizens were desperately waiting for security forces to be deployed from the capital to Lofa by the Liberia National Police. Lofa is a seven-hour drive from the capital on very bad roads. This is the first time we realized the flaw of operating a highly centralized security and law enforcement system. To save the day, we requested assistance from UNMIL, who quickly deployed a Nigerian contingent from Gharnga, an area midway between the capital and Lofa County. The situation was brought under control by the UNMIL before the Liberian police arrived.

From the Lofa experience, the Liberia National Police proposed that we move to decentralize management and operations in the security sector as part of the UNMIL drawdown plan. We could not replace the UNMIL everywhere, but we could increase the presence of Liberian security and law enforcement officers in various parts of the country so that response to emergency situations, as in Lofa, would be more expeditious.

We decided to divide the country into five regions and construct full-service justice and security hubs in each of those regions. Each hub would provide services for three of the fifteen political subdivisions. If there was a riot, for instance, the government would be able to intervene immediately with officers already in the problem area or in a nearby political subdivision. There would no longer be a long wait while the authorities in the capital mobilized resources and transported officers by road for several hours.

We determined that if we decentralized justice and security services and strengthened each hub by building capacity and making available resources for operations, more citizens would have access to justice and security, and, accordingly, security in Liberia would be sustainable. The goal was to construct the first hub in Gbarnga, central Liberia, on several acres of land that had been donated by the citizens of that area.

Accordingly, in May 2010, Liberia requested to be placed on the agenda of the UN Peacebuilding Commission (PBC) to help the government with reform of the justice and security sectors and move the country toward healing and reconciliation. The request was endorsed by the UN in September 2010, and immediately thereafter, the United Nations, through its mission in Liberia led by the special representative, Margarethe Loj, agreed to help raise the funding for construction and training. A peacebuilding configuration (PBC) for Liberia was organized at the UN under the chairmanship of Prince Zeid of the Hashemite Kingdom of Jordan, who was, in 2012, succeeded by Swedish-born Staffan Tillerman. Both men approached their commitment to Liberia with the utmost vigor and sense of purpose with the support of very dynamic members of the commission. Liberia was also fortunate to have one its brightest citizens as permanent representative of Liberia to the United Nations, Ms. Marjon Kamara.

It helped also that President Sirleaf had once worked with the United Nations as a senior official. Everyone wanted to help, including His Excellency, the then UN secretary-general, Ban Ki-Moon, and the UNDP administrator, Her Excellency Helen Clark. On the ministerial level, our two main contacts were Ambassador Tillerman and Assistant Secretary-General Judy Cheng-Hopkins. It signaled that that the UN's role in Liberia was transitioning from peacekeeping to peacebuilding.

In February 2012, we inaugurated the first justice and security hub in Liberia. The police, immigration, and corrections (including a Probation Services Department) had a physical presence on the hub, although detention facilities for corrections were located in another area away from the hub site. A courthouse, managed by the judiciary, was also included on the site. The United Nations and other partners had done a lot to assist the government to achieve this important milestone, but all along, we were reminded by our partners that we had to take the lead and we had to claim ownership. I think this was very important for a country coming out of a civil war, and we did just that.

With an identifiable plan in place for sustainable security in Liberia, we could then turn our focus to the drawdown plan of the UNMIL, which was designed to be gradual so that the negative impact, if any, would be at a minimum.

By early 2012, a new SRSG (special representative of the secretary-general), Her Excellency Karin Landgren, was assigned to Liberia by the United Nations. Ambassador Landgren, a Swedish national and an astute diplomat, quickly joined the team and provided support for what we already had in place. But additionally, she wanted to see the reconciliation component of the peacebuilding plan gain more traction, and the pervasive corrupt practices in the public sector alleviated.

In February 2012, President Sirleaf announced publicly, at the Armed Forces Day Program, that the minister of defense would be the Liberian government official responsible for the UNMIL drawdown plan. I did not see this coming and wondered how much thought had been put into this decision. *How did she arrive at the decision?* I asked myself quietly. After the security retreat in 2010, it was determined that at least 90 percent of the UNMIL tasks would be handed over to the police and immigration services, both of which agencies fall under the purview of the Ministry of Justice. Therefore, the Ministry of Justice had integrated the drawdown or transition plan into its daily operational activities for both the police and immigration. In order to effectively manage the UNMIL transition plan, the minister of defense would have to provide supervision and direction of these agencies almost on a daily basis. This would be the first setback for the drawdown plan.

Most of the time when the minister of defense cited the Ministry of Justice to discuss the transition plan, he was not present himself. Instead, the meeting was often conducted by one of his deputies. After two of such meetings, I did not attend but encouraged the heads of the police and immigration services to attend. They also had difficulty taking direction from the Ministry of Defense and designated lower-level officers, who could not make decisions on critical matters, to attend. It appeared that the UNMIL was frustrated by the internal politics, but there was nothing we could do. We did not want to disrespect the decision of the president. We figured sooner than later the president and the minister of defense would figure out the glitches and make the necessary adjustments.

Then there was another setback to the drawdown plan: the delay in the commencement of the construction of the other four hubs. The plan was to begin construction of hubs two and three in 2012 by raising $2 million. This time the government was asked by the UN to contribute $1 million as seed money, and the UN would match that amount. This made sense to me. To take ownership, it is important to also take financial responsibility. Donor money is supplemental and temporary and should not be relied on to build a country. The government needed to commit some of its own resources to show that it was serious about putting in place a sustainable security system in anticipation of the UNMIL exit. The minister of finance attended many meetings of the UNMIL transition team, and each time he made a firm commitment to provide the seed money to commence the construction of the next two hubs. The funds were never released as far as I know.

Yet another setback to the UNMIL drawdown was the psychological security we felt by the presence of the UN in Liberia, to the extent that we had become complacent. It was easy to contact the UNMIL when there was a problem because UNMIL had the solution and the resources. But we soon realized that the longer the UNMIL remained in Liberia, the more we would become dependent on its presence; therefore, it was important, I felt, for us to work hard in the government to regain the confidence of the citizens in our ability to provide for their safety after UNMIL was gone.

The UN, on its part, decided that it would stick to its timetable for the transition. This decision put pressure on the government of Liberia to focus on the transition. In 2014, the president reassigned the responsibility for implementation of the UNMIL transition plan to the Ministry of Justice. The United Nations Mission in Liberia (UNMIL) scaled down its operations in 2015 and formally withdrew from Liberia in 2018 after a difficult but successful assignment.

CHAPTER 32

The 2011 Presidential Election and Its Aftermath

orking in the security sector is very stressful in that one has to make critical decisions on a 24/7 basis. One has to monitor everything on a daily basis, pore over intelligence information constantly flowing in, and shift gears or revise strategies as required. That was the situation during the days following the October 2011 elections where President Sirleaf and Winston Tubman had emerged as the two front-runners. Neither one had won the required "50 percent + 1" majority of votes; therefore, the Elections Commission scheduled a runoff for November 8, 2011. We developed pre-election, election, and postelection crisis-intervention plans for the security sector without really expecting to implement those plans. We relied on firm hope there would be no violence during the runoff elections. The general elections had been conducted without any problems, leading the international observers to conclude that the process was free and fair.

Madam Ellen Johnson Sirleaf had run in the 2005 presidential election and defeated the popular soccer player George Weah in the second round, recovering from her loss against Charles Taylor in the 1997 election for president. She decided to run again in 2011, for a second term. Her rivals were Charles Brumskine, a lawyer and former president pro tempore of the

Liberian Senate, and Winston Tubman, a lawyer and former UN official who chose George Weah as his running mate on the ticket of the Congress for Democratic Change (CDC). The majority of the supporters and potential voters for the CDC candidates were young adults between eighteen and thirty-five years old.

I had hoped that we would not have to conduct a runoff election because of the additional costs to the government, as well as the physical drain on security officers who were already exhausted from the challenges of a general election. But the voters decided otherwise.

The Congress for Democratic Change (CDC) was unhappy with the results of the general election, claiming that it was not fair. Consequently, the CDC Party felt it could challenge the government and the ruling Unity Party by asking its supporters to boycott the ensuing runoff election in November 2011. On November 5, 2011, the police received reports that an unusual number of young people had gathered at the headquarters of the CDC, drinking alcohol and cavorting. The partying apparently continued throughout the night to the next day. On the sixth, the police again received reports that the young people had increased in numbers at the CDC Party headquarters, and the crowd had become louder and unruly. The police did not bother the young people as long as they confined themselves within the fence of the CDC compound and there was no official complaint of violations. However, when the police received and confirmed reports that some of the young people had left the CDC compound, and were attempting to scale the fence surrounding the president's residence, which was less than a quarter mile from the CDC compound, the police were compelled to intervene and make arrests to prevent any security threat. Apart from that incident, the rest of the evening was quiet.

The next day, November 7, 2011, around noon, the president called a National Security Council (NSC) meeting. The NSC, which is higher than the Joint Security Committee, is usually convened by the president when national security issues require the attention and decision of the president. This meeting was to ensure that we had properly developed plans to secure the country and maintain law and order for the runoff election on November 8. Shortly after the meeting ended, my security detail informed me that there was a standoff between the riot police and hundreds of CDC partisans at the CDC headquarters in Sinkor, a suburb a couple of miles or so outside the city center. Apparently, the problem had developed just before the NSC meeting ended.

I immediately rushed to my office and began calling the police director,

Marc Amblard, for updates. I did not hear from him but concluded that he, too, was trying to conduct inquiries into what had occurred, since he had also been at the NSC meeting.

I sat in my office from around two in the afternoon to seven that evening consulting with members of the Joint Security Committee, officials of the Ministry of Information, officials from the Liberia Telecommunications Authority, and the solicitor general at the time, Counselor Micah Wright. We were brainstorming on how to handle what had already occurred and how to ensure that the situation did not escalate. I just sat there listening and thinking about the 1979 Rice Riots and all that went wrong in the mishandling of the situation by the officials at the time, especially the security officials. I recalled that everyone blamed the then minister of justice for not properly managing the situation at the time. As is often said, history is the best teacher. For me, it was important to ensure that we did not violate the fundamental rights of citizens in the process of maintaining law and order, and this position was supported by the solicitor general.

Interrupting the radio frequency was appealing because that way we would avoid a physical confrontation with citizens, but we were not equipped to carry that out. I was not interested in filing petitions to close down the four radio stations identified for inciting the public because no one had presented the evidence I needed to support that decision. Everyone repeated the inflammatory and inciteful pronouncements on the radio, but no one had given me a recording or transcripts to support the allegations.

Knowing that as minister of justice I would ultimately be responsible for how this incident was handled, I was determined to be guided more by reason rather than emotions. I knew that my main support would come from the solicitor general, the police director, and the commissioner of immigration because they were heads of institutions under the supervisory authority of the Ministry of Justice, and because we needed one another to be able to work effectively.

Although there was pressure from other members of the Joint Security for the director of police, Marc Amblard, to marginalize my position, he did his best to cooperate and exude diplomacy and team spirit. Although he did not rise through the ranks of the police and was considered by the public to be a political appointee, he did his utmost to manage an organization as massive and as complex as the Liberia National Police.

Counselor Micah Wright, the then solicitor general was a team player and sometimes joined the JSC meetings to assist with issues that required court actions. The then commissioner of immigration, Chris Massaquoi, was also a team player and very knowledgeable in security matters. Outside of the Justice Ministry family, I could count on the director of the National Security Agency, Fombah Sirleaf, to cooperate where his expertise or support was needed.

We decided we would hold a press conference at 7:00 p.m. We would inform the public what had happened, express condolences to the families of the deceased and those who suffered injuries, and provide assurances to our citizens that the whole matter was under control, and therefore they did not have to worry about their safety. We would also assure them the government would conduct a thorough investigation of the matter and take appropriate action against those responsible for the violence and the attending consequences.

Meanwhile, while members of the Joint Security Committee sat at the table answering questions for the journalists, someone whispered to me that the CDC Party officials were on the radio telling the public the president had instructed the Liberian security to arrest and summarily execute certain CDC officials and members later that night. Again, my mind went back to April 1980 when Baccus Matthews was indicted for sedition. The news quickly spread that the government had planned to execute Mr. Matthews, a false piece of information that emotionally charged the grassroots population. A couple of days later, the government was toppled in a military coup. It may not have been the reason for the coup, but the dissemination of false information that a folk hero would be executed certainly energized an already angry public. Therefore, I knew we had to act quickly to defuse the effect of the misinformation out there.

I kept a calm composure and concluded the press conference within five minutes, dismissed members of the media in attendance, and quietly walked out. The director of police and I headed directly to the solicitor general's office and decided that we had to develop and implement an emergency plan of action immediately. We recovered transcripts of the inflammatory recordings and filed petitions to the court for closure of the radio stations involved under Chapter 11, section 11.11 and 11.12 of the Liberian Penal Code, Criminal libel against the President and Sedition, respectively. We declared the CDC compound a crime scene and asked the UNMIL to secure the area since the latter was a neutral party to the crisis. We developed an enforcement plan for police officers to carry out as soon as the court issued the order for closure. The enforcement order from the judge was not to be staggered but, rather, enforced against the four radio stations simultaneously.

The international community was not too happy with the decision, but I held my ground. I did not think that people outside of the country were entirely familiar with the historical context of violence in Liberia. There was no abuse of the constitutional rights of free speech and free press here. We wanted the public to understand that we had to draw the line between individual rights guaranteed by the Constitution and actions of citizens that tend to undermine national security interest. Our responsibility as a government was to make sure all citizens were safe rather than promote the individual freedom of a few.

We implemented the entire plan within two hours. I called the president around 10 o'clock post meridian p.m. to give a briefing and assured her the justice and security sector had taken steps to ensure there would be no further disturbance. I said that the JSC wanted her to appoint an independent body to thoroughly investigate the incident and bring the responsible party or parties to justice, especially since the incitement of the public had caused a young man to lose his life and several others (including police officers) had suffered injuries. Within a few days, the president appointed a committee under the chairmanship of Sister Mary Laurene Brown, a renown Liberian Catholic nun and educator, to investigate the incident of November 7, 2011.

On November 8, 2011, the day after the violent incident between the CDC partisans and the police, I had to travel more than fifty miles into the interior to cast my vote. Three women in the cabinet (Ettie David Tarpeh, Miata Beysolow and Florence Chenoweth) and Christine Tolbert Norman had asked to travel with my convoy because they had also registered to vote in the same area. They called me on the night of November 7 to ascertain whether I would still be able to travel out of town at five o'clock the next morning, after everything that had occurred on the seventh. My answer was emphatic, "Yes." Some of the security officers worried that an angry mob might ambush us because of the swift and decisive stance we had taken earlier that evening to quell the violence. The women concluded that if I was willing to go out of town under the circumstances, they would follow me. At five thirty in the morning, we pulled out of my residence, in a convoy, stopping at numerous checkpoints that had been set up the night before by the UNMIL and our joint security force. We arrived at the voting precinct at 7:30 a.m. to be the first in line when the polls opened at 8:00 a.m. Everything went well, and we returned to the city before noon without incident.

The judge, His Honor, the late James Zotaa, conducted a preliminary hearing and gave a stern warning to the young men involved in the incitement of violence on the radio to desist from such action in the future. Accordingly, the Ministry of Justice did not pursue prosecution. For us at the Ministry of Justice, we were not interested in a trial, as every action does not necessarily require a punishment. For us, it was important only that our young people understand that they cannot say or do as they please in a society where the rights of everyone should be respected. It was important for them to understand that certain actions carry consequences under the law.

As a result of the post-election violence, growing out of the clash between the police and partisans of the CDC, the president relieved the director of police of his post. After the Laurene Brown Committee completed its investigation, it made several recommendations, which included the dismissal and prosecution of some police officers and the suspension of others.

CHAPTER 33

The Unconstitutional Crisis

Once you agree to accept to serve in a public office, especially in a high-profile position, you always must be prepared for the unexpected, for dramas and battles, even those someone else has chosen for you. Such was the case one afternoon as I sat in a meeting at the National Investment Commission.

My cell phone vibrated, and I could see that it was the number of the president's brother-in-law, Estrada Bernard. He was one of the few people, other than the president, whose call I would accept in the middle of a meeting. I took his calls not only because he was a part of the Joint Security Committee but also because he was one of the few persons alive who knew both of my parents and had known me since I was a toddler. His family's homestead is on the same block as ours in the center of the city.

When I answered the phone, Mr. Bernard announced his name. "I know it is you," I said. "I stepped out of a meeting to take your call. Anything?"

Then Mr. Bernard continued, "Have you heard anything about a constitutional crisis?" I stood for a few seconds, trying to figure out what he was talking about, but I had no idea. Then he said, "Clarence tells me that there is a constitutional crisis. I don't know where he got that." Clarence Simpson Jr. was an attorney general of Liberia in the nineteen seventies and a friend of the president. For that reason, any information from Mr. Simpson was not taken lightly.

I said to Mr. Bernard, politely, "After my meeting, I will inquire and let you know what I find out." I spoke with two lawyers after the meeting, and neither one had any idea what Mr. Bernard was alluding to.

Then the following evening, on a Friday, around eight o'clock, I received a call from a broadcast journalist whom I know very well. After the usual greeting, he asked, "Minister, do you know that the Supreme Court has issued a writ of summons requesting you to show cause why you should not be held in contempt for granting compassionate leave to the journalist, Rodney Sieh?" He went on to say that as he was about to leave work earlier that evening, one of the justices of the Supreme Court of Liberia called to say he had an important announcement and wanted the broadcaster to wait for him. The justice wanted this specific broadcaster to read the document on the radio all weekend. The broadcaster went on to say that he was puzzled by the fact the justice had driven himself to the radio station with the document.

I had not seen or heard of the writ of summons from the Supreme Court before the young man called me. I learned on Monday that the document was delivered to the security officers guarding the Justice Ministry building at 6:00 p.m. the same Friday evening the justice delivered it to the radio broadcaster. I was attending an official reception away from the building, and my staff had already gone home since they did not expect me to return to the building on a Friday night.

To put this narrative into perspective, it is imperative that we go back and review the events that led to what I believe is an unfortunate political drama.

A former minister of agriculture, Chris Toe, brought an action for "damages for wrong" against Rodney Sieh, the *FrontPage Africa* newspaper, *FrontPage Africa* online, and Samwar S. Fallah, collectively the defendants, in May of 2010. The publication by the defendants alleged former Minister Toe was engaged in corruption in his capacity as minister of agriculture. The circuit court ruled in favor of the former minister and awarded damages for USD$1,500,000 as damages. LRSC 2 (10 January 2014). Rodney Sieh and other defendants announced an appeal and filed a bill of exceptions but did not perfect the appeal by filing an appeal bond and notice of completion of the appeal, as required by law.

Former minister Toe then filed a motion in the Supreme Court to dismiss the unperfected appeal. The Supreme Court, on July 15, 2013, dismissed the appeal and order the clerk to send a mandate down to the judge of the lower court to resume jurisdiction of the case and enforce the ruling of the lower court. The mandate was sent to Judge Boima Kontoe of the Sixth Judicial Circuit Court of Montserrado County on July 19, 2013. The Sheriff attempted to enforce judgment but subsequently made returns to the effect that Mr. Sieh had "refused and/or failed to identify any property whatsoever", for which the judge held Mr. Sieh in contempt of court and ordered him remanded to the Monrovia Central Prison on August 21, 2013 until the judgment was satisfied. (Culled from LRSC 2 (10 January 2014). Apparently, the Judge's decision to send Mr. Sieh to prison until the judgement was satisfied was based on a provision in the Civil Procedure Code, I LCL Revised, subchapter C, section 44.71, subsection 2 (e), which reads as follows:

> *2. Judgments enforceable by imprisonment if execution not satisfied.*
> Judgments in any of the following actions shall be enforceable by execution, but if the judgment debtor cannot or will not pay the full amount of the judgment together with interest and costs, the sheriff shall arrest him and the court shall order him imprisoned for a period sufficiently long to liquidate the full amount of the judgement, interest, and costs at the rate of twenty-five dollars per month:
> (a) Adultery;
> (b) Seduction of wife or child;
> (c) Illegally taking away or harboring a wife or child or ward under twenty-one years of age;
> (d) Enticing an incompetent away from his legally appointed trustee or guardian; or
> (e) **Injury to the reputation when the words spoken or written are actionable per se.** [emphasis added]

Somehow, during the public sector reform, when government repealed most obsolete laws, this law remained on the books. I believe the repeal of this law was inadvertently overlooked because it was a law that was hardly ever used.

It is important to note Rodney Sieh, as a journalist, often writes about corruption in the public sector and has written numerous articles not only about corruption in the executive and legislative branches of government but also about corruption in the judiciary.

A few days after Rodney Sieh was committed to prison, the prison authorities reported to my office that he was on a hunger strike. We asked the staff to observe him closely. Six days after he had begun the hunger strike, I received another report that Mr. Sieh's health was deteriorating, that he was weak and disoriented. I instructed the prison authorities, as a matter of policy, to contact the John F. Kennedy Memorial Hospital (JFK) to send medical personnel to the prison to assess the condition of Mr. Sieh, and they did. Upon the doctor's advice, Mr. Sieh was transferred to JFK for further examination, as the prison did not have the facilities to conduct the proper tests. Because of his condition, Mr. Sieh was hospitalized and remained there for treatment for the next three weeks and then returned to prison. He was guarded by corrections officers while in the hospital.

Again, Mr. Sieh went on a hunger strike several days after his discharge from the hospital. And again, we requested the JFK to visit the prison, conduct an assessment, and advise us accordingly. The hospital informed us he was "weak and lethargic," had lost a lot of weight, was probably dehydrated, and should be hospitalized. Accordingly, Mr. Sieh was admitted to the medical facility, in the company of corrections officers who remained with him at all times.

By mid-September 2013, President Sirleaf had traveled to the United States to attend the UN General Assembly in New York and to deal with a few personal matters after that. She called me, expressing concern about Mr. Sieh's health and his continued incarceration and wanted to know if anything could be done to have him released. She was concerned that the Committee for the Protection of Journalists (CPJ) and other human rights organizations were advocating for the release of Mr. Sieh and wanted her to grant interviews to answer questions along those lines. She did not want to grant interviews while Mr. Sieh was still behind bars.

During the last week of September and the first week of October 2013, the president and I spoke almost daily on the Rodney Sieh matter. She wanted Mr. Sieh released to rid herself of the pressure from these various international human rights groups. I mentioned under the corrections laws, the minister of justice has discretionary power to grant a "compassionate leave," but that would be temporary. I worried if Mr. Sieh was as ill as the doctor had reported, then we had to do our utmost to ensure that he received proper care, as his death in prison would pose a serious problem for the government and would be a bigger problem than the persistent media advocacy. Before the conversation ended, I added that, as minister, I could not *sua sponte* (on my own accord) grant the leave; Mr. Sieh or his lawyer(s) would have to initiate the request. Kofi Woods, one of Mr. Sieh's lawyers, was communicating directly with the president on this matter, while Counsellors Beyan Howard and Fonati Koffa, his other two lawyers, were in direct contact with my office.

On September 30, 2013, Counsellor Howard sent a formal letter to my office requesting compassionate leave for Rodney Sieh. During the following week, the assistant minister for the Bureau of Corrections, and I spent time reviewing the current regulations we had on file governing furlough of prisoners in general, which included compassionate leave as well. I kept the president informed of every action that was taken. The Ministry of Justice proposed a fifteen-day compassionate leave, but after negotiations with the lawyers of Mr. Sieh, we agreed to grant a thirty-day compassionate leave with specific regulations provided to him through his lawyers. Before the Ministry of Justice sent out the formal response to Mr. Sieh's lawyers, I made the following telephone calls:

1. I called President Sirleaf, who was still in the United States, so that she would be aware that we had reached an agreement on the release, as per all of our previous conversations leading up to the decision. She was very pleased and quite relieved, and she thanked me.
2. I called Dr. Amos Sawyer, the head of the Governance Commission, because I was told that he was actively negotiating a resolution of this matter between former Minister Chris Toe and Rodney Sieh. He thanked me for the call.
3. Finally, I called Counsellor Emmanuel James, the lawyer for former Minister Chris Toe. I wanted him to be aware of the decision since his client had a direct interest in the matter. He told me that he had no objection.

On October 8, 2013, I wrote a formal letter to Counsellor Beyan Howard, the lawyer of record for Rodney Sieh, granting the compassionate leave in keeping with volume I of the Liberian Code of Laws Revised, chapter 34, section 34.20 (1), which states:

> *Compassionate Leave.* The Minister of Justice shall formulate rules or regulations governing compassionate leave from institutions and, in accordance with such rules and regulations, may permit any prisoner to leave his institution for short periods of time, either by himself or in the custody of an officer, to visit a close relative who is seriously ill, to attend the funeral of a close relative, to return to his home during what appears to be his own last illness, **or to return to his home for other compelling reasons which strongly appeal to compassion.** [Phrase in bold for emphasis.] The rules or regulations shall provide for the manner in which compassionate leave shall be

granted, for its duration, and for the custody, transportation, and care of the prisoner during his leave. They shall also provide for the manner in which the expense connected with such leave shall be borne and may allow the prisoner, or anyone on his behalf, to reimburse the State for such expense.

The preceding narrative is the basis, to my certain knowledge, why the Supreme Court of Liberia issued the citation requesting me and co-respondent Beyan Howard to appear and show cause why we should not be held in contempt.

The first person I thought to call was the president, since we spent nearly two weeks meticulously trying to unravel the whole Rodney Sieh matter. When we met to discuss the upcoming contempt proceedings, the president said, "The Supreme Court justices claim that you have disrespected them by releasing Rodney Sieh, so you need to apologize to them." I was confused. Why would the Supreme Court want me to apologize for doing nothing wrong? And why would the president, who was completely informed and had asked for my intervention to release Rodney Sieh, ask me to apologize? It seemed hypocritical.

The court scheduled the hearing for the afternoon of October 21, 2013. The former solicitor general, Micah Wright, and current solicitor general, Betty Lamin Blamo, would represent me in court. The Supreme Court had appointed three lawyers as amici curiae (friends of the court): Counsellor David A. B. Jallah, dean of the law school at the University of Liberia; Counsellor Cyril Jones; and Counsellor Negbalee Warner.

The courtroom was unusually crowded on the afternoon of the hearing. A few of my relatives, friends, and staff had come to give moral support, but the majority of the more than one hundred persons in the court were present out of curiosity or, perhaps, for some other reason best known to themselves. As for me, I was in attendance first and foremost because the court had summoned me. It would be disrespectful not to appear even if I believed I had done nothing wrong. But I was also in attendance because I was curious to find out firsthand the real reason why these proceedings had been instituted.

Solicitor General Blamo argued on my behalf. She tried to stick to the contents of the returns (my response to the contempt citation), which essentially stated, among other things, the attorney general / minister of justice was acting under the firm belief section 34.20(1) of the Liberian Criminal Procedure Law applied to the circumstances of this case. She argued that the the decision to grant compassionate leave to Rodney Sieh was temporary and in keeping with Liberian law, and, was not intended to disregard the order of the court. Solicitor General Blamo went on to state the attorney general / minister of justice was the dean of the Supreme Court Bar and would do nothing to undermine the court or "bring disrepute to the judiciary."

Unfortunately, Solicitor General Blamo was hardly allowed to complete a sentence due to the volleys of questions and comments coming from the justices who appeared angry and frustrated by her presentation. I believe they expected her to simply concede that I had done something wrong and offer an apology. I sat there watching what seemed to be a surreal event. When the former solicitor general, Micah Wright, went to the podium, he spoke briefly and then apologized on my behalf, which seemed to calm the justices somewhat but did not placate them.

As for the amici curiae (friends of the court), they presented four issues:

> 1) Whether the Supreme Court of Liberia, having rendered a judgment in a case before it and issued a mandate which was served and returned served, can exercise original jurisdiction for contempt over an act impending or tending to frustrate enforcement of its judgment and mandate?

> 2) Whether Section 34.20(1) of the Criminal Procedure Law applies to civil cases and assuming it is, any of the reasons provided thereunder for releasing a prisoner was satisfied in the instant case?

> 3) Whether co-respondent Counsellor Beyan Howard's September 27, 2013, letter to the Minister of Justice requesting that his client is granted compassionate leave to him to serve his indefinite term of imprisonment at home had no reasonable legal basis and can be fairly construed as intended to circumvent enforcement of the Court's judgment and order?

> 4) Whether co-respondent Counsellor Christiana P. Tah is in contempt of Court for her conduct in releasing, without reference to the Court, a person imprisoned as a result of contempt of Court?

The amici curiae were also passionate in their presentation but enjoyed the warmth and civility of the justices. They essentially concluded in open court that section 34.20 (1) did not support the action of the attorney general and her co-respondent, Counsellor Howard. The amici curiae concluded that if the contemnors continued to challenge the court rather than ask for forgiveness, then it was their position that the court should impose the "harshest punishment" on the contemnors.

The fact was we had not challenged or disrespected the court. We only tried to respectfully explain why we believed our decision to grant compassionate leave was supported by Liberian law. The court reserved its ruling for a later date. After that, the hearing was adjourned.

So far, I have reserved my comments on the legal positions expressed by the court and the amici curiae for the ensuing chapter 36; where the points raised by all parties within the context of the Supreme Court opinion will be discussed further.

CHAPTER 34

The Hour Just
before Dawn

After the contempt hearing in October 2013, I knew now the court's reaction to my decision to grant compassionate leave to a journalist who had a medical emergency in prison was not purely legal. There were political and personal dimensions as well. Robert Sirleaf, the president's son, told me on more than one occasion that he had asked the president to relieve me of my post since 2012 because I was an obstacle to his legacy. According to him, his legacy would be the reform of the petroleum sector. I was confused. Where did he get the idea that I was obstructing his legacy?

God knows the last thing I wanted in my life was to get involved in a fight with the president or members of her family. She had all the machinery of government at her disposal, and most of all, she had the unflinching support of the international community. Besides, to fight the president would mean a show of disrespect for the highest office in the land, something I would not do as an advocate for adhering to the rule of law.

At the same time, the president was fully aware I would always be forthright on issues that were critical to the security and well-being of the Liberian people and would not mislead her out of fear or greed.

When I accepted the position as attorney general in 2009, I intended to join the government, make my contribution to the administration of President Sirleaf, make a difference in the lives of ordinary people, and then take my exit in early 2012. However, I had delayed my plan to leave for three reasons:

1) I wanted to make sure the president had a replacement for me, as I did not want to abandon the job while she was in the midst of a search for a new minister of justice;

2) I wanted to make sure that we laid the proper foundation for building a holistic criminal justice system so peace and security would be sustainable; and

3) I wanted to make sure I left the government on amicable terms with the president.

That said, I traveled to Abidjan on October 28, 2013, to attend a meeting of ministers of justice of ECOWAS countries, which convened under the sponsorship of the United Nations Office for West Africa (UNOWA). The purpose of the meeting was to conclude the draft documents for the formation of the ECOWAS Parliament. Liberia's participation in these meetings was very important since we had lost prominence in this sub-regional organization due to lack of meaningful participation during the years of the civil war. We needed to start attending meetings regularly and participate fully, in order to regain the stature Liberia once held in the ECOWAS.

When I called the president to inform her I had arrived in Abidjan, she noted that I was out of the country on the day that the House of Representatives was conducting a hearing on the new petroleum law introduced to the legislature by Robert Sirleaf. I explained to her that I did not know of the hearing, as I did not receive a citation from the legislature to attend, as is the usual practice; otherwise, I would have been in attendance or would have designated a deputy. The other four principal officials (The Minister of Finance, the Minister of Lands, Mines & Energy, the CEO of the National Oil Company, and the Chairperson of the National Investment Commission) who should have been in attendance were also absent from the hearing. I suspected they were also unaware of the hearing since the petroleum law had been prepared in secrecy and shared with only a few people, excluding key officials who usually negotiate and sign the oil contracts.

I had only seen the document twice. A few weeks before the hearing, the president had asked me to review the document and give her my sincere comments. Two days later, her secretary called me to retrieve the document, explaining that Mr. Robert Sirleaf did not want the document "widely circulated." Although I was minister of justice, Mr. Sirleaf placed me among those who should not have access to the draft petroleum law. He disregarded that it is one of the statutory functions of the of Justice Ministry to review and comment on such documents. I returned the document.

The second time I saw the document was sometime in early October 2013 when one of the three senators selected to review the document, Senator Frederick Cherue, called and asked if the ministry could assist him with the review. I informed him that I did not think that the Ministry of Justice was among the select few to have access to the document, but he insisted that he needed our assistance. We told him that there was a petroleum expert currently in Monrovia conducting workshops for the ministry's staff, and we could ask her to assist with the review. He agreed.

A few months before, when we had commenced negotiations with a foreign oil company for a Liberian oil block, we requested a grant from the United Nations Development Program (UNDP) to hire a petroleum law expert to train our staff in the negotiations of production sharing contracts. The expert, who was then in Monrovia on her contractual assignment, met with the senators and made some very minor suggestions. Apparently, she did not want to become engrossed in the review process since it was not a part of her terms of reference. I was very relieved when she told me that she had not made any drastic recommendations. The senators seemed very pleased. After that, we heard nothing more from the senators. In fact, we heard nothing more about the mysterious draft petroleum law until October 28, 2013, about two weeks later, when the House Committee on Energy convened the hearing on the draft law.

I could tell from the tone of the president's voice she was upset her officials had not gone to the hearing to defend the document. She claimed that this was her son's legacy, and we were deliberately placing roadblocks for him to fail. I was baffled. How were we to participate in a process from which Mr. Sirleaf had excluded us? Even if I had been notified to attend the hearing, I would not have been prepared to participate since I had not reviewed the document. The fact is the president had allowed her son to take over the reform of the petroleum sector singlehandedly. He had sidelined all the key officials, including the CEO of the National Oil Company, Dr. Randolph McClain, and had selected to work with a few of his friends and a couple of public officials who did not have authority to defend the document before the legislature. Instead of blaming her son for going about the process the wrong way, she blamed the government officials for not accommodating him.

We were now in the second term of the Sirleaf administration, and she had nearly made a 360-degree turn on everything. She listened more to gossip and rumors. She allowed relatives and friends to interfere with the work of government officials more. It is one thing when as a government official you incur the wrath of an ordinary citizen, and quite another when you incur the wrath of the president or that of her family member or her close friend, especially if the relative is the president's favorite son.

In November 2013, the president asked if I would be traveling out of the country for the Christmas holiday, as I normally did every year. When I answered in the affirmative, she asked if we could meet before my trip, which we did on December 17, 2013, one day before I left the country. I was not sure what the meeting was about, but I suspected it had to do with my job.

A few months earlier, when President Sirleaf was looking for a chief justice of the Supreme Court of Liberia to replace the retiring chief justice, Johnnie N. Lewis, she called me to a meeting. She had a two-day unofficial engagement in London and asked me to join her on the trip, as she would have time for us to sit and discuss what she had on her mind. At the meeting in London, she told me I was the popular pick for the position among both the Liberian and foreign communities, but she was not inclined to nominate me because I was too "headstrong." When she clarified what she meant by headstrong, it all had to do with instances that required me to take a firm stand as attorney general to minimize criticisms of the government and ensure the rights of ordinary citizens were not trampled on. Besides, most of the specific examples she gave, where she believed I had been difficult, were instances where it was important for me to take a strong stand to protect her legacy.

For example, I did not think it was a good idea for the president to include on her official delegation to the UN General Assembly a man who had been charged and indicted by the Justice Ministry for economic sabotage. I did not agree with the president's son, Robert Sirleaf, that the president should sign a major oil contract without proper negotiations between the investor and the relevant government agencies. I did not agree with the president and her sister that government should hold on to the prime real property of a Liberian family and, in turn, lease it out to private businessmen in violation of the constitutional requirements for eminent domain. The property in question was not used for a public purpose, and the family was not compensated for the taking, as required by the Constitution. Therefore, I felt that the allegation that I did not always act in her best interest was unwarranted.

I thanked the President for inviting me on the trip to England and informed her that I did not lobby for the Chief Justice position because it was not part of my immediate plans. In any case, I expressed the view that the

Acting Chief Justice and she would work well together. Within days after we returned from London, the Acting Chief Justice was nominated by the president for the position of Chief Justice.

At the December 17, 2013, meeting in her office, she proceeded to inform me that in early 2014, she would carry out a reshuffle of government and that the Justice Ministry would be affected. She went on to say that she had had no reason to question my integrity or competence. "In fact," she said, "I am told that you are a very good negotiator of contracts on behalf of the government."

"It is all about teamwork, Madame President," I interjected quickly. "I have been fortunate to be on negotiation teams with some of the brightest Liberians like Richard Tolbert, Eugene Shannon, Randolph McClain, Seward Cooper, Elfrieda Stewart Tamba, Patrick Sendolo, Binyah Kesselley, and quite a few other individuals."

Then she went on to say, "As for the matter of the contempt case before the Supreme Court, I will do what I can to see that it comes to a positive end."

The president struggled to continue the conversation. She looked exhausted and frail. At one point, she nodded and must have taken a ninety-second cat nap before she caught herself.

When she was done speaking, I told her how working with the government as the attorney general since 2009 had been a great opportunity not only to help my country but also to broaden my perspective, given the array of issues and challenges that prevail in a post-conflict environment. I pledged that even as a member of the private sector, I would continue to do my utmost to contribute whatever I could to the rebuilding efforts being carried out by the government. I thanked her for including me on her journey, if even for a short while, and wished her and her loved ones a wonderful and happy holiday season, and then I asked to take leave. As I walked out, she asked that I extend her holiday greetings to my family.

After the meeting, I called my husband immediately and told him what had transpired between the president and me and went on to state that I was very pleased with the prospect that our working relationship would most likely end on amicable terms.

CHAPTER 35

The Power Circus

The United Airlines flight landed in Brussels just before 6:00 a.m. local time on January 10, 2014. I headed to the business class lounge to freshen up, get some rest, and do some work (in that order) during the nearly six-hour layover before boarding Brussels Airlines for Monrovia. As I entered the lounge, I ran into Robert Sirleaf, the president's son; we exchanged pleasantries and began a conversation. During the conversation, he let me know that he was not pleased with me because I am "very controlling" and had blocked his attempt to change the petroleum law, the legacy he had planned to leave for himself. He repeatedly said loudly and firmly, "Ellen" (as he calls the president) "has not been forthright with you." I quickly concluded that it was best for me to listen out of politeness, as it was pointless to engage in a conversation. Then, in a few seconds, he calmed down and asked whether we could have a joint press conference in Monrovia to talk about the new petroleum law. I was noncommittal and just simply excused myself.

I recalled that sometime back in 2011, just before the elections, Mr. Sirleaf, Christopher Neyor (the then CEO of the national oil company of Liberia) and I were having a telephone conference with a British law firm and as I tried to make a point, Mr. Sirleaf rudely interrupted and said, "Minister Tah, you have your marching orders." His comments were followed by silence on the line. After a few seconds, Mr. Neyor asked if everyone was still there.

When we answered in the affirmative, he tried to recommence the meeting, but it ended shortly after it recommenced. As soon as I got off the line, my phone rang; it was Mr. Neyor offering his apology for the behavior of Mr. Sirleaf. My response was, "It is your board chairman who should apologize, but thanks anyway." I said further, "I don't think the British firm will continue to work with the oil company after what just happened." I was right.

I was so thrown off guard by the outburst that I could not speak or think for a few seconds, especially since this occurred in the presence of total strangers who also must have been appalled. Sometimes it was unclear to me who was running the country, President Sirleaf or her son Robert. He was senior adviser to the president and chairman of the board of the National Oil Company (NOCAL), but you would have thought he was the de facto president. Because of his abrasive behavior, many officials of government simply avoided him if they did not have reasons to deal with him directly; others manipulated him to gain access to and favor from the president or obtain his blessings to go after an enemy.

During the flight, I thought of how this man reminded me of all the reasons why nepotism is a bad thing for good governance. To think that he impudently declared that he had wanted me dismissed a long time ago but that his mother had "not been forthright" with me was mind-boggling. Did he ever stop for one moment to think that his mother needed me in her government more than I needed the job?

I decided for the rest of the flight to Monrovia, I would focus on drafting a brief proposal to submit to President Sirleaf and the minister of health regarding the mental health issues in Liberia. While I was in the US, a Liberian named Moses Saygbe had arranged a conference call with former US congressman from Rhode Island, Patrick Kennedy, to follow up on the expressed interest of the congressman to help revitalize the mental health–delivery service in Liberia based on a request from some Liberians. Too many young people in Liberia with mental health issues end up in the criminal justice system. Mr. Kennedy gave some advice on how we, as Liberians, could jumpstart the process, and how important it was that the Liberians take ownership of this initiative, with which I wholeheartedly agreed. Upon my return to Monrovia, it would be my mission to convince the president and the minister of health to embrace this new venture.

We arrived at the Roberts International Airport around seven in the evening on January 10, 2014. As soon as I disembarked from the airplane at the international airport in Liberia, one of my security officers said, "Honorable Snowe wants you to call him; he said it was urgent." Edwin Snowe (popularly called "Snowe") is a member of the House of Representatives, and like quite a few other legislators, now and then he would contact me about some matter of concern to him. I was tired from traveling and wanted to wait until the next day to contact him, but I remembered that the security officer had used the word "urgent." He might have a problem that required immediate attention, I reasoned, so I called.

On the other end of the phone, Snowe said, "The Supreme Court of Liberia has unanimously voted to suspend your law license for six months." I was surprised at how well I kept my calm. I thanked him for the information and clicked off the phone. I sat in the SUV, still waiting for the security officer who had gone to retrieve my luggage and began to process the information. First, I wondered why Mr. Snowe had called to give me this information and not one of my deputies in the ministry, or a relative, or a close friend. Why was he so concerned that he called my security officer to try to find me to deliver the news? Second, I thought about the justices on the Supreme Court bench and wondered, *What is going on with these people?* It was not so much about what they were doing to me as it was what they were doing to the judiciary as an institution. To hold an attorney general in contempt and punish her for doing her job was a gross injustice and a blatant abuse of power.

I asked the security officer to drive directly to the home of Estrada and Jennie Bernard. They were the ones, among the president's family members, with whom I had the closest contact, especially since Jennie had recommended me for the position of attorney general. When I sat down and explained what I had heard from Mr. Snowe, the couple expressed utter surprise and dismay. Jennie assured me that the president, who was then on a short visit to La Cote D'Ivoire, was completely unaware of what was going on and that she would communicate to her the information I had shared. She went on to say, "Ellen has never hurt a fly since she was born and would never join these people to do such a thing."

Just then, my phone rang, and a friend on the other end said, "I just heard that you had returned to Liberia. Where are you right now?" When I told him, he said, "Be careful what you say so it does not come to haunt you. Leave as soon as you can and call me when you get in the car."

A few of my friends followed the contempt matter from the beginning and tried to keep me apprised of what was going on behind the scenes even when I was out of the country. The man who called was one of those individuals; he seemed to have been acting out of his conviction. He was also well connected with people in the Executive Mansion, the judiciary, and people in the private sector who had strong connections with government officials. Therefore, for all these reasons, I was inclined to believe what he was about to say. He spoke on the phone in a monotone: "Look here, madam, that couple is completely aware of what is going on. The husband was the emissary of the president to the judiciary during the past couple of weeks while you were away. Jennie is no longer supporting you because of a decision you gave against some of her foreign business partners. They all want you out, and they feel that this very stupid contempt charge has finally given them an opportunity."

I listened intently, and then I said, "You are making my head spin, but thank you for the information. I will touch base with you tomorrow. Good night."

I recalled the case the caller was referring to. President Samuel Doe's Government decided in the mid nineteen eighties that a certain real property taken from a Liberian family by government several decades prior, and leased out by the government to some foreign businessmen for commercial purposes, was in violation of the Constitution of Liberia since the government had not compensated the family for the taking as required under the doctrine of eminent domain. After careful examination of all the documents in this matter, I concurred with the decision of the Doe Government and, accordingly, advised the Government of President Sirleaf to enforce it.

Notwithstanding I trusted the credibility of the caller, I still felt that I should give Jennie the benefit of the doubt. After all, it was Jennie who had recruited me to work for the Sirleaf Government, and both she and her husband had done their utmost to provide moral support over the years I had spent at the ministry of justice. Therefore, I was reluctant to conclude that they would participate in a conspiracy against me. But then, with Liberian politics, you just never know.

During the seven-minute ride back to my house, I relaxed and took a quick nap. I was too tired to think about the hurdles that waited ahead with this contempt matter. I promised myself that as I arrive at each hurdle, I will muster all the strength in my body to jump over it. Usually when I am faced with a huge task or problem, I approach the solution in small manageable segments. In Liberia, we say "small, small" or "little by little." That way, I am most likely to overcome my challenge without realizing that I have figuratively climbed a mountain.

When I got home, I decided to get some sleep and await the president's return to Liberia the following day to pursue this matter further. A few minutes after nine o'clock post meridian, the phone rang; it was the former solicitor general, Micah Wright. He said he was calling from the Supreme Court, that the court had just announced the decision to suspend me. I said,

"Yes, I know." He was surprised that I already knew. "I have known since around seven o'clock this evening."

He was silent for a while. Then he said, "That is strange! The court was still reading other opinions at seven o'clock; your opinion was the last. In fact, the court just delivered it a few minutes ago." I thanked him for representing me and went to sleep.

The President returned late afternoon, and on the way from the airport, her protocol officer called and set up an appointment for me to meet with the president at her home later that evening. The president appeared to have already heard what the Supreme Court decision was. All she said was that she did her best to bring this matter to "a positive end" but that the justices were determined to "punish" me. The only advice she had to give was that I simply go to the justices and apologize and beg for forgiveness. I almost fell off the chair. "Madame President," I said, "what would I be apologizing for?"

She looked at me as though she had not understood what she had just said to me. Then she said, "I am tired. Let me confer with some lawyers in the private sector, and then we can talk some other time."

I did not present the mental health proposal I had scribbled on the flight back to Monrovia. I thought it would be a good idea to put it on hold for a while. Little did I know that this unconstitutional crisis that had begun six months ago would overshadow this rare opportunity to address mental health issues in the country. But it did.

CHAPTER 36

The Opinion

I was curious to read what the Supreme Court had written in its opinion regarding the contempt charges against me. It would be the first time that I would get to know what I had done and why the court had suspended my law license. I had never thought there would be a written opinion because there was nothing to write about. But since this matter, from the government's standpoint, was so grave that it had required the attention of the full bench of the Supreme Court of Liberia and ultimately resulted in a written opinion to become a part of the Liberian case law, I could not wait to read it.

Throughout the court's opinion, it became clear that those of us in Liberia, both lawyers and nonlawyers, still struggle with the distinction between the judiciary and the criminal justice system. Although the judiciary is one of the three distinct branches of government (the other two being the executive and the legislative branches), it is an integral component of the criminal justice system. The four components of the criminal justice system consist of law enforcement, prosecution, courts, and corrections. And although the components are expected to work collaboratively, the legislature had been very meticulous in crafting the laws to ensure that actors in the criminal justice system did not disregard the doctrine of separation of powers by crossing the lines of distinction between the judiciary and the executive branches.

First, there was the question of jurisdiction. Rodney Sieh, the journalist, had first announced an appeal in the libel case to the Supreme Court but had not perfected the appeal; in other words, he had not complied with all the legal steps required under the law for the Supreme Court to hear and decide on his appeal. Consequently, the appeal was dismissed by the Supreme Court, and the case was remanded to the civil law court so that the latter could enforce its judgment. Therefore, at the time the contempt charges were brought against me, as attorney general, the matter was before the civil law court. It means, if my decision to grant compassionate leave to the journalist was contemptuous, then it should have been a matter taken up by the civil law court and not the Supreme Court. On page 10 of its opinion, culled from the brief of the amici curiae, the Supreme Court justified its claim to jurisdiction. It reasoned that after issuing a mandate to a lower court, which had been served and returned served, the Supreme Court had the right to "exercise original jurisdiction for contempt over an act tending to frustrate and impede enforcement of its judgment and mandate."

Also, on page 10 of the Supreme Court opinion, the court cited *Glassco v. Thompson 30 Liberian Law Reports*, 670 (1983), which states: "This Court has also held that a contempt proceeding is a *sui generis* action. Thus, the Court, without a complaint, may, on its own motion, institute proceedings to punish for offenses against its own dignity and authority." In the succeeding paragraph, the Court went on to say the fact that the main case was before the Civil Law Court "does not preclude the Supreme Court, the head and parent body of the Judiciary from instituting these contempt proceedings **to protect the dignity and authority** of the Civil Law Court, the Supreme Court, and the Judiciary as a whole." The bold is added for emphasis, as in many places in the opinion, the court tended to focus on the protection of its "dignity and authority." It is still not clear to me how granting compassionate leave to an inmate by the attorney general, in keeping with the statutes, would undermine the dignity and authority of the Supreme Court. Moreover, the decision to grant leave to a prisoner is an administrative function exclusively within the purview of the executive branch, just the same as providing medical services, security, food, and lodging to prisoners.

On page 11, the court opined the following:

> Section 34.20(1) of the Criminal Procedure Law upon which the contemnors relied does not state, on its face, that it is also applicable to a civil case; and we know of no statute or decisional law of this Court that says that Section 34.20(1) is also applicable to civil cases ... To the contrary, Section 34.20(1) only authorizes the Minister of Justice/Attorney General to

formulate rules or regulations governing compassionate leave for prisoners who are sentenced to terms of imprisonment in criminal cases to which the Republic of Liberia, represented by the Ministry of Justice, is or was a party. This conclusion is supported by the fact that the Republic of Liberia has no vested interest in a civil contempt imposed by a court to force compliance with its order, mandate or ruling.

I was appalled by the fact that an otherwise plain and clear statute would be deliberately misinterpreted by an august body of the Republic of Liberia to undermine the doctrine of separation of powers. This position by the court was so abhorrent that Kate Chang, a human rights advocate and an international law practitioner based in the United States, was compelled to write an open letter to President Ellen Johnson Sirleaf, in which she stated, inter alia:

All parties agree that Section 34.20(1) of the Liberian Criminal Procedure Code governs this dispute. It is clear that the statute vests unequivocal, exclusive, and final authority in the Minister of Justice to establish and oversee the administration of compassionate leave and other decisions for prisoners. It appears that what the parties disagree on is whether Sieh was eligible for the leave approved, and whether the Minister of Justice should have first obtained the approval of the Justices before granting the leave. The Justices claim that because the statute regarding leave is set forth in the Criminal Procedure Code, it only applies to criminal prisoners, rendering it inapplicable to Sieh, who was detained for a civil offense.

It is untenable and without concrete basis to claim that the administration of civil prisoners is governed by a body of law distinct and separate from the comprehensive guidelines provided by Chapter 34. Chapter 34, Section 2, expressly applies to all individuals held in custody including those incarcerated "under civil commitment." It, therefore, stands to reason that Sieh, who was imprisoned for libel, which is a civil matter, was eligible to be considered for compassionate leave. Accordingly, it was valid for that prisoner to petition the Minister of Justice. As stipulated in 34.20(1) of the Liberian Criminal Procedure Code:

"The Minister of Justice shall formulate rules or regulations governing compassionate leave from institutions and, in accordance with such rules and regulations, may permit any prisoner to leave his institution for short periods of time … to return to his home for other compelling reasons which strongly appeal to compassion."

As a lawyer and a student of corrections, I found the law to be clear in its applicability; it applied to all prisoners irrespective of whether the case was civil or criminal. There was no law on our books that provided for distinct treatment of inmates in civil cases from those in criminal cases. All inmates were subject to the laws that provided for the custody and care of prisoners, meaning anyone who was locked up in facilities operated by the correctional system under the Ministry of Justice was governed by the correctional statutes.

The court, on page 12 of its opinion, stated that "the framers of our law intended compassionate leave to afford a prisoner the opportunity to attend a pressing matter of serious or critical nature involving himself or his family for a short period." In my view, the serious medical condition of Rodney Sieh ultimately justified the action taken. Besides, chapter 34: 20 (1) gives the minister of justice discretionary power to grant compassionate leave in that the section states, among other things, the minister of justice may grant compassionate leave "for other compelling reasons which strongly appeal to compassion."

It is noteworthy that on page 12 of its opinion, the court concluded: "Notwithstanding, this Court recognizes that where, growing out of actions of contempt of court or any civil matter, compelling reasons(s) exist for the provisional release of a prisoner from a detention center, an application may be made in every such case to the court by the Minister of Justice, as custodian of the prisoner, or by the prisoner himself or herself. The application may be granted under conditions laid down by the court."

The court, in the preceding paragraph, effectively devolved upon itself the authority to administer functions delegated by the legislature to the executive branch of government. What if an inmate's family files an application on behalf of a prisoner in an emergency that arises on a Sunday morning? Would the court convene on Sunday morning to review and act upon such application? The power conferred on the Supreme Court, by law, is to interpret the law. The existing law is clear on who is responsible for the care and custody of inmates. If the Supreme Court had determined that it should share the responsibility with the executive, then the legislature should have been asked to amend the existing law or enact a new law to that effect. First, the Supreme

Court interfered with the functions of the executive, and second, it created a law to justify its unlawful action. It was an outright disregard for the spirit and intent of the doctrine of separation of powers among the three branches of government.

To quote Kate Chang again, "It is one thing to concede that the Judiciary may well be the arm of government best equipped to interpret the Constitution and underpinnings such as the separation of powers doctrine. It is another thing to act as if this fiduciary capacity entitles the Judiciary to truncate the values of the Constitution, let alone trump the powers of the corollary arms of government. In the realm of objective reasoning it is neither for the Judiciary to arrogate to itself the authority to circumscribe an act of the Legislature, nor is it for the Judiciary to appropriate the powers of the Executive."

The Rodney Sieh case is a clear reminder of why the government should not engage in the practice of incarcerating citizens involved in civil matters and should, accordingly, take steps to repeal all such archaic laws. Until we do so, it is expected that the executive branch of government, through the Ministry of Justice, will continue to allow prisoners to avail themselves of the most favorable provisions of the law. We need to be vigilant in finding a way to release from incarceration all those prisoners who should not be in prison in the first place, as well as those who pose no apparent risk to the safety and well-being of the society. The only danger Rodney Sieh posed to society, from the standpoint of this government, was his audacity to write about the pervasiveness of corruption in the public sector, especially in the hierarchy of each of the three branches of government.

It is noteworthy that the justices on the Supreme Court of Liberia at the time this contempt case was heard and decided were: Francis S. Korkpor (Chief Justice); Kabina Ja'neh; Jamesetta Howard Wolokollie; Philip A.Z. Banks, III; and Sie-A-Nyene G. Yuoh.

CHAPTER 37

The Aftermath of the
Court's Opinion

I went to work on Monday, January 13, the week after the suspension of my law license by the Supreme Court, not knowing what to do since I controlled both the justice and security sectors and, consequently, most of what I had to do in security and law enforcement did not require a law license. After about a week, the president called and said that the justices did not want me in the office at all. Suspension of my license meant suspension from the job. My staff did not know what to do, as no one had seen this coming. Our foreign partners were a bit confused about the status of various projects and wanted to know whether I would return to the office after the suspension was over. I went home as the president had requested, but I also went home to think about what I wanted to do for the rest of my life.

In the meantime, Counsellor Varney Sherman, someone I have known most of my life, stopped by my office to ask what I was doing about the Supreme Court ruling against me. I did not see him often; therefore, I was a bit surprised but very pleased to have his support. He was then chairman of the president's Unity Party. He was someone the president deferred to from time to time for legal advice on political and personal matters. He offered to help me prepare and file a petition for re-argument before the Supreme Court.

"We have to protect the integrity of the judiciary," he said. "The re-argument will provide an opportunity for both the justices and you to reframe the legal discourse and correct the record for posterity."

I was aware that a few others, including Senator Frederick Cherue, Charles Walker Brumskine, Binyah Kesselley (the then Commissioner of the Liberian Maritime Authority), and Counsellor Fonati Koffa had gone to see the president, on separate occasions, to convince her that there was a similar situation in the mid nineteen eighties where the late President Samuel K. Doe intervened to resolve a matter between the Supreme Court and the then Attorney General, Jenkins K.Z. B. Scott. But from what was recounted to me, she did not budge.

Instead, the president asked me to meet with her so that we could determine what to do to get the Supreme Court to work with us to resolve this matter. When we met, she insisted that once I "begged" the justices, the whole matter would be over. Of course, I was astounded and could not believe that the president appeared not to have remembered how the whole Rodney Sieh saga developed. She told me that it was my fault that I had made a poor decision, and as a result, it had created a constitutional crisis.

What the president did not recall was that it was the court, and not the ministry of justice, that had sent Rodney to jail on a civil charge. Notwithstanding the ministry of justice position may not have been consistent with the court's position on this matter, we did not release Mr. Sieh from prison. That would have been disrespectful to the court. Instead, we granted Mr. Sieh a temporary leave from prison for thirty days because of his medical condition. The ministry simply afforded Mr. Sieh the service he was entitled to under the law as an inmate. We granted him compassionate leave, a temporary relief, but he continued to remain under the supervisory custody of the correctional system.

I explained to the president that it was best, at this point, to pursue the legal route since the court had already released its opinion. It would be more prudent, I asserted, to file a petition for re-argument, that apologizing, or "begging" as she had suggested, would not destroy the record the court had made by issuing a written opinion in this matter.

Counsellor Sherman and I worked on the petition for re-argument the next day. We agreed that it would be prudent to rely on the law to support our position, for the simple reason that the law was on our side. On the day Counsellor Sherman was to file the petition, he called to say that he had received a request from the legal adviser to the president that the petition was first cleared with his office in the Executive Mansion before it was filed with the court. "What!" I exclaimed. Then Counsellor Sherman said calmly, "You are the client; it is only my duty to inform you of the request from the Mansion." By now, I was at my wit's end. I said, "Hell no," and he said, "Okay," and clicked the phone off.

When a lawyer from Sherman's office went to file the petition, the legal adviser to the president was in the office of one of the justices. We did not know what it meant and decided not to speculate. In any case, the court did not accept the application that day; one of the justices complained that her name was misspelled on the petition. My special assistant, Edward Dillon, retrieved the document, went to the Sherman & Sherman Law Firm to make the correction, and took the document back to the Court to be filed. When the petition was finally accepted and a hearing was scheduled, Counsellor Sherman did not come to court that day; only Counsellor Cherue showed up. I had a gut feeling that something was wrong. I was right; the court denied the application for reargument.

Tuesday, January 21, was the first day I officially remained home under the so-called suspension. With all the support that I had, I still turned to God for help, as always. As I sat on the couch in my study, drinking a cup of coffee, I recall thinking that I had been let down by the highest person in the land, the president. The only place to turn was to the God we serve; He would be the primary source of my strength. Although in my adult years I have not been as active in church as I should be, I continue to be deeply spiritual and often call on God for wisdom and protection. Once again, God would be my greatest source of strength. As is written in Proverbs 3:5–6, "Trust in the Lord with all thine heart, and lean not unto thine own understanding. In all thy ways acknowledge him, and he shall direct thy paths."

Suddenly my phone rang, startling me. It was my special assistant, Edward Dillon; he called to say that there were some people who wanted to see me, but they were not sure whether it was appropriate to come to my home. Among the visitors, he named the head of the United Nations Missions in Liberia, the then United States ambassador to Liberia (Deborah Malac), the head of the European Union Delegation in Liberia, heads of other international organizations with offices in Monrovia, journalists, and a host of others. My classmate from Yale Law School, Professor Leslye Obiora, flew in from Arizona; she would later report back to one of our favorite former professors, Michael Reisman, who had encouraged me to serve my country. Then Joseph Bell, board chairman of the International Senior Legal Project (ISLP), who had worked closely with the Ministry of Justice in his role as ISLP's senior legal adviser to the government of Liberia, flew in from Washington, DC. I told my special assistant to go ahead and make the appointments. I would see them at my home in separate time slots. They all simply wanted to know what was going on and whether there was anything they could do.

Some Liberians called to thank me for my courage but hastened to tell me that they could not show support publicly for fear of reprisal from the government. Nevertheless, I was appreciative of their thoughtfulness. In addition to my immediate relatives and the Ministry of Justice staff, others, I am grateful to the many Liberians, including Rev. Emmanuel Bowier and Rev. Kortu Brown, who called and/or stopped by and remained consistent in their support as I transitioned from public to private life. Additionally, Rodney Sieh of the *frontpageafricea newspaper* and Henry Costa of Roots FM radio talk show, were very persistent in keeping my story alive, and for that I thank them,

I did not know what to explain to my visitors. Other than recounting the facts briefly, I could not say more. Although I appeared to be very composed, I was just as disconcerted, disappointed, and perplexed as they were. It was left up to each of my visitors to determine whether the granting of compassionate leave, under section 34.20(1), to an ailing prisoner was contemptuous and, hence, justified the action taken by the Supreme Court.

There was also a flurry of emails from the international legal community, including Liberians practicing abroad, offering support of some kind or the other. One former attorney general in a West African country offered to represent me at the ECOWAS Court (the sub-regional judicial body) if I was willing to bring human rights abuse charges against the Liberian government. By then, the country was overwhelmed with issues surrounding the outbreak of the Ebola virus, which I will cover in a later chapter, and I felt it would be insensitive to file a lawsuit against the government amid the calamity.

CHAPTER 38

Taking Control of
My Situation

Just after the February 10, 2014, publication by the *FrontPage Africa* newspaper of an open letter to the president from a Californian attorney, Kate Chang, the president asked me to come in so we could talk. She wanted me to know that she was still consulting with the justices of the Supreme Court as well as eminent Liberian lawyers in the private sector to resolve the matter with the Supreme Court once and for all. She also wanted to know whether I had anything to do with the Liberians and foreigners, both at home and abroad, who were publishing articles criticizing the decision of the Supreme Court and the government of Liberia regarding the contempt case.

The president appeared to be more perturbed about the bad publicity she had received on this matter than the unnecessary tarnishing of my reputation by the Supreme Court. What concerned me even more, neither the president nor the Supreme Court justices seemed to have understood the implication of this whole matter and how the international community viewed our judicial system. It bothered me that the Liberian judiciary had become a laughingstock around the world.

In the meantime, I learned that sometime in February 2014, the president had asked the vice president to convene a meeting at his home with the justices and her to discuss a resolution to my matter. Although I was the subject of the discussion, I did not receive an invitation to be present. When I spoke with the vice president afterward, it appeared that the meeting was more about justifying the action that had been taken against me than an effort to resolve the matter. The Supreme Court had denied my application for a re-argument. Therefore, to me, the matter was over. The court was acting deliberately and had no intention of changing its position. I often wondered why they had become so emboldened and so purposeful in their action. The judiciary is supposed to be an independent branch of government, but the president was taking the lead on this matter.

At this point, I did not expect anything from anyone. I was tired of the charade and had determined that I simply needed to serve out the six-month suspension and decide on what I wanted to do going forward. Do I return to government, or do I formally tender my resignation and move on with my life? It was time for me to take charge of my situation, even if it did not go in the direction I anticipated.

What was very clear in my mind up to this point was I would resign from the government at the end of the six-month suspension. My only concern was how to carry out my plan with the minimum amount of impact to my reputation. All the meetings of "eminent" justices and lawyers meant absolutely nothing to me anymore. The opportunities we all had to have an amicable resolution had passed. It was clear to me that there was no intention on the part of the president or the justices to resolve this matter justly. Everything seemed to be proceeding according to their plan, except that they had not been successful in beating me into submission.

I heard from various sources that the president had already decided to replace me with the deputy minister of justice for economic affairs, Benedict Sannoh. I was not surprised because he spent more time in the Executive Mansion than the Ministry of Justice. Mr. Sannoh and I graduated from the Louis Arthur Grimes School of Law, University of Liberia Law School, with our first law degree the same year. I graduated as valedictorian, and he was second in a class of thirty students. Therefore, I was confident that he was competent to hold any position in the ministry.

Back in 2013, Counsellor Sannoh stopped by my office to see me and told me that he had been in the employ of the United Nations Missions in South Sudan, but he was undecided at the time as to whether he should remain in Liberia or seek reassignment with the UN. I convinced him to remain in Liberia and join the Ministry of Justice, as the country desperately needed qualified people. I recommended him to the president to fill the vacant post of deputy minister for economic affairs, and she approved.

After the first six months of his appointment, I hardly ever saw him in the office, especially during the latter months of 2013, except for once or twice a week. One of my intelligence officers, who was apparently preoccupied with this man's movements, told me that the deputy spent most of his time in the office of the legal adviser to the president in the Executive Mansion, in the private office of a downtown lawyer, and in the Temple of Justice. I was aware of his many visits to the Mansion because, on one occasion when the president's secretary could not find him, she called me out of desperation to track him down.

This was one time, since my appointed as attorney general, I wrestled with the idea of whether it is better to choose loyalty over competence, although all of my staff had been selected based on their professional qualifications.

The Supreme Court opened in March 2014, and nothing about my matter was on the docket, as I had correctly predicted. Then on March 30, 2014, the president called me to her house for a meeting. In essence, she said that she wanted the position of attorney general vacated, as she needed to appoint her new attorney general. It was news to me, since only the week before she had told me that she was still seeking a resolution. At the end of the meeting, I told her that I would resign on the following day. On March 31, 2014, I wrote and dispatched the following letter:

Republic of Liberia
Ministry of Justice
9th Street, Sinkor
Monrovia, Liberia

Office of the Minister/
Attorney General

March 31, 2014

CPT/MOJ/AG/RL/696/13

Her Excellency Madam Ellen Johnson Sirleaf
President of the Republic of Liberia
The Executive Mansion
Monrovia, Liberia

Dear Madam President:

I have the honor, most respectfully, to refer to our conversation last evening regarding the status of my suspension from the practice of law by the Honorable Supreme Court for a period of six months predicated upon my decision as Minister of Justice/Attorney General, R.L. to grant Rodney Sieh, formerly an inmate at the Monrovia Central Prison on a civil charge, a 30-day compassionate leave in keeping with my understanding of the authority vested in the Minister of Justice/Attorney General, R. L. under Section 34.20 of the Criminal Procedure Law.

When I was approached by Your Excellency in 2009 to return to Liberia to assume the position as Minister of Justice/Attorney General, R.L., you were unequivocal that your decision was based on my ability and integrity. Indeed, over the years I have worked unrelentingly and assiduously with international and local stakeholders to re-establish the rule of law and build a holistic justice and security system in our country. I believe that I have discharged my duties in a manner to ensure that the Ministry of Justice is not impugned by unsavory scandal and charges. Most importantly, the justice and security team and I have worked to ensure that our citizens receive access to justice and enjoy the human rights protection the law guarantees, which was essentially the crux of Rodney Sieh's matter.

As regards the Supreme Court's decision to suspend my license from the practice of law for six months, I again state emphatically that this was an unfair and unjust decision which, I believe, has done serious damage to the status of the rule of law in Liberia. Initially, I am on record for refusing to get involved in the Rodney Sieh matter as I knew that it was an issue between two private individuals and did not concern the Liberian Government as a party. But when Mr. Sieh was remanded to custody, and the matter of his human rights came into play, I was compelled to take action to avoid international embarrassment to the Government and people of Liberia. I did not act to gain any personal benefit or to accord to Rodney Sieh a privilege that had no basis in law. I acted based on my understanding of the law at the time; which is the responsibility entrusted to the Minister of Justice/Attorney General, R.L., by the Executive Law. Besides, my involvement with Rodney Sieh's matter was done after due consultations with you, Madam President, as I do on all matters of significance. Certainly, I did not act to disrespect or disregard the Supreme Court; I never intended to bring this eminent Body into disrepute; that is not my character.

You have said, Madam President, the Supreme Court has categorically stated that my sanction must be served to its fullest and that I cannot under any circumstances serve as Minister under a suspended license, even if the task is non-legal. You have also stated that you cannot accept that the Ministry of Justice will be run for three more months with the Minister under suspension.

Given your position expressed in the preceding paragraph, it is unmistakably clear that you, as the Chief Executive, do not intend to defend the office of the Minister of Justice/Attorney General, R.L. Therefore, it is my position that in the best interest of the people of Liberia I should tender my resignation. Accordingly, Madam President, please accept this letter as my resignation from the position of Minister of Justice/Attorney General, R.L., effective immediately.

I thank you for the opportunity given me to serve my country.

Very respectfully yours,

Cllr. Christiana P. Tah
MINISTER/ATTORNEY GENERAL

I dispatched the letter on the afternoon on March 31, 2014, and when the president received it, she called and wanted to know whether I sent a copy to the press. "No, Madam President," I said. "The letter was addressed to you and not the press."

"Well then," she continued. "I am traveling to Paris tomorrow for a week. Can we talk when I come back?" I answered affirmatively.

Three days later, the legal adviser, Seward Cooper, who was part of the president's delegation to Paris, called me from Paris about the letter. I was certain that the president had had some discussion with him prompting him to call me. The call was intended to dissuade me from publishing the letter, which I had no intention of doing at that time. He promised to have a meeting with me upon his return from Paris to see how he could help reduce the mounting tension occasioned by the Supreme Court action. I never heard from him again.

With this letter out, both the president and I now understood the real status of our relationship.

Since the president had not accepted my resignation letter of March 31, 2014, I continued to remain in the employ of the government under the suspension status. However, I now knew that she did not accept the resignation because she wanted control over how I left the government.

Therefore, it was now left with me to chart my exit carefully.

CHAPTER 39

Tough Times: Ebola Outbreak and Death of a Friend

In the meantime, while I was dealing with my own issues, Liberia was suddenly plunged into an outbreak of the Ebola virus. The virus, the Ministry of Health explained, was transmitted by a two-year-old child from neighboring Guinea to a Liberian woman in Lofa County, Northern Liberia, sometime in February 2014. The information became widespread in March 2014. The woman's sister traveled from Firestone, a rubber plantation not too far from the capital, to Lofa County to care for her sick sister and contracted the virus. The sick sister died, and her caregiver returned to her residence in Firestone, but the caregiver also died within a few days of her return home. By then, only a few citizens and a few people in the health care area knew what this virus was and the real danger it posed to the population.

From what I read in the 1990s, the virus is carried by contaminated monkeys and chimpanzees and is passed on to humans who either come in physical contact with a contaminated animal or consume its flesh. The virus starts to manifest itself with flu-like symptoms and, in a matter of hours, progresses to vomiting, fatigue, diarrhea, and bleeding.

With help from the international community, such as the World Health Organization, the Ministry of Health began a massive public awareness campaign and simultaneously began a tracking of all citizens who may have come into contact with the two women. Journalists and private nonprofit organizations, such as the Angie Brooks Center and the Urey-Foundation) owned and operated by Benoni Urey and his wife, Mae Bright Urey) provided public education and raised money to assist with food and health care supplies for individuals placed in isolation for observation or treatment. A member of the House of Representative, Honorable Solomon George, provided ambulances he had received from donor organizations to help transport the sick. The Firestone natural rubber farms, where the first known contact resided, took all measures possible, including the burning of the residence of the caregiver after her death, to bring the virus under control.

As the news dribbled from the Ministry of Health, the country first went into denial. Those who contracted the virus told relatives that they had malaria, a common ailment transmitted by mosquitos. Then misinformation flooded the airways as conspiracy theories filled the living rooms and restaurants of Liberian citizens. A lot of people threw caution to the wind, while others limited their social contacts and placed chlorine water in pails at the front and back doors of their homes and offices, requiring visitors to wash their hands before entering the premises.

Somehow, between March 2014 (when the public first heard of the virus) and June 2014 (when the first case was reported in Monrovia, the capital, everyone seemed to think that the virus had been brought under control.

I spoke with the minister of health, Dr. Walter Gwenigale, back in March 2014. I told the good doctor that I had followed the story of Ebola outbreak in the Democratic Republic of the Congo (the DRC) back in the mid-1990s and was afraid that we had a serious problem on our hands. I said to the minister I could not understand why we did not close the border with Guinea so we could contain the outbreak in Northern Liberia. Dr. Gwenigale, age eighty-one at the time, was very sharp and feisty and a very good team player. "I am taking advice from the experts, baby girl," he said. "I am a doctor, but this disease is very new to me."

In March 2014, I was already on the six-month suspension, and, therefore, it was easy to reduce contacts, as everyone was being advised by the government to do. I did not have to attend meetings and did not have to receive visitors if I did not want to. I reduced my security staff by half, retaining those whom I believed were not high risk. High risk involved those who lived in an area where an outbreak of the virus had been reported or who had to use public transport to come to work. Some officers had motorcycles assigned to them.

Ebola had made life very difficult for Liberians. You had to be mindful not to touch another person in a society where people like to touch. In an ordinary conversation, a Liberian would slap you on the arm or the back to make a point. Liberians shake hands and often hug to greet, console, or show affection.

Although I was on suspension and did not go to the office, at some point I was compelled to call a meeting at my house with senior staff, including the heads of immigration (Lemuel Reeves) and police (Chris Massaquoi), to discuss the role of the ministry in the fight against Ebola. We needed to establish standard operating procedures for border crossing, especially for traders. We needed to determine how to protect health workers who were being stoned by angry citizens when they tried to bury those who had died from the virus. We needed to decide how to enforce the laws against citizens whose cultural practices of washing the dead had been temporarily banned. We needed to discuss how to protect police officers exposed to the virus in the course of carrying out their duties.

After the meeting, I traveled to the United States in April for a family emergency unrelated to Ebola. It was the first time since the 1980 military coup and the Charles Taylor incursion of 1990 that a trip out of Liberia was such a psychological relief. Even though I was not physically in the office, somehow the stress from the Ebola outbreak had taken its toll on me. I was so glad to see my family. I was so glad to touch another human being without worrying that I might likely be dead the next day because of a hug or a simple handshake.

Just before I returned to Monrovia in mid-May 2014, I went to visit my friend Marie Parker in Silver Spring, Maryland. She had retired from the oil company in October 2013, where she had served for several years with distinction as vice president of finance. She had been in the States since November 2013 and wanted to stay on until the Ebola virus was brought under control, but I assured her that it was possible to live in Liberia in spite of the virus. I asked her to promise that she would return to Liberia soon. She promised, with a smile, that she would return in June 2014.

I left for Monrovia on May 22 and called Marie on May 23 to inform her that I had arrived. I spoke with her a week later, on Friday, May 30, and asked her to follow up on a scholarship we were trying to secure from the National Oil Company of Liberia (NOCAL) for a promising young student. She promised to call first thing on Monday, June 2. I called her on June 2 at 10:00 a.m. Liberian standard time (it was a 6:00 a.m. eastern time in the United States). The phone rang off the hook. I decided that I would call back two hours later when I thought she was awake. In less than two hours, a friend called and said, "Marie Parker has just died." It was so surreal to think that Marie had died so suddenly. I thought my head was about to explode. I thought my friend would call me back to say that it was just a joke. But no, it was not a joke. She had died in the hospital on June 2, 2014, after a brief illness. Her body was brought to Liberia for burial the following week. She returned in June, as she had promised, but not the way I expected. May her soul rest in eternal peace.

I felt like my world was crumbling: the suspension, the Ebola outbreak, and now the death of Marie, the person who did the most to help me readjust in 2009 when I agreed to return home to accept the appointment as attorney general.

In mid-July 2014, I returned to the office. I forwarded a letter to the president, formally informing her that I was back at work, and she replied welcoming me back. I was touched by a personal handwritten note from Vice President Joseph Boakai welcoming me and expressing his sincere delight that I was back at work. He has always come across as a very sincere person.

I hit the ground running. Ebola was too serious a matter to be inactive. A nurse at the Redemption Hospital, a small clinic on the outskirts of Monrovia, contracted the Ebola virus on the job. She returned home from work, and within a few days, she and her entire family of seven were all dead. A prominent Liberian doctor, Samuel Brisbane, affiliated with the John F. Kennedy Hospital, the major government hospital in the capital, died in July after unknowingly treating a patient with the Ebola virus. I believe, as a government, we became more serious when health care workers began to die from the virus.

Two American doctors, who contracted the virus while treating patients in Liberia, were airlifted on a special medical plane to the United States for treatment. They were treated at Emory University Hospital in Atlanta, Georgia, with an experimental drug called ZMapp, available in very limited quantity. They survived. Another Liberian doctor who contracted the virus survived after being treated in Liberia. A few citizens also survived.

Unfortunately, more than five thousand Liberians died from the virus over a six-month period (between March 2014 and September 2014). During that period, two Liberians carrying the virus traveled separately to Lagos, Nigeria, and Houston, Texas, USA. They both died but not without spreading the virus. Two nurses in Texas, who came in contact with the Liberian traveler, contracted the virus, were treated, and survived. Unfortunately, a few of the contacts in Nigeria, including a doctor who treated the afflicted traveler, died of the virus before it was brought under control.

I joined the barrage of daily meetings at the Executive Mansion, at the Ministry of Justice, and the Ministry of Health. The health officials, including Minister Gwenigale, Deputy Minister Bernice Dahn, Assistant Minister Tolbert Nyensuah, John Sumo (in charge of data at the Ministry of Health), and others at the Ministry of Health seemed to have been working around the clock. Dr. Wani-Mai Scott McDonald, head of the J.F.Kennedy Hospital, and her staff also worked relentlessly. The ELWA Hospital, the Carter Center, Doctors Without Borders, the World Health Organization, the International Red Cross, USAID, the United Nations, and Samaritan Purse were among the many organizations involved in determining how best to bring this malady under control.

The cabinet met with the president to decide whether we should declare a state of emergency under the Constitution but was also concerned about the implications it might have on the economy. First, we declared a national emergency as provided for under the public health law to test the water. Under the public health law, the minister of health is given sweeping powers to take actions necessary to prevent and control an epidemic. Therefore, the executive branch already had broad powers to prevent the spread of the disease.

After a few days, when we realized that investors who want to leave the country would leave no matter what decision the government made, we decided to elevate to a state of emergency under the Constitution to expand the authority to protect citizens. The basic difference was that the state of emergency curtailed additional fundamental rights, such as free speech and the freedom to assemble. For instance, the people were dissuaded from meeting in large groups solely to socialize; they were also dissuaded from distributing misinformation about the cause and treatment of Ebola.

We also met to discuss the burial protocols. Up to July, bodies of Ebola victims were being buried all over the place, mostly in neighborhoods where children played, and women made gardens. We needed to designate specific burial ground to reduce the exposure of residents in the various communities to the virus. Besides, a dedicated burial ground would make it easier for the police to protect health care workers who went out to bury corpses and reduce the cost of deploying police officers at multiple burial sites at the same time. The decision under the new protocol was to cremate the bodies, rather than bury. The minister of internal affairs was asked to identify a suitable location and handle all matters relating to Ebola burials. The police would continue to provide security.

Implementation was always difficult because of the resistance from the public. The public resisted cremation because it was new to most Liberians. Old practices die hard. The citizens did not want to be told that they could not wash the dead, lay hands on the sick to pray, or eat bush meat as they had done before the Ebola outbreak. The public was stressed and depressed. Here, we were struggling to recover from a fourteen-year-old senseless civil war, and now this, Ebola. I could completely understand the pain, anger, and frustration of the public. I was afraid myself. I wondered whether we could ever bring this virus under control with an already weak health care system.

In the meantime, on July 17, 2014, a friend called me to turn on the radio. The minister of information, on behalf of the executive branch of government, was responding for the first time to the Supreme Court opinion in my contempt case. He talked about how I was just "an angry and bitter" woman and that the executive branch was in complete support of the opinion handed down by the Supreme Court. The opinion had been handed down since January 10, 2014, and now the chief executive, through her minister of information, was finally stating her position publicly.

The government's reaction hit me like a ton of bricks. Here, I had returned to the job and plunged myself into the work after the president refused to accept my resignation dated March 31, 2014. Now, out of the blue, I am being insulted on the public radio by the chief spokesperson for the government of Liberia. It was hard to believe that with all that the country was going through at the time, there were people who had time to be pernicious. It would have been more prudent for the president to have simply accepted the resignation letter when I submitted it back in March.

I thought about the Liberian people and the crisis we were all facing with the Ebola virus and decided it would be too insensitive to resign or even react to spiteful statements. I ignored them all and continued to go to work.

Someone once said that when life throws a curve ball at you, you have to get up and keep going.

The July 28, 2014, report from the Ministry of Health showed the cumulative number of confirmed, probable, and suspected cases of the Ebola virus to be one hundred in Montserrado County, where the overcrowded capital (Monrovia) is situated. That was not good news. One case of Ebola in an overcrowded urban area is bad enough; one hundred is catastrophic. Of the fifteen counties, the virus hit Montserrado and Lofa Counties the hardest. There were a few cases in Bong, Nimba, Margibi, and Bomi. The other counties, especially the eastern region, seemed to be faring well.

In August 2014, the United States government deployed the 101st Airborne of the US armed forces to Liberia to help establish treatment centers for the growing number of Ebola cases and to help bring the virus under control. Representatives from the Center for Disease Control and the National Institute of Health also traveled to Liberia to join the fight against Ebola. Temporary treatment centers were established throughout the country by the American military, relieving the disconcerting sights of Ebola patients lying on the side of the streets or the lawns of the various hospitals and clinics.

CHAPTER 40

Ebola Politics

In early August 2014, I had to travel to Washington, DC, for five days to attend a conference, during which time I received a call from the solicitor general, Betty Lamin-Blamo. She informed me that when I was away from the office, sometime between January and July 2014, the police referred a case to the Ministry of Justice, alleging that certain officers of the National Security Agency (NSA) had extorted nearly a quarter-million United States dollars from Korean investors in the country to buy gold. The deputy minister of justice for administration, who was acting in my absence, had written a letter to the director of the NSA (the president's stepson) requesting him to turn over the money in question while the Ministry of Justice investigated the matter.

The NSA took offense to the tone of the letter, claiming that it presupposed that the NSA had taken money from the investors as alleged. The solicitor general and I both agreed with the position of the NSA director. On the phone, we decided that we would ask the head of the Independent National Human Rights Commission to take over the investigation since we did not, as yet, have an oversight body for the law enforcement and security agencies. She promised that the letter would be sent out before my return to Liberia.

As soon as I returned to Liberia during the second week of August, the Liberian Senate summoned me to explain how the fundamental rights of citizens would be affected by the state of emergency declared by the president in July 2014 due to the Ebola outbreak. I assured the legislature that law enforcement officers would not do any more than was required to protect the welfare of citizens. For instance, the limit on public gathering was to reduce the likelihood of the spread of the virus through physical contact.

The President also summoned me to let me know that during my trip to Washington, she had decided to appoint the Minister of Defense as the "head of Ebola security," an action she said was necessary since I was out of the country. The minister of justice is head of security of the country, and in the absence of the minister, the deputy (or acting minister of justice) assumes that role. I wondered how the minister of defense would be able to direct activities of the Liberia National Police (LNP), an internal law enforcement institution under the supervisory authority of the Ministry of Justice. But then I determined that the President was Commander in Chief of the Armed Forces of Liberia and leader of the country, therefore I complied.

I learned that the funding for Ebola security was disbursed directly to the Minister of Defense, the Director of Police, the Commissioner of Immigration, and other members of the security apparatus while I was away from the country. The staff of the Bureau of Corrections complained that it had not received any funding although it had been asked to provide segregated quarters for inmates who showed early symptoms of the Ebola virus. Both the Police and Immigration organizations complained of receiving inadequate funds. My staff did not seem to understand that I was not in charge of security when it came to Ebola, and that included funding as well as supervision. Others in the Liberian community inquired about psycho-social services for families that had been devastated by the virus. Although I was not responsible for psycho-social services, I was aware that funds had been allocated for those services but did not know why the program had not been established, even up to the time I left government in October 2014.

This was one of those times when I felt that my presence in government was hurting more than helping the institutions under my supervision. In any case, I continued to do whatever I could to assist with the Ebola crisis without appearing to interfere with the role of the Minister of Defense as head of Ebola security.

The usual meetings at the Ministry of Health continued. We were especially worried about news of an outbreak of the Ebola virus in West Point, a large, overcrowded ghetto just outside the center of the capital city, Monrovia. Residents from West Point worked and attended school throughout the capital. Therefore, the threat that the disease could spread ferociously in the densely populated capital was real and frightening.

We conferred with the president about the possibility of a quarantine of West Point for a short while to contain the virus and ensure that those who were already infected or exposed to the virus would be identified and isolated to receive proper care. The president agreed.

We met immediately after that at the Ministry of Health to work out the conditions for the quarantine. The government would provide care centers in West Point for those who were already infected and monitor those already exposed to the virus in their respective homes. The government would provide food and basic supplies for the community (especially the sick) since they could not leave the area. The markets, convenience stores, and other businesses in the area would continue to operate so that residents who were well would be able to move about within the West Point community and acquire their basic needs. Further, the government would provide a medical team, through the Ministry of Health, to assess the residents and treat those diagnosed with the virus. Lastly, the government promised to provide security so that residents of West Point would not attack government workers who went in the area to provide health services and ensure that residents would not break the quarantine by leaving the community at will.

The day the operation was launched, only the security personnel consisting of soldiers of the Armed Forces of Liberia (AFL) and officers of the Liberia National Police (LNP) showed up. There was no drinking water, and there were no supplies and no medical workers. Apparently, the other agencies were still coordinating their activities for logistics and services. The delay caused agitation among the residents of West Point, most of whom were not sick and, therefore, wanted the freedom to leave West Point at will.

As tension mounted in West Point, some of its residents, out of frustration and stress, stormed an Ebola treatment center, drove out the sick patients, and stole their mattresses and food. Within a couple of days, we learned that nearly all the thieves had contracted the virus and had begun to die off. It was sad, but it was a rude reminder that we (meaning the government) had fallen short on educating the public on the unmerciful consequence of disrespecting this deadly virus.

In the meantime, sometime in mid-August, I received a telephone call from the president informing me that she had decided to have an independent body investigate the matter involving the NSA and the Korean investors. I replied that I agreed with her and had, in fact, asked an independent group to conduct the investigation. Before I could complete my sentence, the president explained, "I do not want your committee nor the Ministry of Justice to investigate this matter. I do not trust the Ministry of Justice. In fact, the national security adviser tells me that you will be biased against my son. He has suggested that we set up a committee under the chairmanship of the dean of the law school."

All I could say after that was "That is fine with me, Madam President."

From my understanding, the Ministry of Justice was not investigating the Director of the NSA. Rather, the investigation involved certain officers of the agency. After having worked with the Director, Fombah Sirleaf, for a few years, I did not doubt that he would cooperate with the Ministry of Justice on a matter like this. We collaborated with him on many assignments and found him to be a very good team player; so, for me, the reaction from the President was unexpected and somewhat confusing.

After my conversation with the President, I sat there thinking for a while. My mind went back to the meeting with the president on March 30 that led to my letter of resignation dated March 31, 2014. I thought about the official statement of the government, released by Mr. Lewis Brown (the minister of information) on July 17, 2014, affirming the executive support of the Supreme Court ruling in the contempt matter. Now this. *Well*, I thought, *I have to start thinking seriously about my exit.* I promised myself to go back and take a look at my letter of resignation dated March 31, 2014 and begin updating it. At this point, it was no longer when to exit; it was how.

A few days later, around August 20, 2014, I received an unofficial report from a citizen that the crowd in West Point had grown unruly, and, as a result, the security personnel had opened fire. I was completely shocked. The caller said the shots were fired by the soldiers, and bullets hit two teenage boys. He said one of the boys, bleeding profusely from a gaping wound to the leg, was taken to a nearby hospital. We later learned that the young boy bled to death, as no one would attend to him, thinking that he might have the Ebola virus.

We received reports yet again that a police officer may have also fired his weapon. It is always difficult to carry out duties and responsibilities when you have two distinct institutions in the same place at the same time trying to enforce what are exclusively police functions.

As was expected, the minister of defense, head of Ebola security, first pulled his soldiers from West Point and then set up a committee under the Ministry of Defense to investigate the incident. I recall that the Ministry of Justice and the Liberia National Police were appointed members of the committee as well. When I left government, the investigation was ongoing, and I did not follow its outcome.

The president appointed the dean of the law school, Counselor David A.B. Jallah, to investigate the allegations of the Korean businessmen against the NSA. The committee decided the matter in favor of the Korean investors and, accordingly, recommended that the government restitute the full amount of US$247,000. As of this writing, I do not believe that the investors have received any money from the Liberian government.

CHAPTER 41

The Final Straw

Sometime around the third week of September 2014, I sat in my study at the desktop computer updating my resignation letter of March 31, 2014, which the president did not accept. I had planned to tender my resignation, again, by November or December 2014, expecting that the Ebola virus would have abated by then.

It was apparent that my continued presence in the government was hurting those institutions under my supervision, especially the police and the immigration services. By then, I was barely receiving the required financial support, and there was certainly no cooperation from the president, the judiciary, and other security agencies. The funding for security operations for the Ministry of Justice had decreased considerably, to less than 25% of the original budget amount. I discharged most of the intelligence agents due to lack of funding, and the few who stayed on did so out of loyalty.

The president was now managing the justice system through her legal adviser, the deputy minister of justice for economic affairs, the solicitor general, and the police director. The police director began to act on certain matters unilaterally. For instance, he commenced an investigation of the vice president merely because the latter was making preparations to contest the upcoming 2017 presidential elections. The minister of defense, the director of the National Security Agency, and the national security adviser advised the president regularly on security matters.

When I learned that the vice president was of the impression that I had ordered the director of police to investigate him, I called him and made an appointment for the director and me to meet with him early one morning at his house. The vice president invited four other persons to be present, including a family member, office staff, and close associates. I explained to the vice president that I did not order the investigation and did not know who ordered it, and that I was just as curious to get to the bottom of this as he was.

During the meeting, it was established that I did not order the investigation of the Vice President and I felt vindicated.

Within a couple of days after the meeting with the vice president, I received a telephone call from Jennie, the president's sister. She wanted to talk to me about a very important matter, so we arranged to meet. This time she was advocating for the release of a foreign businessman who had been convicted just the month before for human trafficking.

The eighty-year-old businessman and his son, forty-four, were convicted of trafficking nine young women from North Africa to Liberia to work as prostitutes, after misleading the women to believe that they were traveling to Liberia to work as waitresses in a restaurant for US$1,000 a month. They had appealed their conviction to the Supreme Court of Liberia. Jennie wanted to know if I could advise the president to grant a presidential pardon to these two businessmen.

My response was simply, "No, I cannot help in this matter."

"Who do you think can help?" she asked.

"I suggest that you confer with the chief justice and the president," was my response. The very next day, I received a letter from the late Honorable Edward B. McClain, the minister of state for presidential affairs, asking me to provide an opinion on whether the president should grant the two convicted human traffickers pardon.

The law on pardons and reprieves in the Liberian Criminal Code Revised Volume I, chapter 25.1 states:

> The President has the sole power to grant or deny applications for pardons, reprieves, and commutations to persons convicted of public offenses. To assist in his determinations on such applications, the President may request the Board of Parole to investigate the merits of the applications and make recommendations thereon in accordance with the procedure prescribed in this chapter.

Surely the president of Liberia has the sole power to grant pardon but not when the defendant chooses to appeal his conviction, effectively placing the matter under the jurisdiction of the Supreme Court. The defendants should have withdrawn the appeal if they wanted to request a presidential pardon. Alternatively, the defendants' counsel could have worked with the court to advance their case for hearing since the court was scheduled to officially open in three weeks for its October term. In the latter scenario, if the court had affirmed the conviction, the defendants could have then requested the presidential pardon. At that point, the conviction would have been final, and the matter would no longer have been under the jurisdiction of the court.

My decision to advise the president not to grant a pardon at that time was underpinned by two concerns: (1) The granting of a presidential pardon to defendants convicted only one month earlier for trafficking in persons would certainly reduce the seriousness that the government attached to combating human trafficking. (2) The granting of a presidential pardon to defendants whose matter was pending before the Supreme Court of Liberia would undermine the authority of the court and, hence, the doctrine of separation of powers.

I am always in support of any decision that would improve the life or well-being of another human being. Corrections is all about giving someone who has violated the law a second chance. Each year, the Ministry of Justice approaches the president to grant pardons and reprieves to deserving inmates. In 2011, the Ministry of Justice established the first Board of Parole in Liberia and the President appointed Joyce Frankfort, Kahn Kennedy, and Fatu Daramy Mensah as its first members. The principle mandate was to review applications from inmates for parole with the view to shorten the incarceration of well-behaved inmates and allow them to serve the rest of their sentences in the community in keeping with the law. Therefore, the decision in the matter of the two human trafficking defendants was not personal but, rather, based on what would be in the best interest of society.

On October 2, 2014, the president sent me a letter acknowledging my legal advice on the matter but hastened to state that she disagreed with my position and had conferred with "other lawyers" who had advised that as president of Liberia, she had the power to grant a pardon *at any time.*

It was disheartening to see that people out there were deliberately misleading the president, but it was even more disheartening and quite disappointing when she went along with it.

The letter sent to me by the president on October 2, 2014, was evidence that she had drawn a line in the sand. The message could not be any clearer.

Once the president stated that there were lawyers out there whose opinion she preferred over mine when it came to issues that concerned the Ministry of Justice, there was no longer a need for me to continue to be the attorney general in her government. It was time for me to step aside so that she would have the benefit of counsel of her choice.

CHAPTER 42

My Resignation

I took the letter the president had written to me on October 2, 2014, home and, again, spent all weekend updating my draft resignation letter. I did not discuss the letter with anyone in Liberia. At least four people knew that I would eventually resign but did not know when and how: one of them lived in Liberia, and the other three lived in the United States.

On Saturday, October 3, 2014, I attended two meetings, both of which were chaired by the president. The one in the morning involved the transparency agencies of government, and the topic centered around the fight against corruption. The president ranted about the escalation of corruption and how the Justice Ministry was not doing anything to bring corruption under control. I listened to the heads of two of the agencies impressing the president about what they would do to stamp out corruption. The two lawyers from the Ministry of Justice who attended the meeting with me later told the staff how they were shocked that I had sat quietly in the meeting while all kinds of insults were hurled at me indirectly. They were right; I was also surprised at myself, but at this point, there was no need to fight. All the zest in me was now gone.

In the afternoon, I attended another meeting in the Cecil B. Dennis auditorium at the Ministry of Foreign Affairs. By now, the president hardly included me in activities that had to do with the Ebola virus. My presence there was merely perfunctory. I did not want to disrespect the president by sending a deputy, especially when she knew that I was in the country. I had nothing to say about security, which would have been the main reason for being there; that would be the role of the minister of defense since he was the official head of Ebola security.

As I sat at the computer to finalize my letter of resignation late Saturday afternoon when I returned home from my meetings, my heart was laden with grief for Liberia. I worried about the future of the country and the future of the young people. For nearly a half of a century Liberia has been embroiled in internal turmoil: young people have developed more interest in politics than education; citizens have taken to violence to resolve minor disputes; the pen and the tongue have become just as harmful as the gun and knife; money has become more important than human life; and mentorship has been disregarded by most of the youth; when they do decide to choose a mentor, they tend to choose those whose behavior they should not emulate.

The Sirleaf government was the first light I saw at the end of the tunnel for Liberia; it was the closest to normality since the rice riot of 1979. The support from the international community was astounding. Therefore, it was no mistake on my part when I left my family and my job abroad to join the Sirleaf government. To me, it was realistic to be hopeful.

I sat there thinking about some of the things we had accomplished in the short time we had spent in the Sirleaf government. We tackled and won some of the corruption cases, one of which had to do with corruption in the forestry development authority; we introduced probation and parole to help reduce prison overcrowding and to give offenders a second chance; we conducted a major criminal justice retreat to convince the government and our partners that it was important to develop the criminal justice system in a holistic manner; we built the first of five justice and security hubs to decentralize the service delivery to citizens after the exit of UNMIL; we conducted a national conference to determine how best to harmonize the informal and formal justice systems; we sponsored two prosecutors to attend school in the United States under our capacity building plan, and were in the process of sponsoring two Liberian doctors to travel to the Republic of Ghana to specialize in pathology to reduce the cost of contracting the services of foreign pathologists for the prosecution of major cases; we have established a specialized court for the prosecution of gender-based and sexual violence crimes; we recruited and trained more police and immigration officers than we had at the beginning of the Sirleaf administration, consequently mob violence and other violent personal crimes were under control and our borders were less porous; we worked with other agencies of government to conclude concession agreements that would provide more jobs for citizens in the rural parts of the country; we worked along with agencies of government to tackle illegal fishing activities within the Liberian territorial waters, and so forth.

But then, here I found myself embroiled in this asinine contempt case when the court could have simply disagreed with me. Legal institutions and legal practitioners around the world disagree all the time.

I recall one of my colleagues, Tilman Dunbar, Jr., a practicing attorney in the United States and Liberia, said to me back in October 2013 after the first contempt hearing, "this Court is setting a bad precedent in your case. If they take such serious action against the Attorney General, who is also the Dean of the Supreme Court Bar of Liberia in a matter like this, then they are opening the door wherein high profile lawyers in the Liberian Bar, and even themselves, might fall victim to abuse of power of this nature."

Oh well, I thought, *all of this is water under the bridge now. I need to move ahead with the resignation. The justice ministry has a strong team, and all will be well.*

I called the president's protocol officer during the evening of Sunday, October 4, 2014, and asked for an appointment with the president on Monday, October 5, 2014; she said that she could confirm an appointment for 11:30 a.m., and I accepted.

On Monday morning, October 5, 2014, I arrived at my office at seven o'clock, two hours earlier than usual; my secretary was waiting for me. I asked her to make the necessary corrections I had highlighted and print out the document on the letterhead of the Ministry of Justice. Before she left my office, I explained what document I had on the USB and made her promise not to discuss it with anyone until I released it to the public. She immediately broke down and started crying. I begged her to be strong for me and assured her that I was confident that my action was necessary at this time.

The only other person I needed to confer with before my appointment with the president was my lawyer. If he had any comments, I wanted to know before I took this bold step and not after the fact. At 10:30 a.m., I was seated next to the lawyer in his living room while he read the two documents: one, a resignation letter, and the other, a press statement. He showed no emotion or expression after reading the document. My guess was I caught him by surprise. He simply said, "When do you want to do this?"

"Within the next hour," I responded, and then I walked out and left in my vehicle. As we drove out of the yard, I turned to look back at the lawyer's house; interestingly, the lawyer was still standing at his front door watching the vehicle drive away.

On the way to my appointment, which was ten minutes away from the lawyer's house, I called at least six different journalists and asked them to meet me at my office at one o'clock for a press conference. No one asked me about the purpose of the press conference. I guess they assumed I wanted to talk about the Ebola situation.

I arrived at the office of the president a few minutes early and sat in the office of the minister of state for presidential affairs, which I normally did when I had appointments with the president. Minister McClain (now deceased) had always been one of my favorite colleagues. He was bright, civil, and always in a jovial mood. I was naturally drawn to him when I joined President Sirleaf's cabinet in 2009 because I grew up in a boarding school with four of his younger brothers. To me, he was a big brother. But that day, I had to do everything I could to contain my emotions and keep from telling him the real reason I was there to see the president. I do not doubt that he always had my interest at heart, but there was no mistake that he had a stronger bond with the president and would likely place her above all others except his immediate family. Therefore, I concluded that it would be naïve and downright stupid to disclose the purpose of my visit to him.

When I finally arrived in the office of the president, we greeted each other cordially with a handshake, and before she could offer me a seat, I asked her permission to have the minister of state present in the meeting. "But you asked to see me," she said. "Why does Minister McClain have to be present?"

I hesitated and took a deep breath and said, "I am here to tender my resignation, and I just think it would be a good idea to have your minister of state and confidant present." For some reason, I felt that his presence would put both the president and me at ease, knowing that she would not accept the letter without a short discussion.

The president's reaction appeared to be a mix of shock and relief. Initially, she appeared shocked, and after what I said sank in, she appeared relieved. After all, this was what she had wanted to accomplish for the past ten months. It was the minister who was shocked. I had just left his office in high spirits and had not given a hint of what I was about to do. In any case, I figured he would eventually understand.

We spent about fifteen minutes discussing many things that had brought us to where we were in our relationship, but we especially spent some time on the human trafficking issue. When I stated why I believed that the decision to pardon an inmate while an appeal in the matter was pending before the

Supreme Court would undermine the doctrine of separation of power, she asked, "But why didn't you advise me? You are the minister of justice."

I said, "I did advise, Madam President. My advice was in response to the minister of state's request for an opinion." But a reply came from the president herself stating that "other lawyers" had advised differently and that she preferred to go along with their opinion. They both were silent. It then occurred to me that someone else, perhaps a lawyer, had written the response to me for the president's signature. "Wow!" I whispered inaudibly.

Both the minister and the president asked if I could hold over as minister of justice until the end of the week, as all of the deputies in the Ministry of Justice were out of the country. Some were on official assignment, and others were seeking respite from the psychological stress the Ebola virus had rained on us. I agreed at first, but as I approached my vehicle in the parking lot, it occurred to me that I was setting myself up to be fired. That should not be allowed to happen after a carefully crafted exit.

I had planned to return to my office and dismiss the corps of journalists waiting for me to conduct a press conference, but, instead, I called Minister McClain from my SUV and informed him that I would not be able to hold over as I had promised. I would prefer to follow through with my resignation, effective immediately. I would hand over my duties/responsibilities to the most senior official in the ministry on that day, Harriette Badio, the assistant minister of justice for economic affairs. Again, he was stunned.

I called my senior staff members, including the director of police and the commissioner of immigration, as I rode in the vehicle back to the office and simply asked them to join me for a press conference. No one had any idea why I had decided to call a press conference at this time; however, it did not seem unusual since we conducted press conferences regularly.

I started the press conference by saying, "Let me begin by extending my solemn condolences to all Liberians who have lost loved ones to the deadly outbreak of the Ebola virus disease or have been otherwise affected by the epidemic. My prayers remain that all of us will continue to work together with our international partners, who have come to our aid, to remove this scourge from our country and the entire region.

"I have convened this press conference this afternoon to inform the Liberian public that I have respectfully asked President Sirleaf to accept my resignation, which I tendered on March 31, 2014."

The room went silent. I paused for a few seconds and looked around the room at the faces of the journalists and my staff. The expressions I saw on their faces were indescribable and have remained etched in my mind. I sat at the head of the long conference table, and the director of police sat in the chair at a right angle to my left. I could see, from the corner of my eye, that his right hand fiddled aimlessly with his cellphone as though he could not understand why I had not confided in him regarding this decision. I looked to my right and my eyes met the eyes of Kenneth Best, a respected Liberian journalist, and I was pleased that he had honored my invitation.

In giving my reasons for submitting my resignation, I informed the Liberian public that "the landscape of the Liberian jurisprudence is being transformed in arbitrary and inscrutable ways that make it onerous to navigate conscientiously." For instance, "Amidst the prevailing interpretation of the doctrine of separation of powers and the ensuing blurring of the rules and roles of engagement ... The rule of law is being eroded by actions that contradict the values that underpin the fabric of our society." And lastly, I stated that I could no longer "continue to fill the position of minister of justice in name without the substantive support of the chief executive."

At the end of the press conference, I felt an inexplicable calmness overtake my entire body. I felt relieved and did not care what consequences lie ahead. All I knew was that I had finally recaptured and repositioned my sense of self.

Acknowledgements

Writing this book has not been an easy journey for me. It has taken me four years and a lot of rewriting and deletion to arrive at a final product. I am appreciative of those who took time to discuss ideas and issues with me on the telephone and those who read the entire manuscript or parts of it.

I must, however, specifically mention a few individuals who, although very busy, took time to read segments of the manuscript and provided very useful and constructive comments, propelling substantive changes that ultimately improved the quality of the book. They are: Althea Romeo-Mark, Yvette Chesson, Willie A. Givens, Sr., Gerald Padmore, Randolph McClain, Edward Dillon, Carlos Z.B. Smith, Kate Chang, Jim Dube, Fatu Daramy Mensah, Lucelia Harmon, Michen Tah, Calvin Bropleh and George Fahnbulleh.

Special thanks to Alima Joned, Caroline Williams Egbe, William A. Cisco, Jr., Saba and Mildred Kla-Williams, Catherine Elizabeth Reffell, Janet Maxwell, Max Dennis, Gleneda Richards, Edwin Zelee, Rudolph Bropleh, Colin Fraser and Samuel G. Hai for your encouragement.

I wish to especially thank all my friends and acquaintances who stayed by my side during the best of times and the worst of times. It is through my journey that I came to understand the true meaning of friendship.

I thank the LifeRich Publishing Company for its service.

Most importantly, I thank my family members for their love and loyalty, and I thank God for His Blessings.

Photo from my parents' wedding

Harriette E. Hammond (my mother) at age 50

International students at Carson Newman College in Tennessee, USA

At age 17 in Liberia   At age 18 in Liberia

Liberian delegation at the UN in 2009 with UN Special Representative of the
Secretary-General Ellen M. Løj

With Minister of Agriculture Florence
Chenoweth at the 2012 Inauguration
of President Sirleaf

With President Sirleaf welcoming Secretary of State Hillary
Clinton to the Liberian National Police Training Academy

With Minister Chenoweth and Tarpeh in conversation with
President Sirleaf

In conversation with Vice President Joseph N. Boakai
Courtesy of Sando J. Moore Productions

Delivering a speech at the opening of the term of the
Liberian Supreme Court
Courtesy of Sando J. Moore Productions

At age 22 in Wisconsin, USA

On the train in Switzerland on the way to a conference

With Tete Glaypoh (the Bassa Governor for Monrovia) and Doc (my husband) in 1980

With Dr. F. Augustus P. Tah (my husband) at an event in the 1980s

At a Maritime reception in Greece in 1986

In England in 1986

266

At a reception in Monrovia in 2011

At the Ministry of Justice in 2012

Endnotes

1   International Monetary Fund, *Liberia: Poverty Reduction Strategy Paper* (Washington, DC: International Monetary Fund Publication Services, 2008), 15.

2   United States Department of State, Office of the Historian, *Founding of Liberia, 1847*, https://history.state.gov/milestones/1830-1860/liberia (Last accessed: November 10, 2019).

3   Charles Henry Huberich, *The Political and Legislative History of Liberia*, vol. 1 (New York: Central Book Company, 1947), 23-25.

4   Minority Rights Group International, *World Directory of Minorities and Indigenous Peoples - Liberia, 2007*, https://www.refworld.org/docid/4954ce5823.html (Last accessed: November 10, 2019).

5   Tom W. Shick, *Behold the Promised Land: A History of Afro-American Settler Society in Nineteenth Century Liberia* (Johns Hopkins University Press, 1980), 66-75.

6   Huberich, 822.

7   Shick, 108.

8   Huberich, 47.

9   Shick, 28.

10 Shick, 29-31.

11 *The African Repository*, vols. 41–42 (Washington, DC: American Colonization Society, 1865), 236-243.

12 *Liberia*, vol. 12, *The Eighty First Annual Report of the American Colonization Society*, (New York: Kraus Reprint Company, 1969), 3.

13 *Liberia*, vol. 10, *The Eightieth Annual Report of the American Colonization Society*, (New York: Kraus Reprint Company, 1969), 43-45.

14 Shick, 66-67.

15 *Yancy et al v. the Republic of Liberia*, 18 LLR 97 (1967).

16 *Glo et al v. the Republic of Liberia*, 17 LLR 681 (1966).

17 Craig Timberg, "Liberia's Taylor Found and Arrested," *Washington Post*, March 30, 2006.

18 Alpha Sesay, "Charles Taylor Sentenced to 50 Years in Jail," *International Justice Monitor*, May 30, 2012.

19 Republic of Liberia Truth and Reconciliation Commission ("TRC"), *Volume II: Consolidated Final Report (unedited)* (Monrovia, Liberia: 2009), article 4, section 4.

20 TRC Consolidated Final Report, 14-19.

21 Mambu James Kpargoi, Jr., "True Whig Party Suppressed Rights of Liberians … Fahnbulleh at Hearing," *The Liberian Journal*, August 6, 2008.

22 United Nations Security Council, *Fifth progress report of the Secretary-General on the United Nations Mission in Liberia* (December 17, 2004).

23 Daniel Mensah Brande, "Vision 2030: A Plan to Transform Liberia," *UN FOCUS*, vol. 9, no. 2, December 2012 – February 2013, 6.

24 Kirsten Johnson, et al., "Association of Combatant Status and Sexual Violence with Health and Mental Health Outcomes in Post-Conflict Liberia," *JAMA The Journal of the American Medical Association* 300(6): 676-90.

25 Shick, 142.

26 Shick, 142.

27 Robtel Neajai Pailey, "Patriarchy, Power Distance, and Female Presidency in Liberia," in Baba G Jallow, ed., *Leadership in Postcolonial Africa: Trends Transformed by Independence* (New York: Palgrave Macmillan, 2014), 180-81.

Index

Bryant, Charles Gyude, 127, 128, 198
Bryant, Kate, 72, 135, 136
Bryant, Tidi, 135
Budy, Alfred, 116
Budy, Robert, 142
Bull, Pearl Brown, 156
Burrowes, Patrick, 128
Butscher, June Kamara, 136

C

Caesar, Ruth Gibson, 134
Cannon, Louise, 29
Cesaire, Aime, 39
Chang, Kate, 229, 231, 236, 263
Chapman, Peter, 178
Cheapoo, Chea, 76, 77, 82, 83
Chenoweth, Sr., Albert, 17
Chenoweth, Florence, 4, 58, 63, 135,
    189, 195, 207
Cherue, Frederick, 219, 233, 234
Chesson, Leona Tucker, 135
Chesson, Joseph J. F., 63, 76, 77 79,
    84, 110, 115
Chesson, Yvette, 110, 111, 112, 113,
    116, 119, 120, 121, 128, 130,
    131, 132, 133, 157, 263
Cisco, William A., 263
Clark, Helen, 133, 200
Clinton, Hillary Rodham, 154
Clinton, William Jefferson (a.k.a Bill
    Clinton), 116, 117, 119, 120
Cole, Henry B., 54
Cole, Leslie Norman, 111, 117
Coleman, Gerald, 156
Collins, Elizabeth, 135
Conyers, John, 117
Cooper, Dugpeny, 111
Cooper, Edweda Gbenyon, 127
Cooper, Rita, 27
Cooper, Seward M., 221, 240
Costa, Henry, 235

Cox, Ayele Ajavon (a.k.a Ayele
    Ajavon) 111, 128, 136
Cummings, Ayo, 136
Cummings, Catherine Harmon, 135
Cummings, Elijah, 117

D

Dahn, Bernice, 245
Damas, Leon, 39
Davis, Joshua, 46
Dennis, Agnes Cooper, 135
Dennis, Cecil B., 84
Dennis, Ernest, 20
Dennis, Granville, 49
Dennis, Laurinda, 134
Dennis, Maggie, 136
Dennis, Max, 263
Dennis, Yeda Baker, 136
Deshield, Charles, 143
Deshield, Joseph Ellworth, 26
Deshield, McKinley A., 62
Diggs, Rachel Gbenyon, 117
Dillon, Edward, 118, 234, 263
Diop, Binta, 133
Dixon, S. N., 136
Doe, Jackson F., 73
Doe, Samuel Kanyon, 79, 82, 86, 91,
    93, 93, 94, 95, 96, 97, 99, 100,
    102, 103, 104, 106, 108, 109,
    225, 233
Dolopei, Dede, 156
Dube, Jim, 172, 263
Dunbar, Fulton, 53
Dunbar, Jr., Tilman, 112, 259

E

Egbe, Caroline W., 263
Ehanire, Eleanor Neal, 136
Eldrige, Lara, 178
En'tow, Saah, 111, 164

K

L

M

N

Sherman, Theresa Leigh, 112, 113, 127, 134, 136
Sherman, Varney G., 96, 118, 162, 232, 233, 234
Sidifall, Reuben, 48, 76
Siegel, Reva, 191
Sieh, Mona (a.k.a Mona Sieh Brown) 142, 152, 153
Sieh, Rodney, 210, 211, 212, 213, 214, 227, 231, 233, 235, 239
Simon, Paul Martin, 109
Simpson, Jr., Clarence, 73, 209, 210
Simpson, Veda, 133
Sirleaf, Ellen Johnson, 1, 2, 3, 16, 59, 72, 83, 97, 98, 103, 109, 113, 129, 130, 132, 135, 148, 149, 154, 162, 165, 187, 188, 189, 191, 192, 200, 201, 203, 212, 213, 217, 218, 219, 220, 221, 222, 225, 226, 229, 233, 236, 249, 250, 251, 255, 260, 261
Sirleaf, Fombah, 207, 251
Sirleaf, Robert, 217, 218, 219, 220, 220, 222, 223
Smallwood, Ephraim, 76, 94
Smith, Carlos Z. B., 112, 263
Smole, John, 77
Snowe, Edwin, 223, 224
Sonkarly, Wongbeh, 143
Soros, George, 181
Spalton, Natalie Fisher, 133
Speare, Fannie V., 17
Speare, Nathaniel Puo, 17
Stevenson, Eugenia, 96, 117, 135
Stewart, Sr., Frank, 84
Stewart, John H. T., 156
Stryker, Rose, 195
Stubblefield, Samuel, 25
Suah KoKo, 137
Sumo, Luther, 196
Sumo, John, 245

Syllah, Oumu, 156

T

Tah, Augustus, 78, 79, 81, 104, 106
Tah, Michen, 118, 263
Tamba, Elfrieda Stewart, 221
Tarpeh, Etmonia David, 189, 207
Tarpeh, James N., 55, 56
Tarpeh, James T., 95
Tarr, Byron, 83
Tate, Geneva, 33
Tate, William, 33
Taylor, Charles, 102, 103, 104, 106, 113, 115, 116, 126, 158, 162, 165, 166, 203, 243
Thompson, Luvenia Ash, 136
Tillerman, Staffan, 200
Tipoteh, Togba Nah, 59, 83
Toe, Chris, 210, 213
Toh, Elizabeth Catherine, 48
Tolbert, Sr., Frank E., 84
Tolbert, Richard, 221
Tolbert, Steve, 62
Tolbert, Jr., William R., 54, 57, 58, 59, 60, 62, 68, 69, 73, 75, 78, 188
Townsend, E. Reginald, 60, 73, 84
Tubman, Antoinette Padmore, 136
Tubman, Robert C., 98, 99
Tubman, Sr., William V.S., 27, 57, 88, 136, 188
Tubman, Winston, 204
Tucker, Gabriel, 49
Turpin, Eleanor, 39, 40
Tweh, Moses, 53
Tyson, Carole, 133

U

Urey, Benoni, 242
Urey, Mae Bright, 242

276

V

Verdier, Jerome, 156
Victor, Ciata, 133
Von Ballmoos, Agnes Nebo, 135

W

Walser, Emma Shannon, 136
Ward, Amelia, 134
Warner, Bennie D., 73
Warner, Negbalee, 214
Washington, George, 11
Washington, Massa, 156
Washington, Sayon, 48
Waters, Maxine, 117
Weah, Etty, 127
Weah, Joseph, 34
Weah, George Manneh, 159,
    203, 204
Weeks, Sr., Rocheforte, 13
Weeks, Vittorio, 110
Weeks, Vivian Sayeh, 109, 110
Wells, Rebecca, 33
West, Phillip (a.k.a Phil West), 111
White, Sr., Albert T., 50, 70, 71

White, Kate Urey, 50, 70
Williams, Christine Hoff, 111
Williams, George, 110
Wolokollie, Jamesetta, 231
Woods, Kofi, 212
Wotorson, Cletus, 72
Wotorson, Michael, 111
Wreh, Michael, 111
Wreh, Tuan, 89, 93
Wright, Micah Wilkins (a.k.a Micah
    Wright), 142, 173, 205, 214,
    215, 225
Wulu, John, 133
Wureh, Emmanuel, 94, 118, 128

Y

Yancy, Freddie, 48
York, James L., 20
Yuoh, Sie-A-Nyene, 231

Z

Zeid Raad Al Hussein (Prince
    Zeid), 200
Zelee, Edwin, 263
Zotaa, James, 207